The British Labour Movement and Imperialism
(with Foreword by Tony Benn)

The British Labour Movement and Imperialism
(with Foreword by Tony Benn)

Edited by

Billy Frank, Craig Horner and David Stewart

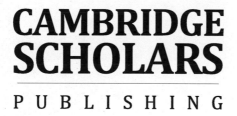

**CAMBRIDGE
SCHOLARS**

P U B L I S H I N G

The British Labour Movement and Imperialism
(with Foreword by Tony Benn)
Edited by Billy Frank, Craig Horner and David Stewart

This book first published 2010

Cambridge Scholars Publishing

12 Back Chapman Street, Newcastle upon Tyne, NE6 2XX, UK

British Library Cataloguing in Publication Data
A catalogue record for this book is available from the British Library

ISBN (10): 1-4438-2220-5, ISBN (13): 978-1-4438-2220-6

This volume is respectfully dedicated to the memory of John Saville (1916–2009), a pioneer of labour history.

TABLE OF CONTENTS

Foreword ix
Tony Benn

Introduction 1
Billy Frank, Craig Horner and David Stewart

Exploited Workers or Agents of Imperialism? British Common
Soldiers in the Nineteenth Century 9
Nicholas Mansfield

Empire before Labour: The "Scramble for Africa" and the Media,
1880–99 23
Christopher Prior

Labour and Empire: Australia and Britain from the Late Nineteenth
Century to the Inter-War Years 41
Neville Kirk

Weaving Tales of Empire: Gandhi's Visit to Lancashire, 1931 65
Hester Barron

Labour, Race and Empire: The Trades Union Congress and Colonial
Policy, 1945–51 89
Mary Davis

Labour's "New Imperialist Attitude": State-Sponsored Colonial
Development in Africa, 1940–51 107
Billy Frank

Labour and the Central African Federation: Paternalism, Partnership
and Black Nationalism, 1951–60 131
Murray Steele

Labour, European Integration and the Post-Imperial Mind,
1960–75 149
C. M. M. Cotton

"A Complex Question about the Remnants of Empire": The Labour
Party and the Falklands War 173
David Stewart

Contributors 191

Index 195

FOREWORD

TONY BENN

The British empire came to an end during my lifetime and its transformation from imperial rule to independence within the Commonwealth was achieved without the bloody wars that occurred in Algeria and Vietnam which put an end to French domination.

Of course Britain fought a lot of actions against those whom they described as terrorists, such as Mau Mau in Kenya, but in general the transition that occurred was made possible because of the links that the British labour movement and socialists had established with colonial liberation movements.

From the time that Annie Besant supported the Indian nationalists in the nineteenth century through to Keir Hardie, Fenner Brockway and the Movement for Colonial Freedom, these links were of great importance for both sides.

British imperialism, like all imperialism, was motivated by the desire for power and resources made possible by Britain's industrial strength as the first country in the world to undergo the industrial revolution.

Being an island with a strong navy we had military support that sustained that empire. This strategy was based upon Britain's attempt to establish economic supremacy, which allowed it to have access to cheap labour and raw materials and create a market for its own goods.

When I was born in 1925 a quarter of the world's population was run by the government in London and although the white commonwealth – Canada, Australia, New Zealand and South Africa – had acquired effective self government, the rest of the empire had no democratic base whatsoever.

It was the internationalism associated with socialism that marked the beginning of the co-operation that made possible a relatively peaceful end to British imperialism.

The Suez war in 1956, engineered by Anthony Eden to gain control of the Suez Canal, was actually brought to an end by American pressure at a time when the United States was anxious to dislodge Britain from the Middle East and establish its own dominance.

We currently hear a lot about globalization as if that word only meant free trade and the domination of the world by multinational corporations, but in a sense empires were early examples of globalization. International socialism has the same perspective but with a totally different interpretation based on the common interest of working people everywhere to establish some control over their own lives free from the landlords, kings, emperors and corporations which have historically controlled them.

It would be quite wrong to say that the post-war Labour government gave independence to India and the colonies, because they won it. However, independence was achieved with the good will of influential socialists in the post-war government of Britain which established a real friendship that has served both very well in the years that followed.

We are now witnessing the decline of the American empire, weakened economically by the financial crisis, overstretched militarily in Iraq and Afghanistan and with its influence having diminished sharply during the Bush presidency.

The Stop the War coalition and world-wide peace movement which grew up after the invasions of Afghanistan and Iraq are an example of a global response to American military interventions interpreted in the occupied countries as a sign of friendship from progressive people here and in the United States.

As the Chinese economy grows, despite its present economic problems, and as India comes into its own, it is likely that this will be reflected in a new balance of power between East and West that could bring its own repression, not unlike the empires of the past.

We are being told that new global financial structures are needed to help us to recover from the global recession. It is easy to see why such an argument should be put forward by the rich and powerful, but the question has yet to be answered: "How will those structures become democratically accountable?" Here we face a challenge as great as that faced by Britain in the 1830s and afterwards when the Chartists and the suffragettes demanded the right to be represented in a political system that had previously excluded them.

When the first reform bill came before the House of Commons – modest as it was – it was seen as a revolutionary proposal that would empower the poor against the rich and was bitterly fought to the point that it was only in 1948 that Britain achieved one man, one woman, one vote at the same age.

With two billion Chinese and two billion Indians and many millions of other people who are grossly underrepresented in the UN and other bodies, the meaning of internationalism has to be seen in a new context.

A world run by corporate interests would be as undemocratic as was the political system of Britain until quite recently.

And the argument against enfranchising the poor is an argument that is still very much on the agenda of the multinational corporations and their political friends.

That is the challenge for this generation to realize the historical perspectives which will help us to make sense of it now.

Working people have always been instinctively internationalist and have come to realize that democracy is the most revolutionary idea in the world. Democracy dissolved the British empire and has to become the instrument that controls the world in which our grandchildren will have to live.

INTRODUCTION

BILLY FRANK, CRAIG HORNER AND DAVID STEWART

Until recently it was widely assumed by historians and labour studies scholars that the British labour movement's concerns with empire were limited. This was deemed to be a reflection of British workers' parochialism, preoccupation with workplace and standard of living issues, and ambivalence towards imperialism. Consequently, labour historians have tended to neglect the labour movement's interaction with imperialism, preferring to concentrate on internal factionalism, the Labour Party-trade union alliance, industrial relations, and economic policymaking.[1] Partha Sarthi Gupta's classic, though somewhat dated, work on *Imperialism and the British Labour Movement* is the only general survey of the British labour movement's relationship with empire. However, John MacKenzie's pioneering research into popular attitudes towards imperialism is also notable for highlighting working-class enthusiasm for empire and labour movement advocacy of a liberal, ethical imperialism.[2] He argues that "by creating a national purpose with a high moral content [imperialism] led to class conciliation".[3] MacKenzie's argument has been challenged by Bernard Porter, who contends that the working classes were either apathetic towards the empire or superficial in their attitude to it, viewing the empire as a concern of the ruling class.[4]

---

[1] Recent volumes of *Labour History Review*, which have focused on transnational ideas, activities, spaces, strategies and organizations since the 1860s, are a welcome exception. See *Labour History Review* 74, no. 3 (2009); *Labour History Review* 75, no. 1 (2010).

[2] Partha Sarthi Gupta, *Imperialism and the British Labour Movement, 1914–1964* (London: Macmillan, 1975); John M. MacKenzie, *Propaganda and Empire: The Manipulation of British Public Opinion, 1880–1960* (Manchester: Manchester University Press, 1994).

[3] MacKenzie, *Propaganda and Empire*, 2.

[4] Bernard Porter, *The Absent-Minded Imperialists: Empire, Society and Culture in Britain* (Oxford: Oxford University Press, 2007), 311.

Although during recent years several scholars have sought to redress the balance by examining the Labour Party's foreign policy and relationship with the world, imperialism has formed only one of several themes within these studies and the wider labour movement has tended to be neglected.[5]

Rhiannon Vickers contends that the Labour Party's policy on imperial affairs was frequently confused and inconsistent with Labour's belief in Britain's continuing world and imperial role.[6] She argues that in the period 1900–51 a form of internationalism underpinned the Labour Party's foreign policy. Labour's internationalism was primarily influenced by radical nineteenth-century Liberal ideas, and comprised support for social justice at home and abroad, opposition towards militarism, the promotion of democracy and human rights, advocacy of collective security, and hostility towards jingoistic nationalism. On the other hand, John Callaghan presents the Labour Party as holding paternalistic views about empire, based upon commitment to the perceived virtues of British government, which led the party to support colonial trusteeship and disassociate itself from anti-imperialism.[7] Callaghan links Labour's advocacy of trusteeship to the popular belief in Britain's imperial destiny, which justified empire as a civilising mission bringing law, commerce, and Christianity to barbaric parts of the world. In effect, many labourites were convinced that the labour movement could use the wealth, institutions and ideas of the British state to improve colonial people's lives. Of the remaining texts that engage with the wider labour movement and imperialism, Stephen Howe's work on *Anticolonialism in British Politics* is the most noteworthy. Howe refutes the concept of voluntary British decolonization by highlighting the role played by left-wing opponents of empire in advancing the case for colonial independence.[8] Analyzing the strategies of radical pressure groups and political parties, he contends that divisions within the Labour Party left over decolonization have been underestimated.

This book stems from a conference on "The British Labour Movement and Imperialism", held at the University of Central Lancashire in Preston

---

[5] The recent edited volume by Paul Corthorn and Jonathan Davis, *The British Labour Party and the Wider World* (London: I. B. Tauris, 2008), is an excellent example of this, as empire is only central to two of the ten chapters.
[6] Rhiannon Vickers, *The Labour Party and the World*, Vol. 1: *The Evolution of Labour's Foreign Policy, 1900–51* (Manchester: Manchester University Press, 2003), 5–9.
[7] John Callaghan, *The Labour Party and Foreign Policy: A History* (Abingdon: Routledge, 2007), 146–48.
[8] Stephen Howe, *Anticolonialism in British Politics: The Left and the End of Empire, 1918–1964* (Oxford: Clarendon Press, 1993), 19–26.

on June 26–7, 2008. The conference was organized in conjunction with the People's History Museum, an institutional partner of the University, and a national Centre for the Study of Democracy. We are extremely grateful to UCLan's former Pro-Vice Chancellor, Patrick McGhee, for helping to fund the conference. Over the course of the two days there were an archive/museum workshop,[9] several stimulating academic panels, and keynote addresses by Tony Benn, Professor Neville Kirk, and Professor Gregory Claeys, the first of which attracted a large public audience. The book, which spans the period between 1800 and 1982, reflects the range of work presented and discussed at the conference. Although it would not claim to be fully comprehensive, the chapters explore the relationship between the British labour movement and imperialism in innovative and challenging ways.

Tony Benn, a veteran Labour Party anti-imperialist, begins the volume with a thought-provoking foreword based upon his personal recollections of the labour movement's interaction with empire. Thereafter, working-class agency emerges as a central theme of Nicholas Mansfield and Christopher Prior's chapters. Mansfield confronts the challenge of incorporating unorganized workers, readily associated with imperial oppression, into labour history by analyzing working-class soldiers' relationships with empire and race during the nineteenth century. He explains that the army's structure closely mirrored the class structure of British society and emphasizes that working-class soldiers were the largest group of Britons that the colonized would encounter. Despite identifying examples of political radicalism and racial tolerance, Mansfield concludes that soldiers' reputations as "ruffians led by gentry" was largely justified. In his chapter on labour movement press coverage of the "scramble for Africa", Prior addresses John Callaghan's call for more research into how the press framed the discussion of empire.[10] Prior identifies a direct correlation between the labour movement's "lack of inclination to go directly for the imperial jugular", limited media access to information about colonial developments, and the perceived popularity of empire

---

[9] We are extremely grateful to Maria Castrillo, National Library of Scotland, Gillian Lonergan, National Co-operative Archive, Darren Treadwell, Labour History Archive and Study Centre at the People's History Museum, and Jim Garretts, formerly of the People's History Museum, for participating in the workshop. We would also like to thank the Working Class Movement Library (Salford), the TUC Library (London Metropolitan University), and Glasgow Caledonian University Research Collections for sending relevant archival listings.

[10] John Callaghan, "Editorial: Imperialism Recidivism", *Socialist History* 31 (2007), 5.

amongst the working-class. In particular, Prior reveals how the interaction between the newly enfranchised working-class electorate, popular culture and nationalism intersected with labour movement fragility to prevent the development of radical left-wing anti-imperialism.

Hester Barron and Neville Kirk further enhance our understanding of working-class and labour movement attitudes towards empire through regional and comparative studies of Lancashire, Britain and Australia. Barron's chapter on Gandhi's 1931 visit to Lancashire, which highlights the goodwill shown towards Gandhi by cotton workers, demonstrates the fragility of popular imperialism amongst Lancastrian cotton workers during the depression, and their varying degrees of commitment to international working-class solidarity. Given the importance of imperial trade to the Lancashire cotton industry, the chapter provides a fascinating case study that encapsulates the dilemma of British workers who were often torn between self-protection, sympathy for the poor and class solidarity. Kirk broadens our understanding of how imperialism shaped the development of United Kingdom and commonwealth labour movements by focusing on the cross-fertilization of ideas between the British and Australian Labour parties. He challenges core-periphery and top-down approaches to imperial history, and calls for new approaches to the subject that fuse historical context with culture and political economy. Emphasizing the dual influences of class and race on British and Australian attitudes towards empire, Kirk contends that British and Irish migrants were pivotal to the growth of the Australian Labor Party, which in turn helped to maintain British Labour Party interest in the Australian labour movement.

The next three chapters concentrate on the Attlee governments' colonial policies. Mary Davis brings into focus the role of the Trades Union Congress (TUC) in developing non-militant trade unionism in the colonies. Presenting the TUC and Labour Party as subscribing to the classic nineteenth-century "white man's burden" justification for the maintenance of empire, she places Labour's colonial trade union strategy in the context of the anti-communist climate of the cold war. Davis concludes by rejecting the Labour Party and TUC's association with anti-imperialism and accusing them of preparing the ground for neo-colonialism. Billy Frank continues the scrutiny of the seemingly "positive" colonial policy that emerged during the war, championed by figures such as Creech Jones and Rita Hinden of the newly formed Fabian Colonial Bureau, through the study of Labour's colonial development policy in Africa. Acknowledging the Labour Party's paternalistic views on race, Frank explains the distortion of Labour's colonial development policy into colonial exploitation as a result of the demands of the post-war dollar shortage and domestic reconstruction. In doing so, Frank provides an insight into Labour's historic difficulties in reconciling the pursuit of radical domestic and progressive international objectives while revealing the weaknesses of a core-periphery approach to imperial history.

Thereafter, Murray Steele's chapter on the Labour Party and the Central African Federation provides a bridge between the colonial and post-colonial eras, which further enhances our understanding of the limitations of the core-periphery model. Outlining Labour's pivotal role in the establishment of the Central African Federation, he highlights the party's refusal to adopt an anti-imperialist posture despite the lack of progress towards racial partnership made by the white-settler-dominated Federation. In particular, Steele's work illuminates Labour's desire to build a strong inter-racial commonwealth, and places this desire in the context of the party leadership's anti-communism and paternalistic view of colonial development in Africa.

The final two chapters extend the chronological sweep of the book into the late twentieth century. They further illuminate the Labour Party's difficulties in reconciling the pursuit of progressive national and international interests, and highlight the extent to which the party was divided over Britain's post-imperial world role. Exploring the debate over membership of the European Economic Community (EEC) in the period 1960–75, C. M. M. Cotton identifies anti-imperialism and support for the Commonwealth as central to the Labour Party's sense of political self. His work shows how Eurosceptics and Europhiles sought to harness anti-imperialist rhetoric to justify their stances towards the EEC, and reveals considerable overlap between the membership and ideas of the Labour Committee for Europe and the Social Democratic Party, formed in 1981. Cotton concludes that the social democrats' rejection of Britain's imperial legacy lends them a serious claim on the mantle of Labour progressivism.

Labour Party commitment to a global role and engagement with supranational institutions also underpins the final chapter on the Falklands War. David Stewart demonstrates how the Labour Party's anti-imperialist, pacifist, and anti-fascist traditions were exposed as inchoate during the conflict. The chapter is underpinned by the contrasting personalities of Tony Benn and Michael Foot. Emphasizing the importance of internal party factionalism and Foot's commitment to the United Nations, Stewart argues that the Labour Party leader's complex diplomatic argument, which contrasted sharply with Margaret Thatcher's populist jingoistic rhetoric, had limited appeal in an increasingly polarized wartime climate. Stewart contends that the failure of both Benn and Foot's strategies weakened the popular appeal of the Labour Party and galvanized Thatcher's post-imperial mission to destroy socialism.

Nevertheless, considerable gaps remain in the historiography relating to the British labour movement and imperialism. One of the most sizeable voids surrounds the co-operative movement's relationship with empire. This movement was closely involved with imperial trade and working conditions through its tea plantations in India and Africa, and in the promotion of colonial education through the Co-operative College. From the early twentieth century, Co-operative produce was marketed as using "non-sweated labour", making it arguably the most progressive wing of the labour movement in this field.[11] Under the Attlee governments, civil servants were compelled to undertake training courses at the Co-operative College, and more recently the co-operative movement has played an integral role in the development of fair trade.[12] Given the Co-operative's unique position as a highly successful business and mass social movement, it warrants more detailed attention from scholars of imperial and labour history.

Further research is also required into the Welsh and Scottish labour movements' relationships with empire. As Kirk demonstrates through the example of Andrew Fisher, an Ayrshire miner who became the first Labor prime minister of an Australian majority government, Scottish, Welsh, and Ulster migrants to the Commonwealth developed a tripartite identity incorporating their nation of birth, Britain, and their host dominion, which strengthened bonds between commonwealth labour movements and their British brothers and comrades. It would be fascinating to investigate the extent to which these relationships influenced the unionism of the Welsh and Scottish labour movements and interpretations of Britishness in the "celtic fringe" of the United Kingdom.[13] This would also complement

---

[11] Stefan Schwarzkopf, "Innovation, Modernisation, Consumerism: The Co-operative Movement and the Making of British Advertising and Marketing Culture, 1890s–1960s", in Lawrence Black and Nicole Robertson, eds., *Consumerism and the Co-operative Movement in Modern British History* (Manchester: Manchester University Press, 2009), 197–206.

[12] Matthew Anderson, "'Cost of a cup of tea': Fair Trade and the British Co-operative Movement, c.1960–2000", in *Consumerism and the Co-operative Movement*, 240–55.

[13] Recent research has tended to focus on the influence of empire in terms of the economy, missionaries, migration, and military service. See T. M. Devine, *Scotland's Empire, 1600–1815* (London: Allen Lane, 2003); and Esther Breitenbach, *Empire and Scottish Society: The Impact of Foreign Missions at Home c.1790 to c.1914* (Edinburgh: Edinburgh University Press, 2009).

Kirk's pioneering work in the area of global labour history, and clearly demonstrates the need for wider exploration in this field.

Preston, March 2010

EXPLOITED WORKERS OR AGENTS OF IMPERIALISM? BRITISH COMMON SOLDIERS IN THE NINETEENTH CENTURY

NICHOLAS MANSFIELD

In his keynote address to *The British Labour Movement and Imperialism* conference of June 2008, Tony Benn referred to the white British working class as "exploited exploiters". The subject of this chapter – the white working class in uniform – might be considered the epitome of this classification. There is now a huge popular literature on the British army and, as a result of their function as quasi-war memorials from 1918, there are still more military museums in the United Kingdom than any other category. Both tend to concentrate on individual regiments and their battles and rarely address more representative issues concerning soldiers' working lives. This chapter forms part of a larger and longer-term project on class and the British army. Whilst the structure of the British army closely mirrored the class structure of British society as it moved through the period of industrialization, few historical accounts of it analyze this blindingly obvious fact. Soldiers' working lives have a potential for enquiry in more detail, in the same way as some historians have applied in more recent years to other groups of unorganized workers such as domestic servants, yet labour historians have ignored them as docile and probably politically suspect. Finding a sympathetic hearing in a conference and book on labour and empire may be hard for a group who might be regarded at best as tools of the ruling class and at worst enthusiastic participants in the oppression against indigenous peoples. In the words of Linda Colley, who has made some groundbreaking reference to the subject:

> But to modern eyes the British or any other imperial soldiery easily appear uncongenial or at best unpredictable. It is assumed that they were violent (which they were) and that they were necessarily and inherently conformist (which they were not)... We need to probe beneath the lush

proconsular and plutocratic chronicles of Indian empire and uncover different, more subterranean, less dignified stories, stories of renegades and deserters, stories around punishment and resistance, stories of those majority of British soldiers who stayed loyal and outwardly obedient but sometimes with gritted teeth: the subalterns with white faces.[1]

Class, Empire and the Army

The British empire was central to the creation and experience of the army for a very long time, from Tangier and Bombay in the 1660s, to Aden in the 1960s, and discussion of the complex relationships between class and empire is potentially fruitful. With a powerful navy strongly allied to commercial interests and a dominant political tradition of distrust for a standing army, the army's main role for over three centuries was as an imperial gendarmerie, defending frontiers won in brief and bloody aggressive wars. The all-volunteer British army was tiny compared to European rivals and the seizure and holding of these immense spaces was an extraordinary technical achievement, based on discipline, bravery and well organized logistic and naval support. Like other imperialisms, the British made extensive use of locally recruited auxiliaries, usually from conquered peoples. Unusually, with one exception – the white regiments of the East India Company – it did not raise specific troops at home for colonial service. By the mid-nineteenth century, most of its core regular soldiers could typically expect to spend much of their service overseas, usually in no bigger units than the individual regiment and often in much smaller postings.

The army's structure closely mirrored the class structure. Officers traditionally came from the gentry or even aristocracy, though with wartime enlargements, more from upper middle-class backgrounds appeared, especially in unfashionable and technical regiments. Until the 1880s, junior officers, except in the artillery and engineers, purchased their commissions and promotions, a system which suited both the families of otherwise unemployable younger sons and the state, which did not have to provide retirement pensions. In contrast with much of post-revolutionary Europe, as a deliberate and class-based policy, very few British officers were promoted from the ranks. Those who were elevated mainly had specialist roles such as paymasters, adjutants or veterinary surgeons,

---

[1] For the discussion on the literature on servants from a labour historian, see John Benson, "'One Man and his Women': Domestic Service in Edwardian England", *Labour History Review* 72, no. 3 (2007), 212; Linda Colley, *Captives: Britain, Empire and the World 1660–1850* (London: Pimlico, 2002), 316.

which enabled the prevailing anti-professionalism in the British officer corps to continue. Even the abolition of purchasing commissions did not change the class-based composition and, except arguably for the two world wars of the twentieth century, it continues to this day.[2]

Common soldiers, by contrast, were nearly all working class, and were traditionally viewed as a dangerous and unsettled class – "the very scum of the earth" in the Duke of Wellington's famous phrase. Even in the more settled working class it is said that "to go for a soldier" brought disgrace to your family. Ruffians officered by gentry became a separate military caste remote from and distrusted by the rest of British society, compounded by long overseas imperial service. This analysis is typical of most military historians – the popular wing (including the museums referred to earlier) seeing common soldiers as ragged heroes not able to control their own destinies and mistreated by government and British society in general. This widespread and simplistic view is reflected when the subject is dealt with (usually tangentially) by academic historians. The subject of soldiers as workers has barely been covered by labour historians, and if it had been considered, it is likely that this "powerless dupes" analysis would also be shared.[3]

---

[2] Colley's recent analysis of soldiers in sections of *Captives*, and in chap. 7 of *Britons: Forging the Nation 1707–1837* (London: Pimlico, 1994), though worthy of expansion, is a refreshing counter-balance to standard accounts like Edward M. Spiers, *The Army and Society 1815–1914* (London: Longman, 1980); and *The Late Victorian Army 1868–1902* (Manchester: Manchester University Press, 1992); or Gwyn Harries, *The Army in Victorian Society* (London: Routledge and Kegan Paul, 1977) which downplay class. Hew Strachan, *The Politics of the British Army* (Oxford: Clarendon, 1997) is more concerned with high politics and even the dated popular iconoclastic account. Corelli Barnett, *Britain and Her Army: A Military, Political and Social History of the British Army 1509–1970* (London: Cassell, 1970) displays the prevailing conservatism of military history. All are influenced by the magisterial and arch-Tory J. W. Fortescue, *A History of the British Army* (London: Macmillan, 13 vols., 1899 to 1930). One exception to the trend is Lawrence James, *Warrior Race: A History of the British At War* (London: Little, Brown, 2001).

[3] Variations in Wellington's comment, which he made several times, are discussed in Elizabeth Longford, *Wellington: The Years of the Sword* (London: Weidenfeld and Nicolson, 1969), 379–80. In a similar way to the academics referred to in fn. 2, contributions, since 1922, to the most serious journal on the British forces, *The Journal of the Society for Army Historical Research*, generally treat class in a tangential way. The main British journal for labour history since the 1960s, *Labour History Review*, has published nothing on soldiers as workers, with the occasional piece on unrest and subversion amongst troops awaiting demobilization after 1918.

However, this common view, shared across the spectrum, has come to be queried recently by academics influenced by the new emphasis on cultural history. Disparate historians like Peter Stanley (working on the white regiments of the East India Company); Roger Norman Buckley in a study of the ethnicity and class of Caribbean garrisons of the Napoleonic Wars; and John Rumsby's recent micro-study of early Victorian enlistment as a career choice, have all begun to nuance the working lives and culture of the rank and file away from a crude caricature. My own work on farmworkers and their trade unions has emphasized the importance of the mass mobilization of the Great War and the particular role of radical ex-service organizations; an emphasis suggested when interviewing many of them in Norfolk a generation ago. This has continued with a class analysis of the county yeomanry emphasising their role as political gendarmerie, which extended into the twentieth century.[4]

Working Conditions of Imperial Soldiers

Soldiers were a huge occupational group throughout the century – indeed, the largest group those being colonized would encounter – for example, in 1830 white troops "made up 90% of all British residents in India". Mass mobilizations against the Napoleonic French, with its partial conscription, gave armies of over 300,000 men. Even the pared down army of the 1820s numbered over 100,000, with countering home-grown radical subversion supplementing imperial garrison duty. The climax came with Victoria's jubilee with a regular British army of 200,000, to say nothing of the other colonial forces in which the white working class played a prominent role,

---

[4] Peter Stanley, *The White Mutiny: British Military Culture in India, 1825–1875* (London: Hurst, 1998); Roger Norman Buckley, *The British Army in the West Indies: Society and the Military in the Age of Revolution* (Jacksonville, FL: University Press of Florida, 1998); and John H. Rumsby, *The 16th Lancers 1822–46: The Experience of Regimental Soldiering in India* (PhD diss., Leeds University, 2004). Peter Linebaugh and Marcus Rediker, *The Many Headed Hydra: The Hidden History of the Revolutionary Atlantic* (London: Verso, 2000) attempts a similar process for sailors. Nicholas Mansfield, *English Farmworkers and Local Patriotism, 1900–1930* (Aldershot: Ashgate, 2001), chap. 5; idem, "The National Federation of Discharged and Demobilised Soldiers and Sailors, 1917–1921: A View From the Marches", *Family and Community History* 7, no. 1 (May 2004); and idem, "Foxhunting and the Yeomanry", in R. W. Hoyle, ed., *Our Hunting Fathers: Field Sports in England after 1850* (Lancaster: Carnegie Publishing, 2007).

a figure which soon doubled as the crisis of the Boer War gave a "dry run" for the Armageddon of 1914.[5]

The regiment was the building block of the army and its structure included large numbers of specialist workers whose daily tasks mirrored wider British society in miniature, usually carrying on trades learnt in civilian life. So officers' needs were dealt with by cooks, grooms, horse-breakers, saddlers and servants of all kinds, and even the rank and files' demands were filled by weavers, barbers, the building trades, gardeners, shoemakers, tailors, teachers and tinsmiths, and by soldiers turned traders, especially sutlers running beer-shops and cook-shops. More specialist military trades were also found such as blacksmiths, gunsmiths, armourers, waggoners and riding masters. Soldiers also worked on constructing fortifications and barracks, either as day-labourers where they were paid extra, and in the absence of specialist troops, skilled and often time-served artificers, engineers, masons and miners were usually found in the ranks of any infantry regiment. Away from the atypical large scale and brutal campaigns, most soldiers' service was spent in boring garrison duty and even after enduring the hours of drill and training, common soldiers still had time for part-time jobs. Where indigenous labour did not exist, in isolated military garrisons, the unit came into its own as a self-contained and self-sufficient society which fulfilled its own European consumer demands supplied by pre-enlistment skills of traders and artisans in the ranks.[6]

---

[5] Colley, *Captives*, 316. The statistics about the size of the army are from Roderick Floud, Kenneth Wachter and Annabel Gregory, *Height, Health and History: Nutritional Status in the UK, 1750–1980* (Cambridge: Cambridge University Press, 1990), 46–8.

[6] The everyday working life of nineteenth-century soldiers is largely yet to be reconstructed, though Buckley, *British Army*, presents an object lesson of how it might be done. See also Jacalyn Duffin, "Soldiers' Work, Soldiers' Health: Morbidity, Mortality and their Causes in an 1840s British Garrison in Canada", *Labour/Le Travailleur* 37 (1996), 37–80. For the spare time available to most imperial soldiers, see, for example, *30th Foot, Standing Order Book, Bermuda, 1835–1838* and *Standard Orders 30th Foot* (Chatham: Burill, 1830), both in Queen's Lancashire Regimental Museum Archive, Preston; and the comments of Sergeant John Pearman in Carolyn Steedman, *The Radical Soldier's Tale* (London: Routledge, 1988), 146–7. For self-sufficient colonial communities see Frank Richards, *Old Soldier Sahib* (Uckfield, Sussex: Naval and Military Press, 2003 edn.), 84–6, 94; and, for example, *The Sentinel* (1878), the journal of the 59th Foot, published in India and containing advertisements for a regimental watch and clock maker, printer, monumental mason and electro-plater: Queen's Lancashire Regimental Museum Archives, Preston.

In the Indian subcontinent where local labour was cheap enough to cover all fatigues, common soldiers could live well – "Princes could live no better than we" according to one Victorian trooper – other opportunities rose for trading or for the growing number of training posts in native regiments and the lower ranks of government service. In all sorts of jobs and especially in isolated posts all over the empire, working-class people could assume positions of responsibility, which would not have been available to them in British civilian life, a phenomenon illustrated as early as the 1780s in William Cobbett's memoirs of his life as a soldier in Nova Scotia.[7]

Living Conditions of Imperial Soldiers

Most of the rank and file in Britain's imperial army endured appalling living conditions. In the United Kingdom, troops were billeted in pubs until the Napoleonic Wars, but in colonial service all lived in barracks which were constructed with no thought for comfort, usually of the cheapest materials and the smallest possible size. These cramped quarters allowed little scope for privacy, even for married or cohabiting soldiers. Poor housing was compounded by extremes of weather unimaginable to most British recruits, and made worse by the need for soldiers to be stationed in the most strategic places, rather than in those with temperate climates. Disease was endemic and the mortality rate for common soldiers was much higher than in civilian life. Though some postings were regarded as healthy, in most, the crowded living conditions were breeding grounds for epidemics which even in wartime killed far more soldiers than died in battle. The Caribbean of the 1790s became the nadir of this, with half of the 89,000 soldiers sent to seize French sugar and slave islands dying of disease. Although diet could be supplemented locally, in some places these opportunities did not exist. The government provided rations, based on salted meat and biscuit, which offered little resistance to disease.

---

[7] Quoted in Marquis of Anglesey, *A History of the British Cavalry,* vol. 3 (London: Leo Cooper, 1982), 141. George Spater, *William Cobbett, the Poor Man's Friend,* vol. 1, chap. 2 (Cambridge: Cambridge University Press, 1982); and Ian Dyck, "Introduction", in William Cobbett, *Rural Rides* (London: Penguin Classics edn., 2001), ix. Richard Holmes, *Soldier Sahib: The British Soldier in India, 1750–1914* (London: Harper, 2006), chaps. 2 and 5; and Richards, *Old Soldier Sahib,* 251. See also Dan Howden, "At the Edge of the World", in the *Independent* (Aug. 9, 2005) on how the colony on Tristan Da Cunha was founded by rankers.

What was always available, though, was cheap liquor, and a culture of hard drinking, alcoholism and violence prevailed.[8]

Soldiers also endured a brutal disciplinary system. Officers believed that their ruffians needed controlling with corporal punishment, which was lavishly applied with official sanction for minor transgressions, a practice abolished in most of post-revolutionary Europe but not in the British army until the 1880s. In contrast, in 1835 corporal punishment was abolished for locally recruited Indian sepoy regiments by the Whig Governor General Lord Bentinck. After his tenure ended, somewhat under a cloud – the first of several liberals in that post despised by soldiers – flogging was reinstated along with much harsher punishments as a result of the violent events of 1857. The lash also continued to be used on West Indian soldiers, many of whom were ex-slaves, and on African auxiliaries. Poor diet, crowded barracks, constant threat of disease, harsh climate, brutal discipline, hard liquor, homesickness, miserable pay and boredom caused mental illness later diagnosed by French army doctors as "Soudanism." One outcome, made easier by the availability of firearms, was suicide. In 1860s soldiers had treble the suicide rate of United Kingdom civilians – the highest occupational group – and this does not include the large numbers of ex-soldiers who today might be diagnosed with post-traumatic stress. Less extreme options might involve self-harm to obtain discharge or deliberate crime (including attempting suicide) to obtain transportation to Australia as a preferred location.[9]

Forms of Resistance

Other forms of resistance were more spirited. Desertion was endemic in the British army. In the melting pot of the industrial revolution in the United Kingdom, this was easier; in 1833 one-in-five soldiers on the home establishment were imprisoned, the vast majority for desertion, with over 10 percent of the army on the run. In the empire, desertion was trickier but

---

[8] See Buckley, *British Army West Indies*; and Duffin, *Soldiers' Work; Soldiers' Health*. The statistic is from Michael Duffy, *Soldiers, Sugar and Seapower: The British Expeditions to the West Indies and the War against Revolutionary France* (Oxford: The Clarendon Press, 1987), 333.

[9] Colley, *Captives*, 332–3. Soudanism was covered in Bertrand Taithe's inaugural professorial lecture "Thresholds of Horror: Massacres in French Soudan in the era of the Dreyfus Affair", University of Manchester, Apr. 10, 2008. John H. Rumsby, "Suicide in the British Army, c.1815 to c.1860", *Labour History Review* 84, no. 340 (2006), 351. For the transportation of soldiers to Australia see Fortescue, *History of the British Army*, vol. 11, 495.

not impossible. Before the 1770s the American frontier offered tempting opportunities to slip away and was reachable from Canadian postings for the next century. In South Africa the Boer republics offered similar opportunities. Though hostile environments and societies difficult to hide in presented problems, these were not insurmountable; in 1790s Jamaica for example, white deserters found refuge in the fierce Maroon societies of escaped black slaves. Other deserters sought to use their military skills as renegade soldiers for Britain's enemies. Examples are known from as early as the seventeenth century in Tangiers and in India. Indeed the post-Mughal successor states offered attractive career opportunities for violent and unprincipled mercenaries well into the nineteenth century. Officer service for a foreign power was regarded as acceptable until the Napoleonic Wars and the rise of nationalism. Intermarriage may also have contributed to such apparently inexplicable episodes as the desertion of British artillerymen to the doomed city of Bhurtopore in the 1825 siege, or Sergeant-Major Gordon serving with the revolted sepoys during the siege of Delhi in 1857. Unlike officers, such rank and file renegades received no mercy if captured by British military authorities. One could argue that this tradition continued as late as the 1960s with British soldiers seconded to friendly powers in Asia and mercenary activities in Africa.[10]

Other resistance was influenced by the pre-enlistment working-class attitudes and culture which soldiers brought with them. Evidence for go-slows and strikes is sketchy and opaque but just as in some civilian working lives, such as agriculture, in the absence of formal organizations like trade unions, informal negotiations seem to have taken place, with NCOs acting as a cross between foreman and shop steward in determining acceptable work loads. The clearest examples of this are from Stanley's work on the white regiments of the East India Company, which were raised as early as the 1660s, alongside sepoy regiments to protect their operations. By offering higher pay and eventual pensions, to offset being based permanently in India, they were able to attract recruits with more skills than the regular army. Their officers, appointed by the Company, were of a lower social class than the King's commissioned officers and

---

[10] Anglesey, *British Cavalry*, vol. 4 (1986), 125; Strachan, *Politics of the British Army,* 89; Fortescue, *History of the British Army*, vol. 8, 567; and vol. 11, 495; Buckley, *British Army West Indies*, 226; Colley, *Captives*, 39, 180, 260, 287, 317; C. Stein, *Bhurtpore, Battles of the Nineteenth Century*, vol. 3 (London: Cassell, 1896), 336; and Christopher Hibbert, *The Great Mutiny* (London: Penguin, 1978), 275, 421. For officers taking service in the armies of other countries see Christopher Duffy, *The Military Experience in the Age of Reason* (London: Routledge and Kegan Paul, 1987).

were allowed to engage in trade, a sideline which was supplemented by even more profitable looting, indulged in by all ranks as the Company absorbed more areas of India in wars of aggression. The more astute Company regiments were versed in contract culture, and throughout their history both junior officers and men engaged in strikes when management attempted to transgress these. This culminated in the "White Mutiny" of 1858–9, when thousands of soldiers took over their barracks (even led by spokesmen quoting radical rhetoric, one named appropriately Benjamin Franklin Langford) refusing their forced transfer to the Queen's army – "A Manchester Strike" in the words of one hostile observer.[11]

The Raj and Racism

By the late nineteenth century India had become central to the working experience of the rank and file. With a considerable British army of up to 90,000 stationed there to avoid a repeat of the 1857 rising, most regular soldiers could expect to serve in the sub-continent, with an average length of service for an infantry battalion of fourteen years. With the abolition of the East India Company, the army and the expanding government became intertwined, creating new career paths for white soldiers which became standardized into a Town Major's List for each cantonment. As time elapsed soldiers were prevented from settling, such jobs being essential for those with Indian families, and absorbed up to 10 percent of British military manpower. These posts encompassed military secondments as instructors to sepoy regiments and to military, technical and medical establishments. There were also postings for soldiers with some education to junior government service of all types and jobs in public utilities such as railways, libraries and museums, plus engineering, telegraph and postal

---

[11] For a short survey of military strikes see Lawrence James, *Mutiny in the British and Commonwealth Forces, 1797–1956* (London: Buchan and Enright, 1987), 14–15. Stanley, *White Mutiny*, chaps. 10 and 11 is a detailed account. For other surveys of the "White Mutiny" – suppressed with minimal bloodshed compared with the black revolt of 1857 – see Fortescue, *History of the British Army*, vol 13, 528–9; and T. A. Heathcote, *The Military in British India: The Development of British Land Forces in South Asia, 1600–1947* (Manchester: Manchester University Press, 1995), 22–3. As late as 1890 a company of the 2nd Grenadier Guards in London refused to parade after what they regarded as excessive night duty, and were punished by six court martials and a posting to what was then regarded as an outlandish station, Bermuda: See Ian F. W. Beckett, *The Victorians at War* (London: Hambledon, 2003), 155.

services. These all brought status, more interesting employment, pensions and the opportunity to stay on in India for those who had married locally.[12]

Whilst in the "white Empire" most government jobs were taken by free settlers, expatriate ex-soldiers were employed in police forces and as instructors for local militias which had replaced British troops by 1870. Probably following the misguided ideas of classically educated civil servants, various attempts were made in Canada, South Africa, and New Zealand to set aside land holdings for ex-soldiers, to provide a caste of "military settlers" as the core of colonial self-defense. During the manpower shortage during the Crimean War there was even an experiment to settle German soldiers – from Hanover and Switzerland – in South Africa. Soldiers, however, did not necessarily make good farmers and these were largely unsuccessful.[13]

A considerable number of rank and file soldiers' memoirs emerged from the Napoleonic wars and some continued to be published during the wars of nineteenth-century imperialism. Just as rankers in the Peninsular war were scathing about their Spanish and Portuguese allies, whilst regarding their honorable French opponents in good light, later casual racism about black Indians or Africans was common. There is also evidence that high-caste Indian soldiers regarded British rankers as disgusting barbarians. Whilst racism was an underlying theme, interactions between soldiers and inhabitants – either indigenous locals or white settlers – varied enormously throughout the empire. Buckley's analysis of the Georgian Caribbean uncovers interracial cohabitation even in a society based on slavery, and the same seems to be true of India in the early days of imperialism before the Memsahibs and the regimental women arrived. The decline in the intimacy between the British imperialists and their host Indian community was a major contribution to the rebellion of 1857. Frank Richards's lively account as an Edwardian private illustrates the total lack of respect with which white soldiers then held Indian civilians. Hostility though could exist between white soldiers and free white colonists, for example in New Zealand, where the refusal of immigrants to subscribe to a war memorial for a departing regiment, caused the soldiers to include a

---

[12] Stanley, *White Mutiny*, chap. 12; and Holmes, *Soldier Sahib*, 149–150, 237–9. The impact of India on the English language is also immense.

[13] Davies, *Army in Victorian Society*, 203; Peter Reese, *Homecoming Heroes* (London: Leo Cooper, 1992); Fortescue, *History of the British Army*, vol. 12, 520; and vol. 13, 227; and Arthur Egerton, "The British German Legion, 1855–1856", *Journal of the Royal United Service Institute* 64 (1921).

dedication to their vanquished, but what they felt were more honorable, Maori opponents.[14]

Part of my wider research concerns soldiers displaying radical political opinions – with a sophisticated analysis of wars of conquest and their place in them, and sympathy for black people is a thread in some untutored memoirs like those of Sergeant John Pearman from the 1840s:

> For Instance when we find a part of the world that would be of use and a profit to us. We at once Covit the same. But then it is peopled - with a dark skinned race Gods people but what of that God as not made their views to meet ours in this he was not omnipotante, So we wish to make them Christians.I. E. Covit their Country it will bring a good return for their outlay – our first step is send out 6 or 8 missionary men...They meadle with the ways and the views that God as given them in his omnipotence. But the Christian do not consider that he as given the right way of thought. Well to bring this our next Step send a few soldiers they will soon show the way to become Christians. The next step is you must pay for the Loss you have put us to by being so stubborn as not to accept our views of religion. So you must pay the cost. now comes the grand step Annexation of their Country and in a short time afew years we send them a Bishop and all his host and you must pay for that likewise O John Bull you are a great rouge.

> India was to the white man a free Country we Could go where we liked no Trespass out there and John Company behaved well to us shared some of the Plunder with us Soldiers I mean in prize money not so the Queens Government and then John Company did not make us work found us plenty of servants plenty of Grog and good living if they were Thieves and stole the Country I must say they gave some of it to the Blood hounds (i. E. soldiers) [sic] who hunted down the rightful owners.

> After Morning Drill was over I was very fond of romeing the Country and Converseing with the natives - a people I Always found very kind if properly treated by us But I am Compeled to say some of our men used the Poor native very bad.[15]

---

[14] Hostility and racism displayed to allies are discussed in Charles Esdaile, *The Peninsular War: A New History* (London: Penguin, 2002), 199–201. Incipient racism is a constant theme in Colley, *Captives*; Buckley, *British Army*; and Richards, *Old Soldier Sahib*. For New Zealand see Fortescue, *History of the British Army,* vol. 13, 399–400, 490–1; and James Belich, *The New Zealand Wars and the Victorian Interpretation of Racial Conflict* (London: Penguin, 1986).

[15] Steedman, *Radical Soldier's Tale,* 146, 196–7, 209 (spelling and punctuation as original). For a wider discussion of nineteenth-century political radicalism amongst soldiers and ex-soldiers see the author's "Military Radicals and the Making of

Working-Class Toryism?

It is tempting to suggest that racism increased later as the empire became larger and more organized, and late-Victorian elementary education underpinned popular enthusiasm for its militaristic trappings. In the same period, with the extension of the United Kingdom franchise, the Conservative Party's imperial policies clearly won favour with many new working-class voters. It is difficult to assess whether these views were shared by soldiers and ex-soldiers. Whilst popular literature may be a confusing guide, it is interesting to find similar – and racist – views expressed in contributions by arch-Tory Rudyard Kipling and socialist Robert Blatchford, the founder of the Clarion movement. Blatchford, an ex-ranker in what had been one of the Company's white regiments, wrote a series of novels in imitation of Kipling, based on his Indian service. Other scholars studying the late-Victorian and Edwardian music hall have made conclusions relating to the impact the imperial military had on political affiliations. Gareth Stedman Jones concludes that it was effective in consolidating working-class conservatism, along with other factors, whilst Dave Russell identifies a class hostility towards "toffs" alongside pride in empire.[16]

Soldiers ("single men in barracks" to use Kipling's phrase) did not qualify to vote until 1918 and there seems to be no historical analysis of working-class voters who had family members serving in the forces. Whilst Frank Richards proudly depicts himself as a working-class Tory and racist, both in and out of the army, he also writes about his older

---

Class, 1790–1860", in Catriona Kennedy and Matthew McCormack, eds., *Men At Arms: Soldiering in Britain and Ireland, 1750–1850* (Basingstoke: Palgrave and Macmillan, forthcoming).

[16] For the importance of empire to popular conservatism see Martin Pugh, *The Tories and the People* (Oxford: Oxford University Press, 1985); and for its impact on popular culture see Michael Paris, *Warrior Nation: Images of British Popular Culture, 1850–2000* (London: Reaktion, 2000). Robert Blatchford, *Tell the Marines* (London: Clarion, 1901) and Rudyard Kipling, *Soldier Tales* (London: Macmillan, 1896). Blatchford's patriotic socialism is discussed in Paul Ward, *Flag and Union Jack: Englishness, Patriotism and the British Left, 1881–1924* (Woodbridge: Boydell and Brewer, 1998), chap. 4. Gareth Stedman Jones, "Languages of Class: Working-Class Culture and Working-Class Politics in London, 1870–1900", in Gareth Stedman Jones, *Studies in English Working-Class History, 1832–1982* (Cambridge: Cambridge University Press, 1983); and Dave Russell, "'We carved our way to glory': The British Soldier in Music Hall Song and Sketch, c.1880–1914", in John M. Mackenzie, ed., *Popular Imperialism and the Military, 1850–1950* (Manchester: Manchester University Press, 1992).

cousin David, whose service in the Boer War encouraged Frank's own enlistment, and who later served as a Labour councillor in South Wales. However it is clear that the officer corps, which had been divided between Liberal and Conservative for much of the nineteenth century, now came down firmly down in favour of the latter. By the end of the century, officers and MPs were nearly all Tory. Duncan Tanner's detailed work on Edwardian voting also indicates that garrison towns like Aldershot and communities dependent on naval or military expenditure like Chatham or Woolwich were invariably Tory.[17]

Conclusion

This chapter contends that labour history has much to teach us in the study of the working lives of soldiers, who made up the largest occupational group involved in imperialism. Just as class has been an important concept in understanding empire, so a new analysis of the importance of class in the structure of the British army can only contribute to explaining imperialism itself. This chapter has outlined some of the hidden working lives of common soldiers and opens the way for further research in this area. It also suggests that the appalling living conditions endured by the rank and file bear comparison with the worst endured by workers in the United Kindom's industrial revolution. Just as industrial workers used and adapted existing forms of resistance to fresh, oppressive circumstances, so nineteenth-century imperial soldiers could be found adopting pre-enlistment working-class mentalities in their own strategies of resistance. These might involve desertion or even suicide, but also yet-to-be-further-uncovered contract negotiations, work-to-rules, and strikes. It is difficult to assess the political attitudes of soldiers, given its opaque and contentious nature. However the subject is more complex than an initial examination would suggest, and there is clear evidence that some rank and file shared the political radical opinions widely displayed by contemporary civilian workers. Nonetheless, as service in the British Raj came to dominate the working lives of soldiers after 1857, racism clearly increased. It is likely that this racism in the context of army service (along with a popularization of imperial campaigns) contributed to the growing strength of late-Victorian working-class conservatism in the expanding democratic system.

---

[17] Richards, *Old Soldier Sahib*, 28–30, 66–7, 78–80. For the increasing political conservatism of the army, its connection with imperialism and its electoral impact, see Strachan, *Politics of the British Army*, chap. 5; Spiers, *Late Victorian Army*, 163, 166, 168; and Duncan Tanner, *Political Change and the Labour Party* (Cambridge: Cambridge University Press,1990), 176, 190.

The concept that British common soldiers in the nineteenth century were merely petty agents of British imperialism needs a more careful and informed analysis. They were capable of displaying ruthless brutality and endemic racism, but over an extraordinarily long period they suffered themselves from gross exploitation and class discrimination, to which they reacted with patterns of resistance learned in their pre-military lives. But to think of working class soldiers as just victims is to deny their free will and knowledge of a wider world on which they based their life decisions, however mistakenly this appears to modern eyes.

EMPIRE BEFORE LABOUR:
THE "SCRAMBLE FOR AFRICA"
AND THE MEDIA, 1880–99

CHRISTOPHER PRIOR

In recent years, much has been written about the stance that left-wing political bodies and newspapers took towards empire following the Jameson Raid. Bernard Porter's *Critics of Empire* continues to hold historians' attentions on this.[1] This has been augmented by a variety of works that focus on the Liberal split between 1899 and 1902.[2] Partha Gupta and, more recently, Stephen Howe, are amongst the many to have taken the discussion on into the Great War and beyond.[3] Less, however, has been said about the world of the left-wing press before the Boer War, and the era before the formalization of the Independent Labour Party in 1893 in particular. This is part of a wider relative neglect of the relationship between the left and empire in this period.[4] In an attempt to

---

[1] Bernard Porter, *Critics of Empire: British Radical Attitudes to Colonialism in Africa, 1895–1914* (London: Macmillan, 1968); see also Richard Price, *An Imperial War and the British Working Class: Working-Class Attitudes and Reactions to the Boer War, 1899–1902* (London: Routledge and Kegan Paul, 1972).

[2] Peter D. Jacobson, "Rosebery and Liberal Imperialism, 1899–1903", *Journal of British Studies* 13, no. 1 (1973), 83–107; John W. Auld, "The Liberal pro-Boers", *Journal of British Studies* 14, no. 2 (1975), 78–101; George L. Bernstein, "Sir Henry Campbell-Bannerman and the Liberal Imperialists", *Journal of British Studies* 23, no. 1 (1983), 105–24; Mark Hampton, "The Press, Patriotism, and Public Discussion: C. P. Scott, the *Manchester Guardian*, and the Boer War, 1899–1902", *Historical Journal* 44, no. 1 (2001), 177–97.

[3] Partha S. Gupta, *Imperialism and the British Labour Movement, 1914–1964* (London: Macmillan, 1975); Stephen Howe, *Anticolonialism in British Politics: The Left and the End of Empire, 1918–64* (Oxford: Clarendon Press, 1993).

[4] For example, in his monumental *British Workers and the Independent Labour Party*, David Howell does mention attitudes towards Home Rule and the Boer War, but little else to do with imperialism; see David Howell, *British Workers and*

redress this, recent work by Andrew Thompson has discussed the relationship between workers and the empire, but only in a very general sense, and without spending any time on the "Scramble for Africa", which is understandable given the broad remit of his study.[5] The present chapter aims to begin to fill this clear gap in the historical record, and it will attempt this by answering two simple questions. Firstly, what was written about the scramble by the left-wing media? Secondly, why did they say what they said? To conclude, the ramifications of this for our understanding of late nineteenth-century society will be examined.

The focus will be upon *Commonweal*, *Reynolds's Newspaper*, and *Justice*. The reason for their selection is that they represented very different points along the left-wing spectrum. As Porter has argued, *Reynolds's Newspaper* is best described as a democratic Republican paper with strong sympathies towards the labour, trade union and co-operative movements, rather than as an out-and-out Labour paper like Robert Blatchford's *Clarion* or Keir Hardie's *Labour Leader*.[6] *Reynolds's Newspaper* sold well, topping 350,000 copies a week in the 1870s with its blend of sensationalism and radical politics. At the other end of the spectrum, the most vocal of all journalist critics of empire in the 1880s and early 1890s was probably William Morris, who used his Socialist League publication *Commonweal* as a mouthpiece for his revolutionary views.[7] This, in contrast to *Reynolds's Newspaper*, was only selling around 3,000 copies per weekly issue in the 1880s.[8] Selling a similar number to this, and lying somewhere between the other two works, is our third publication, H. M. Hyndman's *Justice*, the mouthpiece of the Social Democratic Federation.

In the 1880s, left-wing papers did not cover imperial events as extensively as their more centrist Tory and Liberal peers; this is notable

---

the *Independent Labour Party, 1888–1906* (Manchester: Manchester University Press, 1983),138–43, 345–7; see also Martin Crick, *The History of the Social-Democratic Federation* (Keele: Ryburn Publishing, 1994), chap. 11.

[5] Andrew Thompson, *The Empire Strikes Back?: The Impact of Imperialism on Britain from the Mid Nineteenth Century* (Harlow: Pearson Longman, 2005), 38–95.

[6] Porter, *Critics*, 101.

[7] Morris to Andreas Scheu, Sep. 15, 1883, in N. Kelvin, ed., *The Collected Letters of William Morris*, vol. 2 (Princeton: Princeton University Press, 4 vols., 1987), 230.

[8] In 1887, 52 numbers of *Commonweal* were produced, which sold 152,186 copies in total, making an average of just under 3,000 copies per edition: Henry Pelling, *The Origins of the Labour Party, 1880–1900* (Oxford: Clarendon Press, 1965), 45, n. 3.

even if we take into account the fact that most of the former were printed weekly or monthly, and were therefore physically unable to publish as much news as daily papers like *The Times* or the *Leeds Mercury*.[9] For instance, in Uganda, between 1885 and 1887, forty-five African converts to Christianity, and the Anglican missionary James Hannington, were killed on the orders of the kabaka of Buganda, Mwanga. In comparison with papers such as the *Manchester Times*, the *Derby Mercury* and the *Leeds Mercury*, *Reynolds's Newspaper* made very little of the Hannington case.[10] The one occasion *Reynolds's Newspaper* passed any relatively lengthy comment was when it praised the work Hannington and his followers had been able to do in Uganda prior to Hannington's murder. The paper argued that the missionaries had, for a long time, been quietly getting on with teaching Africans to read and so on, and had not done anything to antagonize Mwanga.[11]

Upon broadening out *Reynolds's Newspaper*'s examinations of missionaries, something interesting can be seen. When it came to specific incidents, the paper was invariably sympathetic in its assessment of the intentions of missionaries and empathetic in its assessment of the dangers missionaries faced.[12] And yet, when it spoke, albeit infrequently, in general terms without naming names, the paper claimed that missionaries were having a negative influence on Africa – that they were turning Africans into drunkards was a particularly frequent refrain, and that money was being spent on Africans when it should have been spent at home, improving the lot of the workers – a sentiment redolent of Dickens in *Bleak House*.[13] Such a disjuncture is interesting; given that the paper viewed itself as being propagandist in tone, one might have assumed that any divergences of viewpoint would not be so great. Whilst *Reynolds's Newspaper* heavily condemned the Boer War in tones much akin to those

---

[9] In the 1880s, both of these publications were published daily, excepting Sundays.
[10] "The Murder of Bishop Hannington", *Manchester Times*, Oct. 30, 1886, 2; the editorial in *Glasgow Herald*, Nov. 2, 1886, 4; "The Uganda Massacres", *Leeds Mercury*, Nov. 4, 1886, 12; "The Terrible Massacre in Uganda", *Derby Mercury*, Nov. 10, 1886, 8; "The Massacre of Christians in Uganda", *The Belfast News-letter*, Nov. 13, 1886, 6.
[11] "Bishop Hannington", *Reynolds's Newspaper*, Jan. 3, 1886, 5; see also "Foreign Telegrams", *Reynolds's Newspaper*, Sep. 26, 1886, 1.
[12] "Massacre of a Missionary Party", *Reynolds's Newspaper*, Aug. 28, 1887, 2.
[13] "The Democratic Show; or, the World we Live in", *Reynolds's Newspaper*, July 25, 1886, 6; "The Democratic Show; or, the World we Live in", *Reynolds's Newspaper*, Aug. 29, 1886, 4; see also Tom Maguire, "A Light on Darkest Africa", *Labour Leader*, May 5, 1894, 7; "Notes and criticisms", *Labour Leader*, Jan. 19, 1895, 7.

of J. A. Hobson, before this conflict there was a lack of inclination to go directly for the imperial jugular.

Therefore, the paper tended to criticize London for policies that were felt to be wasteful or unnecessary, such as the Emin Pasha relief expedition of 1886 onwards, rather than to criticize the existence of the British empire *per se*.[14] In a front-page editorial in January 1880, the paper argued that "The present [Conservative] Government is utterly lost to any sense of shame ... We are destroying every vestige of native Government in Afghanistan and Zululand, and in South Africa we are destroying a republic." This is as one might expect of an "anti-imperial" stance. However, this is immediately qualified by the line "We are creating a necessity for setting up a Government beyond our scientific frontier." The article subscribes to the belief, expressed by many late-Victorian imperial geographers, and by later radical theorists of empire such as E. D. Morel, that there were certain places that the British should be in Africa, and there were certain places that they should not. Rather crudely, the British were fine to occupy the Cape Colony, but to go further north into the Boer republics was to invite disaster for a whole host of reasons, such as indigenous resistance and problems in coping with the climate. The article was evidently taking its cues from the atmosphere that had carried Gladstone along on a wave of public support following his famous Midlothian campaigns of 1879–80, rather than from Cobden and Bright; this was not a critique of imperialism so much as a critique of imperial overstretch. It was a critique that would have appeased those individuals who disliked men such as Sir Garnet Wolseley and, later, Frederick Lugard, who were felt willing to do anything to expand the empire in Africa, whilst simultaneously appealing to those with a sense of pride in Britain's imperial history who maintained that present imperial activity was undermining the efforts of past British heroes.[15]

In his excellent biography of William Morris, E. P. Thompson argues that Morris felt imperialism was the "deadliest enemy to internationalism

---

[14] "Stanley's exploits, and their consequences", *Reynolds's Newspaper*, Apr. 7, 1889, 4. This was an event that met with a barrage of press attention amongst both the Liberal and Tory papers of the day; see, for example, "The Relief of Emin Pasha", *Bristol Mercury and Daily Post*, Dec. 28, 1886, 6; "The Relief of Emin Pasha", *Leeds Mercury*, Dec. 28, 1886, 4; "The Emin Pasha Relief Expedition", *Graphic*, Jan. 29, 1887, 113.

[15] "The Voice of Birmingham", *Reynolds's Newspaper*, Jan. 25, 1880, 1. For Morel, this was because such colonisation led naturally to European tensions and, eventually, outright war; Edmund D. Morel, *Africa and the Peace of Europe* (London: Routledge, 1917; repr. 1998), esp. 21–3, 51–2, 79–115.

and to the cause of the people at home",[16] and this is particularly clear from Morris's private letters. But his public declarations on empire were relatively limited, both in *Justice* and, later on, in *Commonweal*. He did weigh in heavily against British involvement in Egypt and Ireland. In 1884, he argued "[t]he workers have many accounts to settle nearer home, without allowing a Liberal government to promote reaction under the pretence of putting down slave-dealing, or to annex Egypt for the benefit of the upper and middle classes."[17] However, he did not comment on a lot else to do with Africa and, as time went on, his writing became more despondent as to the potential for imperial policy to be altered,[18] as will be discussed later. In fact, Morris went so far as to, on occasion, ask that private comments he made be kept from public view. In an 1882 letter to an old Icelandic friend,[19] Morris remarked of those who denied the existence of the famine going on in Iceland at the time:

> As for these scoundrels, who are of the type of cooly-traffickers & rum & canon missionaries who have disgraced us all over the world, it is of little use noticing them; it only advertises them.

E. P. Thompson argues that "[t]act was never Morris's strong point", pitching him as rather a loose cannon,[20] and yet, at the end of the letter, Morris asked his friend not to publicly disclose the thoughts the letter revealed.[21] Instead Morris's public focus was mainly on a domestic plan of revolutionary socialism.[22] Another prominent writer for *Commonweal* was Ernest Belfort Bax. In 1885, Bax wrote in positive tones about the impact of socialism on empire:

> And now a word as to the attitude of Socialists towards the imperial question. For the Socialist the word frontier does not exist; for him love of country, as such, is no nobler sentiment than love of class. The blustering

---

[16] E. P. Thompson, *William Morris: Romantic to Revolutionary* (New York: Pantheon, 1976), 389.

[17] "The bondholders' battue", *Justice* 1 no. 4 (1884), 4.

[18] See, for instance, Nicholas Salmon, "Introduction", in William Morris (N. Salmon, ed.), *Political Writings: Contributions to Justice and Commonweal, 1883–1890* (Bristol: Thoemmes, 1994), xxxvii.

[19] Morris had known Magnússon since 1870; Morris to Scheu, Sep. 15, 1883, in Kelvin, ed., *Collected Letters*, vol. 2, 229.

[20] Thompson, *Morris*, 229.

[21] Morris to Magnússon, Oct. 2, 1882, in Kelvin, ed., *Collected Letters*, vol. 2, 132.

[22] William Morris, *Useful Work v. Useless Toil* (London, 1885), repr. in M. May, ed., *The Collected Works of William Morris* (New York: Russell & Russell, 24 vols., 1966), vol. 23, 98–120.

"patriot", big with England's glory, is precisely on a level with the bloated
plutocrat, proud to belong to that great "middle class", which he assures
you is the "backbone of the nation". Race-pride and class-pride are, from
the standpoint of Socialism, involved in the same condemnation. The
establishment of Socialism, therefore, on any national or race basis is out
of the question.[23]

For Bax, it was only a brief matter of time before the empire would
fall, which is in line with the sorts of arguments that would later be made
in varying forms by Lenin, Rosa Luxemburg, and so on. But, as time
progressed, Bax became increasingly disheartened about whether the
workers would bring about the end of empire. In 1888 he suggested in one
of his articles that the exploitation of Africa might prolong the life of
capitalism, perhaps by as much as a century.[24] However, yet again, Bax's
comments were largely confined to a few sporadic outbursts.

Those imperial areas that were subjected to the most left-wing scrutiny
in the 1880s and early 1890s were India, Egypt, Ireland and, increasingly,
South Africa.[25] However, even then the coverage was not sustained; for
instance, with the British occupation of 1882 receding into the distance,
1886 and 1887 editions of *Justice* covered Egypt less than had previously
been the case. Elsewhere received little or no attention; across the sweep
of papers there was very little content about sub-Saharan Africa.[26]
Interestingly, C. L. Fitzgerald, writing in *Justice* in 1884, argued that
Britain's involvement in Egypt and Sudan "may ere long cause an outburst
of furious [Islamic] fanaticism which would endanger the safety of every
European settlement in Africa."[27] It was later argued in the same paper
that the fact that the British were displaying their vulnerability in their
defeats at the hands of the Mahdhists was stirring up Islamic activity in
India,[28] and that the "security of the Suez Canal can be attained more
completely without occupation than with."[29] The actions of Hicks and

---

[23] E. Belfort Bax, "Imperialism v. Socialism", repr. in his *The Religion of
Socialism: Being Essays in Modern Socialist Criticism* (New York: Books for
Libraries Press, 1902; 1972), 126.
[24] Bax, "Africa", *Commonweal*, July 28, 1888, 3.
[25] "The Principles of *Justice*", *Justice*, Jan. 19, 1884, 4; H. M. Hyndman, "How we
Govern India", *Justice*, Jan. 26, 1884, 3; Adolphe Smith, "English Workmen and
Egyptian affairs: II", *The Labour Standard*, Apr. 22, 1882, 5.
[26] "Clear out", *Justice*, Dec. 4, 1886, 1; "Man-hunting", *Justice*, Jan. 22, 1887, 1;
Hyndman, "Social Democracy and Home Rule", *Justice*, Apr. 2, 1887, 4.
[27] C. L. Fitzgerald, "England (with Israel) in Egypt", *Justice*, Jan. 26, 1884, 4.
[28] "Indian Curry", *Justice*, Feb. 16, 1884, 1.
[29] Fitzgerald, "Nemesis in Egypt", *Justice*, Feb. 23, 1884, 4.

those like him were being criticized on the basis that they were harming a wider imperial set-up. However, as was noted above, references to empire in *Justice* are notable by their relative absence.

Thus, the period is interesting not only for the presence of material, but also for the absence of material. The lack of sustained interrogations of imperial activities in Africa is notable, both in papers, and in other prominent forms of print media such as pamphlets. For example, one of the more popular Fabian tracts, Sidney Webb's *Socialism: True and False*, makes no mention of empire at all, which is all the more impressive given the length of the tract, Webb's interest in empire, and his later position as secretary of state for the colonies and for dominion affairs in the second MacDonald government.[30] And this is not a pattern limited to the press; it is indicative of a wider approach towards empire across those who constituted the different facets of the diverse labour movement. Whilst the MP for Battersea John Burns spoke in seventy-eight debates in 1893 and 1894, only one of these was in any way related to empire – the speech concerned the Government of Ireland Bill. Similarly, Keir Hardie spoke frequently in the House of Commons. However, the only instance of his mentioning the empire between 1892 and 1895 was when, in 1893, he asked the undersecretary of state for India whether 300 tonnes of plant and machinery for public works in Calcutta had been given to a German-registered steamer and if so, why was this happening in spite of a depressed British labour market?

J. Havelock Wilson, whilst not strictly independent of the Liberals, focused his energies upon speaking on behalf of sea and navy types. George Howell, a "Lib-Lab" MP for Bethnal Green, barely mentioned the empire, and on the rare occasions when he did, he avoided making any contentious points, instead only raising issues that were linked to the labour movement and the working classes in a very direct way. For instance, on March 8, 1892, he spoke about meat being sold in Hong Kong and how this affected the people of Deptford, but he declined to take part in the discussions surrounding the Imperial British East Africa Company that took place only a couple of minutes later. On March 14, 1895, Howell chose to ask three brief questions about trade unions in the colonies and the difficulties they had in depositing money in banks, but he played no

---

[30] The pamphlet was into its seventh reprint by Oct. 1933: Sidney Webb, *Socialism: True and False* (London: The Fabian Society, 1894).

part in the major debate concerning Swaziland that took place a little later in the same session.[31]

And yet at this time there was a good deal of criticism – ranging from vitriolic through to critical but yet still imperialist – that was being aimed at London's imperial policies. It is necessary to set aside the main thrust of the narrative for the moment to evaluate these. There were three overlapping groups of people who attacked governmental policy. Firstly, there were those radical Liberals who went far beyond Gladstone in their condemnation of empire. This includes figures such as Herbert Spencer and Wilfrid Lawson, prominent examples of radical Liberals perpetuating John Bright's extreme free-trader stance. Whilst Lawson was opposed to socialism, adopting the oft-heard Liberal argument that change came primarily from moral reform and self-help rather than alterations to economic structures, he spoke out in support of just about every radical measure going in the late nineteenth century, from the disestablishment of the Irish church to the abolition of alcohol. It is therefore unsurprising to learn that in both the House of Commons and some provincial papers such as the *West Cumberland Times*, Lawson fervently opposed British intervention in the Gold Coast, Fiji, South Africa, Egypt, and so on, arguing that Britain's imperial policy should be one of retrenchment.[32]

Secondly, there were those imperialist figures and papers that had nailed their colours firmly to a particular conception of empire and who were trying to move the whole imperial edifice towards this. The *Morning Post* is a key example. Over the course of the nineteenth century, the paper had gradually dropped both its hostile stance towards the so-called "little wars" in the empire and its admiring attitude towards indigenous peoples, and came to see imperialism in a very positive light, going so far as to excuse the Jameson Raid on the grounds that, because they were such a truculent people, the Boers needed reminding that the British were "in the right in South Africa". Nevertheless, the *Post*'s imperialist correspondent G. A. Henty continually filled his reports with criticisms of the way that the British were conducting their military campaigns; he had very

---

[31] *Hansard Parliamentary Debates*, 4th ser., 2 (1892), col. 315; *Hansard*, 4th ser., 31 (1895), cols. 1051–2; *Hansard*, 4th ser., 13 (1893), cols. 673–7; *Hansard*, 4th ser., 11 (1883) col. 18; on Wilson, see Pelling, *Origins*, 106.
[32] Terry Carrick, "Wilfrid Lawson: Attitudes and Opinions on Britain's Imperial Policy, 1868–1892" (PhD diss., Sheffield Hallam University, 2007); Herbert Spencer, *The Man versus the State* (London: Williams and Norgate, 1894); Bernard Semmel, *The Liberal Ideal and the Demons of Empire: Theories of Imperialism from Adam Smith to Lenin* (Baltimore: Johns Hopkins University Press, 1993), 108–9.

particular ideas about imperial military reform. Elsewhere, his paper pushed ahead of what the British government was doing, for instance in calling for Germany to be brought into a firmer alliance with Britain in Africa.[33]

And, thirdly, there were nationalists who had very particular reasons for criticising certain aspects of imperial policy. For example, the staunchly Unionist *Glasgow Herald*'s belief in the British empire was never in doubt. During the Boer War it went so far as to endorse the breaking up of pro-Boer meetings.[34] But it was prepared to criticize the English when it was felt that they were building empires that shut out opportunities for others such as the French, one "ludicrous" example of which was the refusal to let the French colonize a portion of Western Australia.[35] Furthermore, the paper felt that the Scots deserved a bigger role in running the empire because, they alleged, they possessed a finer social policy mindset than the English, being more egalitarian in their approach to education and espousing Presbyterianism rather than Anglicanism.[36] This desire to reorientate imperialism along Scottish lines was a common thread running through the period and out the other end; it is there, for instance, in John Buchan's writing in the early years of the

---

[33] I am obliged to Thomas de Lucy for discussions with him on this subject; Wilfrid Hindle, *The* Morning Post, *1772–1937: Portrait of a Newspaper* (London: Routledge, 1937), 223–9. In a large number of arenas, antagonism between Britain and Germany was rife; for a comprehensive discussion of this see Paul M. Kennedy, *The Rise of Anglo-German Antagonism, 1860–1914* (London: Allen and Unwin, 1980); on European rivalries in China, see, for example, Peter Cain and Tony Hopkins, *British Imperialism, 1688–2000* (Harlow: Longman Pearson, 2002), 368–71.

[34] Richard Finlay, "The Scottish Press and Empire, 1850–1914", in Simon J. Potter, ed., *Newspapers and Empire in Ireland and Britain: Reporting the British Empire, c.1857–1921* (Dublin: Four Courts, 2004), 70.

[35] Editorial, *Glasgow Herald*, May 15, 1880, 4; see also David S. Forsyth, "Empire and Union: Imperial and National Identity in Nineteenth-Century Scotland", *Scottish Geographical Magazine* 113, no. 1 (1997), 6. If population discrepancies are taken into account, as John Mackenzie has written, the Scots were relatively more involved in the empire than the English; John Mackenzie, "Empire and National Identities: The Case of Scotland", *Transactions of the Royal Historical Society* 8 (1998), 215–31.

[36] This emphasis on equality in education was an essential part of the urban educated middle-class Scotsman's arsenal ever since the 1872 Education Act: Forsyth, "Empire and Union", 7–8. The reality away from the urban centres was, however, not always so egalitarian; T. C. Smout, *A Century of the Scottish people, 1830–1950* (1986; London: Fontana, 1997), 216–7.

twentieth century, which goes above and beyond the declarations of the
likes of Baden-Powell in its espousal of the spartan outdoors life.[37]
The journalist T. P. O'Connor, who combined Irish nationalism and
Liberal imperialism, had a particular conception as to the way imperial
business should be conducted. As befitted a Home Ruler, he used his
papers the *Sun* and the *Star* in an unsuccessful attempt to convince the
British public that an empire-wide decentralization of control would
cement the whole enterprise together. Whilst distasteful of "jingoism", he
believed a rational appraisal of empire would provide a better sense of
where it was best for the British to get themselves involved overseas. So,
for instance, whilst O'Connor thought that Gordon had done great things
to further Britain's influence around the world, he had been sent into an
impossible situation in Sudan, mainly thanks to the machinations of the
rabble-rousing W. T. Stead at the *Pall Mall Gazette*.[38] Measured criticisms
of empire can also be seen in the works of Owen Morgan Edwards
promoting Welsh nationhood via his writings in the paper *Cymru*.[39]

This aside has been necessary to establish the point that, rather than the
1880s and the early 1890s being solely a period of unthinking jingoism,
there were a variety of debates about imperial policies, even if the actual
right of the empire to exist was rarely called into question. And this makes
the nature of the left-wing debate on the issue all the more interesting. The
left was made up of people who often suffered privation, harassment,

---

[37] John Buchan, *The African Colony: Studies in the Reconstruction* (London:
Blackwood, 1903); Buchan, *Prester John* (London: Nelson, 1910); John Buchan,
The Thirty-Nine Steps (London: Blackwood, 1915); John Buchan, *Greenmantle*
(London: Hodder and Stoughton, 1916); John Buchan, *The Island of Sheep*
(London: Hodder and Stoughton, 1936); John Buchan, *Memory Hold the Door*
(London: Hodder and Stoughton, 1940); Andrew Lownie, *John Buchan: The
Presbyterian Cavalier* (Boston, MA: David R. Godine, 2003); David Daniell, *The
Interpreter's House: A Critical Assessment of John Buchan* (London: Nelson,
1975); Juanita Kruse, *John Buchan (1875–1940) and the Idea of Empire: Popular
Literature and Political Ideology* (Lewiston, New York: Mellen, 1989).
[38] Ian Sheehy, "'The View from Fleet Street': Irish Nationalist Journalists in
London and their Attitudes towards Empire, 1892–1898", in Potter, ed.,
Newspapers and Empire, 151–8; T. P. O'Connor, *Memoirs of an Old
Parliamentarian*, vol. 1 (London: Benn, 1929), 302–7. This undermines Brady's
argument that it was only when O'Connor stood on a platform with Winston
Churchill in Liverpool in 1914 and spoke up for imperial solidarity that there was a
"distinct change" in his outlook: L. W. Brady, *T. P. O'Connor and the Liverpool
Irish* (London: Royal Historical Society, 1983), 220.
[39] Aled Jones and Bill Jones, "Empire and the Welsh Press", in Potter, ed.,
Newspapers and Empire, 83–8.

depression and the occasional arrest whilst standing up for what they believed in.[40] So why were they disinclined to make sustained attacks upon empire? Why did self-censorship and the sidelining of empire as a cause for debate prevail? The remainder of this chapter will focus on three potential reasons for why the British left-wing press might have said relatively little about the scramble. Firstly, that there were some on the left who had imperialist tendencies. Secondly, that there was limited access to details of what was going on "on the spot" in Africa. And lastly, that journalists perceived the working classes to be imperialist.

Some on the left at this time were strong believers in the maintenance of the British empire, men such as H. M. Hyndman of the Social Democratic Federation.[41] Hyndman had criticized Stanley's activities in East Africa,[42] later declaring that such a denunciation "did something to check filibustering journalistic missioners in their ruthless destruction of natives of the countries they explore".[43] He did, however, support the annexation of Fiji by the British in 1874 and the wars against the Afghans in 1879.[44] Although his views on empire would later change dramatically, in the 1880s and 1890s he believed that a revolution would solve Britain's problems and allow it to take a stronger stand in holding the empire together.[45] Consequently, in the last quarter of the nineteenth century, the Social Democratic Federation's publication *Justice* reflected Hyndman's

---

[40] T. W. Moody, "Michael Davitt and the British Labour Movement, 1882–1906", *Transactions of the Royal Historical Society*, 5th ser., 3 (1953), 65.

[41] Chushichi Tsuzuki, *H. M. Hyndman and British Socialism* (Oxford: Oxford University Press, 1961), 2.

[42] Henry Mayers Hyndman, *The Record of an Adventurous Life* (London: Macmillan, 1911), 165–6; see also Felix Driver, "Henry Morton Stanley and his Critics: Geography, Exploration and Empire", *Past and Present* 133, no. 1 (1991), 151–4.

[43] Hyndman, *Record*, 166, 176.

[44] Tsuzuki, *Hyndman*, 16, 18–9.

[45] Ibid., 48. Despite his increasing criticism of imperialism after the Boer War, he would still argue for a reformed India policy that attained the "re-establishment of genuine Indian rule throughout Hindustan, under light English leadership ... [would lead to] the terrible drain of produce without commercial return being stanched. Thus India from then onwards would ... have gained steadily in wealth and have become, on friendly terms with us, one of the finest Empires the world has ever seen. That, I say, was my belief then, that is still my conviction now": Hyndman, *Further Reminiscences* (London: Macmillan, 1912), 31, 151–73; see also Hyndman, *Colonies and Dependencies: Report to the International Socialist Congress* (London: Twentieth Century Press, 1904); Hyndman, *The Unrest in India* (London: Twentieth Century Press, 1907).

imperialist viewpoint despite its condemnation of the specific instances of imperial activity in India, Ireland and Egypt.[46] In essence, it rallied against "imperialism", which it equated with capitalism, whilst approving of "colonialism", which it felt had the capability to precipitate the emergence of "socialistic democracies in voluntary connection with the greater democracy of these Islands".[47] The same thing can be said of the approach that the *Labour Standard* tended to take; the paper argued that imperialism was "tinsel" and the opposite of a "true national morality",[48] but that the colonialism of South Africa, like that of Canada, was of a positive benefit for all concerned. In 1881, the paper argued that Boer actions in the Transvaal made for "disquieting news", and that it was "absolutely essential that the parts of South Africa in British possession should no longer be imperilled by quarrels of the Boers with Basutos and Zulus".[49] This qualified support for certain facets of the British empire prefigured other notable examples, such as Blatchford's *Clarion*, which sided with the British against the Boers during the second Anglo-Boer War,[50] and the writings of George Bernard Shaw, who in 1900 argued that a reformed empire would be an effective vehicle for the spread of Fabian socialism.[51]

However, Hyndman was, of course, on the right of the Social Democratic Federation.[52] He made a lot of enemies, most notably Morris, who split from the SDF citing Hyndman's autocratic nature and his alleged jingoism. However, a relative absence of discussions about Africa cannot simply be attributed to imperial sympathizing. There has to be something more. The second potential reason is that there was little news coming out of certain parts of Africa, and that such small amounts were coming out of very few mouths. This is a point that has increasingly been stressed in modern histories of the media. For instance, Simon Potter has argued that the provincial press's reliance on *The Times* for its foreign bare-bones content meant that many papers ended up taking quite non-

---

[46] For interesting displays of this, see "The 'imperial' federation of profit-mongers", *Justice*, Aug. 2, 1884, 1; "Tory Empire", *Justice*, Apr. 25, 1885, 1; "Empire and Freedom", *Justice*, May 9, 1885, 1.

[47] "Plutocratic Imperialism", *Justice*, May 2, 1885, 1; see also "A Communistic Experiment in Africa", *Clarion*, Feb. 13, 1892, 4.

[48] "Lord Derby and Imperialism", *The Labour Standard*, Jan. 14, 1882, 4; Henry Crompton, "Imperialism", *The Labour Standard*, July 23, 1881, 5.

[49] "News of the week", *The Labour Standard*, May 14, 1881, 1; see also "Emigration as a Remedy", *The Labour Standard*, June 10, 1882, 5.

[50] Howell, *British Workers*, 380–3.

[51] [Fabian Society,] George B. Shaw, ed., *Fabianism and the Empire: A Manifesto by the Fabian Society* (London: Grant Richards, 1900).

[52] Hyndman, *Record*, 177–8, 231, 237–8.

Liberal lines on African affairs.[53] This can be witnessed in the Ugandan example noted above; papers such as *Reynolds's Newspaper* did not set the agenda on most imperial issues. They were merely responsive to what more mainstream commentators were discussing, and they were, for the most part, beholden to the sort of information available to all journalists.

However, any access to knowledge or otherwise fails to explain both the existence of self-censorship and why there was less on imperial matters in the leftist press than elsewhere. This tendency would suggest that the relationship of most causal significance was not that between access to knowledge and public dissemination, but that between journalists' private perceptions and public dissemination, which leads to the third potential factor, the matter of working-class imperialism.

Most on the left were disconsolate during the 1880s and early 1890s as to their ability to change workers' perceptions. Morris would privately write that "it is obvious that the support to be looked for for constructive Socialism from the working classes at present is nought."[54] This meant that, as he wrote in the *Hammersmith Socialist Record*,

> the truth is, any approach to Jingoism, however feeble, is certain to be popular with the whole mass of non-political people, i.e. about 999 out of the 1,000; who, though non-political, do nevertheless vote on occasion.[55]

It was such pessimism that marked his attitudes towards the British workers and helps account for why he felt that anti-imperial rhetoric had failed to have the desired effect. Joseph Burgess, press editor of various small publications such as *Workman's Times*, was continually pessimistic about the ability of socialists to win workers away from the Liberals,[56] while in 1893 *Reynolds's Newspaper* was remarkably blunt in its assertion that the "English people are naturally inclined to Conservatism".[57]

---

[53] Potter, "Empire and the English Press, c.1857–1914", in Potter, ed., *Newspapers and Empire*, 45.

[54] Morris to Georgiana Burne-Jones, Aug. 26, 1883, in Kelvin, ed., *Collected Letters*, vol. 2, 219; see also Morris to Jane Morris, Feb. 25, 1884, in ibid., vol. 2, 265.

[55] Morris, untitled article, *Hammersmith Socialist Record*, Feb. 1893, 1.

[56] Kevin McPhillips, *Joseph Burgess (1853–1934) and the Founding of the Independent Labour Party* (Lewiston, New York: Edwin Mellen Press, 2005), 60. Similarly, Hyndman would remark in 1912 that "the Trade Unionists, unfortunately, have not ceased to grovel before the Liberals": Hyndman, *Further Reminiscences*, 104.

[57] "Reform the Constitution", *Reynolds's Newspaper*, Sep. 24, 1893, 1.

Simultaneously, newspapers on the left frequently found it hard to make a profit and to keep going. For instance, despite Joseph Burgess's national prominence due to his notable role in the establishment of the ILP, he suffered great difficulties in trying to get any of his papers to pay their way, and so they did not last long.[58] Similarly, as noted above, both *Commonweal* and *Justice* sold poorly, and had to be kept afloat by a few generous donors.[59] There was at this time a distinct fragility about the labour movement as an organizational phenomenon.[60] By 1880 there was already a history of failure on the part of left-wingers attempting to rouse labour movements in support of the rhetoric and ideas that would become widespread during the course of the Boer War. For instance, the positivists repeatedly attempted to try and lift trade unionism above its concerns with local and craft allegiances, but in the end, activist intellectuals such as Henry Crompton had to admit defeat.[61] More specifically, many leftist journalists despaired of working-class attitudes, feeling that as a whole they were either enthusiastic or, at the most, apathetic about empire, but

---

[58] His *Workman's Times* only lasted from 1890 until 1894: McPhillips, *Joseph Burgess*, passim, and esp. 71–87.

[59] Pelling, *Origins*, 30, 32; Thompson, *Morris*, 463; see also Morris to Burne-Jones, Dec. 29, 1883, in Kelvin, ed., *Collected Letters*, vol. 2, 252; Morris to Jenny Morris, in ibid., vol. 2, 261.

[60] This is a matter that has already received sustained scholarly scrutiny. For example, see Andrew Thorpe, *A History of the British Labour Party* (Basingstoke: Palgrave, 1997; repr. 2001), 1–4; Martin Pugh, *The Making of Modern British politics, 1867–1939* (Oxford: Blackwell, 1982; repr. 1993), 79–80. Whatever problems the Liberals were having on both a national stage and in local regions such as Manchester, these cannot compete with the troubles facing the Independent Labour Party, even if the 1890s saw the laying of the groundwork for the successes that were to follow the Gladstone-MacDonald pact of 1903; for one case study of how the Progressive Alliance of the 1890s harmed the Liberals by causing their retreat into their middle-class electoral heartlands, see James Robert Moore, "Progressive Pioneers: Manchester Liberalism, the Independent Labour Party, and Local Politics in the 1890s", *Historical Journal* 44, no. 4 (2001), 989–1013. Even then, the 1900 election saw support for the Conservative "anti-Boer" stance from all sections of British society; Paul Readman, "The Conservative Party, Patriotism, and British Politics: The Case of the General Election of 1900", *Journal of British Studies* 40, no. 1 (2001), 107–45.

[61] Royden Harrison, *Before the Socialists: Studies in Labour and Politics, 1861–1881* (Aldershot: Gregg Revivals, 1965; repr. 1994), 311–2; see also Pugh, *The Making*, 78; E. S. Beesly, "France and Tunis", *Labour Standard*, June 11, 1881, 4–5; "Professor Beesly Sees which Way the Cat Jumps", *The Workers' Herald*, Jan. 16, 1892, 4.

that they were rarely opposed to it.[62] Once again, Morris's letters are particularly illuminating for their castigation of the masses for failing to appreciate the supposedly dangerous implications of empire for workers' wellbeing.

What does all of this tell us of the relationship between left-wing journalists and the "masses"? The most immediate conclusion to make is that, during the 1880s and early-to-mid 1890s, left-wing newspapers tended to avoid making controversial statements on empire when these could not be demonstrably linked to the immediate aims of the labour movement. This is not to say that all on the left were completely quiet. As noted above, there were some persistent denunciations of British actions; these, however, tended to concern particular areas, most notably Egypt, Ireland, India and, a little later, South Africa. Journalists on the left were only prepared to mount a sustained attack on imperial actions in instances when they felt that the British public already perceived such actions to have been the result of capitalism and not philanthropic intent. For opening up this debate, radical Liberals must take a great deal of the credit. Intervention in Egypt was already widely felt to have been due to the interests of large European banks and "bondholders". British policy in Ireland was often seen as a means of sustaining or bolstering the rights of landowners at the expense of the workers. The actions of the British in relation to the Boers, particularly those of the Transvaal, were widely viewed as predicated on the need to maintain the profits of the gold and diamond miners.

The British left played up those instances that were felt most pertinent to the domestic political struggle by highlighting the supposed universality of capitalist evil. Where there was less known about a particular region, and where it was harder for papers to provide tangible evidence that capital was the sole or paramount deciding matter in such a region, the left did not seek to potentially antagonize its followers by criticising the empire. The popular view went that Britain was primarily involved in tropical Africa as a means of preventing slavery, saving souls, and making geographical and scientific discoveries. The left, weakened and fearful as to the longevity of their groups and publications, avoided issues for which they felt themselves unable to construct a powerful counter-charge to mainstream opinion at a time when they were, after all, more concerned with the immediacies of domestic change. This then, restores the agency of the working classes, with press silence indicative of the existence of

---

[62] See, for example, Kenneth O. Morgan, *Keir Hardie: Radical and Socialist* (London: Weidenfeld & Nicolson, 1975), 34.

working-class voices. And such voices indicated that the empire was widely seen as the prime source of Britain's "greatness" and, more often than not, considered valid as an ideal, even if the finer points of its actual manifestations were open to debate.

How does this impact upon existing historical ideas? In socialist history circles, tales of the difficulties that the left faced are nothing new. This fits into David Howell's description of local ILP activists as "pragmatic visionaries".[63] They had to adapt to survive in an unforgiving political climate. But in imperial history circles, the conclusions of this chapter have implications for the arguments that have been made by the key recent discussants on the impact of empire upon British society. For John Mackenzie, the omnipresence of empire in working-class culture shows that the working classes were imperialist. They went to colonial exhibitions, they enjoyed imperialistic music-hall displays, they devoured imperial texts, ergo they were imperialist. This is a rather crude generalisation – Mackenzie does provide testimonies, personal recollections and other snapshots "on the ground", so to speak, to support his case, but these are frequently overshadowed by a discussion of the content of these cultural products.[64] It is naturally easier to discuss the content of such cultural products than it is to prove such content's resonance amongst working-class audiences. Porter has exploited this chink in the methodological framework to good effect, by arguing that the presence of some imperial cultural products does not necessarily prove that workers were imperialist, that they did not necessarily absorb all that was presented to them.[65] Little by way of meaningful response to Porter has yet to materialize; this work has suggested one way that such a response can be framed.

The Jameson Raid of 1895 undermined the reliability of the alliance between the working classes and imperialism. This, and the following slow move towards war, became the most dominant topic in metropolitan discussions of empire to have emerged since the Indian Rebellion of 1857, and the left seized upon it as proof of the atrocities of war-mongering capitalist imperialists. When this took centre-stage, and when the war proved a long and difficult one, it played into the left's hands, uncoupling a sizeable number of the working classes away from an affiliation to

---

[63] Howell, *British Workers*, 339–42.
[64] Mackenzie, *Propaganda and Empire: The Manipulation of British Public Opinion, 1880–1960* (Manchester: Manchester University Press, 1984).
[65] Bernard Porter, *The Absent-Minded Imperialists: What the British Really Thought About Empire* (Oxford: Oxford University Press, 2004).

empire. In the end, the mine-owners and the politicians proved their own worst enemies.

LABOUR AND EMPIRE:
AUSTRALIA AND BRITAIN
FROM THE LATE NINETEENTH CENTURY
TO THE INTER-WAR YEARS

NEVILLE KIRK

The concerns of this chapter are both general and specific. It begins by exploring some of the historiographical, methodological and conceptual issues involved in the study of labour and empire both generally and in Australia and Britain. It then engages with these issues and presents findings in terms of ongoing comparative research into Australian and British labour movement attitudes and practices towards empire. This specific research focus is part of a wider comparative and trans-national exploration of the effects of empire, nation, race and class upon the twentieth-century development of the Australian Labor Party and the Labour Party in Britain. The chapter is intended to raise both specific and general issues and questions which can usefully be fed into discussions about the ways in which historians may further advance the study of imperial, comparative cross-national, trans-national and ultimately "global" labour history.[1]

Historiography and Methodology

The national, comparative and trans-national study of labour and empire in Australia and Britain from the late nineteenth century to the inter-war years has been badly served by labour and other historians. This neglect has been particularly marked in the British case. Most British labour historiography has been rooted in the assumption, so common within the

---

[1] Jan Lucassen, ed., *Global Labour History: A State of the Art* (Bern: Peter Lang, 2006); Neville Kirk, *Labour and the Politics of Empire: Britain and Australia from 1900 to the Present* (Manchester: Manchester University Press, forthcoming, 2010).

national labour movement, that the overriding and "essential" concerns of the "pragmatic", "pioneering" and "core" British movement have traditionally rested, and continue to rest, with "bread and butter" issues of a local, regional and national kind.[2] Impressive contributions to the study of British labour and empire in the period under review have undoubtedly been made, either directly by scholars such as Henry Pelling, Richard Price, Partha Sarathi Gupta, Stephen Howe and Andrew Thompson, or more indirectly by Catherine Hall, Hugh Cunningham, Paul Ward, Miles Taylor and Raphael Samuel.[3] From a wider social history perspective, John Mackenzie and Wendy Webster are prominent among the small group of historians who have written innovatory accounts of the effects of British imperialism upon various aspects of the daily lives of the British "people", including men and women of the mainly unorganized British working class.[4] Yet as Mackenzie and others have pointed out, questions of empire have been assumed, in most of the labour and much of the general British historiography, to have held little appeal for, and exerted marginal overall influence upon, the structures, consciousness and development of the domestic British labour movement and the wider British working class. Apparently so removed from and largely incidental to the all-consuming daily struggle to "make ends meet", the influences of

---

[2] Henry Pelling, *Popular Politics and Society in Late Victorian Britain* (London: Macmillan, 1968); Kenneth O. Morgan, *Keir Hardie: Radical and Socialist* (London: Weidenfeld and Nicolson, 1975), 178.

[3] Henry Pelling, "British Labour and British Imperialism", in his *Popular Politics*, 82–100; Richard Price, *An Imperial War and the British Working Class* (London: Routledge and Keegan Paul, 1972); Partha Sarathi Gupta, *Imperialism and the British Labour Movement 1914–1964* (New Delhi: Sage, 2002); Stephen Howe, *Anti-Colonialism in British Politics: The Left and the End of Empire 1918–1964* (Oxford: Oxford University Press, 1993); Andrew S. Thompson, *The Empire Strikes Back?: The Impact of Imperialism on Britain from the mid Nineteenth Century* (Harlow: Pearson Education, 2005); Catherine Hall, *Civilising Subjects: Metropole and Colony in the English Imagination 1830–1867* (Cambridge: Polity Press, 2002); Hugh Cunningham, "The Language of Patriotism", in Raphael Samuel, ed., *Patriotism: The Making and Unmaking of British National Identity*, vol. 1 (London: Routledge, 1989); Paul Ward, *Red Flag and Union Jack: Englishness Patriotism and the British Left 1881–1924* (Woodbridge: Boydell Press, 1998); Miles Taylor, "Imperium et Libertas? Rethinking the Radical Critique of Imperialism during the Nineteenth Century", *Journal of Imperial and Commonwealth History* 19, no. 1 (1991), 1–23; Samuel, *Patriotism*, vol. 1, introduction.

[4] John Mackenzie, ed., *Imperialism and Popular Culture* (Manchester: Manchester University Press, 1986); Wendy Webster, *Englishness and Empire 1939–1965* (Oxford: Oxford University Press, 2005).

empire and imperial consciousness have paled before the irresistible pulls of a "local" sense of place and belonging within the British nation state.[5]

There has, furthermore, been precious little interest in, and recognition of, the fact that labour movements and workers in the British empire's formal dependencies, "settler colonies", dominions and more recently commonwealth countries, could and undoubtedly have influenced the nature and development not only of the metropolitan labour movement, but also the nation state of Britain itself. All too often the complex circuits of encounters, exchanges and reciprocal, but not necessarily equal, influences within the British empire have been eschewed, in both the labour and general historiography, in favour of an inward-looking, blinkered and deeply flawed "core-periphery" approach positing a largely *one-way* flow of ideas, people, cultures and institutions from the metropolitan "core" to the colonial "periphery".[6]

By way of qualification, it is true that at various points in time Britons, including British labour leaders visiting or residing in Australia and New Zealand, took a keen interest in, and derived domestic British "lessons" from developments in the antipodes. For example, the "advanced" nature of social-welfare provision and state regulation in Australia and New Zealand in the late nineteenth and early twentieth centuries attracted the interest and reinforced the collectivist views of Sidney and Beatrice Webb.[7] During the same period of time the "world touring" Keir Hardie, the visiting Margaret and Ramsay MacDonald and the visiting and resident Tom Mann and Henry Hyde Champion commented upon and were

---

[5] MacKenzie, *Imperialism*, 1–2; Kirk, *Labour*, introduction; Bernard Porter, *The Absent-Minded Imperialists: How the British Really Saw their Empire* (Oxford: Oxford University Press, 2004).

[6] Kirk, *Labour*; Catherine Hall, ed., *Cultures of Empire: A Reader* (Manchester: Manchester University Press, 2000), introduction; Bernard Porter, "Further Thoughts on Imperial Absent-Mindedness", *Journal of Imperial and Commonwealth History* 36, no. 1 (2008), 111. For examples of the "core-periphery" approach see David Cannadine, *Ornamentalism: How the British Saw their Empire* (London: Penguin, 2001); Niall Ferguson, *Empire: How Britain Made the Modern World* (London: Penguin, 2003).

[7] A. G. Austin, ed., *The Webbs' Australian Diary* (Melbourne: Pitman, 1965); D. A. Hamer, ed., *The Webbs in New Zealand, 1898: Beatrice Webb's Diary with Entries by Sidney Webb* (Wellington: Price Milburn for Victoria University Press, 1974); Sidney Webb, "Some Impressions of Australasia", *Labour Leader*, Aug. 26, 1899.

impressed by the "advanced" state of democracy and standard of living in Australia.[8]

The "precocity" of the infant Australian Labor Party (ALP) also drew much comment from, and acted as a "beacon" for, "new" and "old world" socialists and labourites alike. Formed at the federal level in 1901, it became the "the first workers' party anywhere in the world" to form a minority national government, in 1904. Four years later it went one better in its achievement of majority federal rule under the leadership of Andrew Fisher, a former Ayrshire coalminer. The ALP largely ruled the federal roost up to 1916 and made substantial gains at the state level. By the end of the war Australians also lived in "the most unionised country in the world". Fisher and other Australian labour leaders also took the opportunity to familiarize British activists with the impressive "forward march" and seemingly inevitable triumph of the Australian movement in their correspondence and on visits to London, Scotland and other parts of Britain.[9] More recently, of course, the architects of "New Labour" in Britain drew much inspiration from the ruling "third-way experiments" of the Hawke and Keating Labor governments in Australia.[10]

There was, therefore, far more than a one-way flow of ideas and influences at work. But the crucial point to note here is that this flow was not conducted upon an equal basis. The balance lay far more with the perceived outward flow from Britain rather than inward movement from Australia. For most of the period from 1850 to the inter-war period British labour leaders, albeit with an initially powerful but increasingly diminished basis in fact, viewed their movement not only as the pioneer, but also as the "true" home of "labour" – the "essential" source of the ideas, practices and personnel which had inspired, and continued greatly to influence, labour movements on an international and global scale.[11] In addition, British interest in Australian matters often derived from prevailing "Little Englander" or "Little Britisher" "domestic issues and concerns", such as

---

[8] Morgan, *Keir Hardie*, chap. 9; Neville Kirk, *Comrades and Cousins: Globalization Workers and Labour Movements in Britain, the USA and Australia from the 1880s to 1914* (London: Merlin Press, 2003), 62, 64, 70–2, 81–3, 107–11; John Barnes, *Socialist Champion: Portrait of the Gentleman as Crusader* (Melbourne: Australian Scholarly Publishing, 2006), part 2.

[9] Kirk, *Comrades*, 101–111.

[10] Chris Person and Francis G. Castles, "Australian Antecedents of the Third Way", *Political Studies* 50, no. 4 (2002), 683–702.

[11] Kirk, *Comrades*, 30–7.

living and working conditions, relations with employers, government officials and the condition of their own labour movement.[12]

Many within the British labour movement and the wider working class were also affected, albeit to varying degrees and levels of consciousness, by the imperial ideas, practices and symbols which they routinely encountered in their daily lives – in comic books, in the press, in public ceremonies and monuments, in architecture, in the music hall, the cinema and radio and in their personal and domestic memorabilia. Along with the "official" view presented by the state and governments, these daily ideas and practices tended to highlight notions of British superiority and Britain's global "civilising" "duties" and "mission", especially to "lesser" and "darker" "races". Priority was given to the benefits rather than the costs of the empire to both rulers and ruled, conflict downplayed and consensus and stability highlighted. This bundle of daily and official ideas and practices contained within itself complexities and contradictions. But it was also the ruling "commonsense", the hegemonic view of empire. Despite its historically subordinate position within British society, traditions within its ranks of anti-imperialism and class-based support for labour movements and subaltern groups abroad, the British labour movement was simultaneously subjected to and at times significantly influenced by this ruling "commonsense". It thus occupied a contradictory position within the nation state and the empire. Subordination and a critical reception to imperialism were part of a wider picture which also involved the labour movement and the working class as constituents of the ruling imperial nation. As a consequence British labour and British workers exhibited at various points in time not only opposition to, but also endorsement of, the empire and imperialism.[13]

Furthermore, while expressed in an official, "top down" rather than unofficial and "bottom up" form, a predominantly conservative, beneficent and consensual view of empire and imperialism has, in conjunction with a "core-periphery" approach, continued strongly to inform recent and current influential works concerning the empires of Britain and other western powers. Of special significance for labour historians is that these works ignore or marginalize voices, especially critical and oppositional voices and actions, "from below".[14]

---

[12] Mackenzie, *Imperialism*.

[13] Mackenzie, *Imperialism*; Stuart Ward, "Echoes of Empire", *History Workshop Journal* 62 (2006), 264–78.

[14] Frederick Cooper, "Empire Multiplied: A Review Essay", *Comparative Studies in Society and History* 46, no. 2 (2004), 247–72; Richard Price, "One Big Thing:

The Australian labour movement and Australian workers also occupied a complex and somewhat contradictory position within the British imperial system. They traditionally had and often maintained strong personal, family- and class-based labour movement ties with Britain. Yet in their roles as subordinate "colonials" and workers, especially if Irish, they often, but not invariably, expressed stronger opposition to the ruling British nation and the "imperialist" ruling classes of *both* Britain and Australia than their counterparts in Britain. They widely embraced a form of radical nationalism rooted in class and sought to create a "new world Workers' Paradise". At the same time, however, the labour movement's very close attachment to the ALP could not conceal the extent to which the inter-war conservative Nationalists appealed to "loyalist" workers, both organized and unorganized. Moreover, the labour movement and its supporters overwhelmingly defined themselves as "white", predominantly male, and claimed superiority over "coloureds" throughout the empire. As noted below, they excluded the latter from their "white" "Workingman's Paradise". Their attitudes towards "coloureds" in "their own" country, the Aboriginal people, while more complex, were also separatist and superior. In sum, while mainly less contradictory in radical class-based and national terms in the period in question than their British counterparts, they expressed the "settler consciousness" of exclusionary white racism far more explicitly and strongly than their "comrades and cousins" in Britain. Although racism was at times a feature of British workers, especially the unorganized, sections of the British labour movement developed an impressive class-based critique of racism, while the movement formally supported Britain's traditional "open door" policy towards intending immigrants, irrespective of "race", from within the British Empire.[15]

Like their British counterparts, Australian labour historians have set their work largely within a "bread and butter"-based national framework. However, they have more strongly contested the "core-periphery" model than their British counterparts and, as reflected in the pages of the leading Australian labour history journal, *Labour History*, have demonstrated a much keener awareness of, and interest in, questions of empire, nation, "race", trans-nationalism and cross-national comparisons.[16] As suggested above, an important reason for these differences may be sought in the

Britain, its Empire and their Imperial Culture", *Journal of British Studies* 45, no. 3 (2006), 602–27.
[15] Neville Kirk, "'Australians for Australia': The Right, the Labor Party and Contested Loyalties to Nation and Empire in Australia, 1917 to the early 1930s", *Labour History* 91 (2006), 95–111.
[16] *Labour History* 71 (1996); 76 (1999); 88 (2005); 95 (2008).

different locations and experiences of the two countries, their labour movements and their working classes in the British imperial system, with the seemingly autonomous, secure and self-confident British "centre" being set for much of the period against the dependent, subordinate and insecure Australian "periphery".

While Australian influence upon the history of the British metropolis has appeared to many Britons to be remote and slight, the reverse is manifestly not the case. The "marks" of Britain upon Australia and what Australia's most famous historian, Manning Clark, termed the facts and symbols of "dual loyalty" among Australians to their own country and to Britain, were both widespread and palpable during our period. For example, many white "independent Australian Britons"[17] saw their country as a remote and beleaguered island outpost of "Britishness" and "whiteness" in the southern hemisphere. They expressed concern and often anxiety to remain closely tied to Britain, while entertaining, to say the least, ambiguous feelings towards the "mixed race" character of the British empire. The vast majority of them opposed Britain's official "open door" policy towards "coloured" imperial subjects. They excluded the indigenous aboriginal people from citizenship under the terms of the New Commonwealth, believed them to be on the verge of extinction and adopted attitudes and actions towards them combining fear, coercion and, especially in the case of the labour movement, "protection", separation and paternalism. They were further characterized by a chronic fear of invasion by "non-white" Asiatic "others". This fear underpinned the introduction of the "White Australia" policy as a cornerstone of the New Commonwealth in 1901. Designed to preserve the "racial purity" and "homogeneity" of Australia by means of a dictation test and the exclusion of all intending "non-white" immigrants, "White Australia" was supported very strongly by the vast majority of those in the labour movement. The policy lasted officially up to the early 1970s.[18]

"Race" thus constituted a key feature of Australian experience and its historiography. In contrast, in Britain, notes Wendy Webster, "until recently" it was widely assumed, in official, academic and daily circles that "race", especially up to the post-World War Two period of more extensive black and Asian migration to Britain, was a feature of British imperial rather than domestic history. Whereas the latter was assumed, "naturally", if often more implicitly than explicitly, to be homogeneous

---

[17] Gavin Souter, *Lion and Kangaroo: the Initiation of Australia* (Melbourne: Text Publishing, 2000), preface.
[18] Gwenda Tavan, *The Long Slow Death of White Australia* (Melbourne: Scribe Publications, 2005).

and "white", "race" and racial difference were believed to be the preserves of empire – a separate place "where non-white people belonged ... under British colonial rule".[19]

In terms of further British "marks" upon Australia, it is important to record that the federation of the six Australian colonies into the New Commonwealth, in 1901, took place under the Crown. British agreement to federation in turn played an important part in sharply reducing republican and anti-British sentiments in Australia from the later 1890s up to the early period of World War One. In addition, the British monarch remained Australia's head of state with power to appoint the Governor General and, as demonstrated in highly successful royal visits and, albeit highly contested, celebrations of Empire Day, retained impressive support in Australia. Although seeking greater independence within the imperial system and developing its own navy, Australia remained heavily dependent upon Britain for defence purposes and, as seen in the case of World War One, was committed in practice to actively supporting Britain in the event of the latter's declaration of war.[20]

As reflected in the currency (the coins minted in 1911 had a map of Australia on one side and the king's head on the reverse side), the design of the national flag (a combination of the Union Jack, the Southern Cross and a six-pointed star representing the six federated states of Australia was approved by the king) and postage stamps (the royal face being "the main official emblem" of the Commonwealth's first stamp issue in 1913), in "all walks of life" the "visible signs of national identity" preserved "the dual image of being both British and Australian".[21] Moreover, "Australia had no national song, no national heroes, no national literature, and no national days of commemoration".[22]

The experience of World War One, especially during the Australia and New Zealand Army Corps' (ANZACS') campaign at Gallipoli in 1915, combined with the proud radical nationalism and mounting anti-imperialism of the war-time and post-war labour movement. In addition, a growing sporting self confidence and a strong desire to "put one over" on the "Poms" in cricket during the inter-war years signified that important radical and independent changes were increasingly evident in Australia

---

[19] Wendy Webster, "Transnational Journeys and Domestic Histories", *Journal of Social History* 39, no. 3 (2006), 653.

[20] Souter, *Lion and Kangaroo*, chap. 6, conclusion.

[21] Charles Manning H. Clark, *A History of Australia*, vol. 5: *The People Make Laws, 1888–1915* (Carlton: Melbourne University Press, 1999), 331.

[22] Loc. cit.

from 1915 onwards.[23] Furthermore, as part of the transformation of the Empire into the Commonwealth from the mid 1920s onwards, Australia and the other dominions (now deemed by Britain to be "mature") were, in conjunction with Britain itself, officially defined as "autonomous communities within the British Empire, equal in status, in no way subordinate to one another…though united by a common allegiance to the Crown". Yet many leading figures in the labour movement continued to maintain that in practice, as demonstrated, for example, in patterns of trade and economic responses to the depression and in the dismissal of Jack Lang, premier of New South Wales, by the state's governor, British-born retired Air Vice-Marshal, Sir Philip Game, in 1932, Australian interests continued to be subordinated to those of Britain.[24] In these ways questions of "outside" imperial "rule" by Britain, domestic maturity, independence and autonomy and highly racialized notions of nationhood and patriotism, constituted inescapable "facts of life" for many Australians in our period.

As we will see below, the labour movements of both countries also strongly saw empire and nation through the lens of class. But the purpose here is to contrast the more outward-looking viewpoint of Australian labour with the far more insular and "local" outlook of many within the British movement. This contrast is also strongly evident in the labour historiography of the two countries. To paraphrase Michael Davie, Britain and the Empire figured much larger in Australia and Australian consciousness than Australia did in Britain and British consciousness.[25]

Engagement

In its engagement with the methodological and historiographical issues outlined above, my current research into labour and empire in Britain and Australia seeks to achieve three goals. First, it aims to provide a convincing critique of the "core-periphery" model by investigating not only the discrete nature of labour movement attitudes and practices towards questions of empire and imperialism in metropolitan Britain and colonial Australia, but also their connections, exchanges, reciprocal influences, similarities and differences.

In terms of these areas of investigation, I have benefited greatly from the fact that the "ties of empire" between Australia and Britain were deep

---

[23] Kirk, "'Australians for Australia'", 99–102.
[24] Kirk, "'Australians for Australia'", 103–4.
[25] Michael Davie, *Anglo-Australian Attitudes* (London: Secker and Warburg, 2000).

and enduring, politically, economically, culturally and socially. For example, in addition to the connections identified in the first section of this paper there also existed close economic ties, the considerable influence of British-born labour leaders upon the institutional and ideological character of the Australian movement,[26] and the fact that approximately 98 percent of the enumerated Australian population of 3,825,000 in 1901 (excluding approximately 100,000 Aborigines) were emigrants from Britain and Ireland. As late as 1933 this figure still stood at 97 percent.[27] The overwhelming presence of Anglos and Celts in the Australian population also means that labour movement sources are mainly written in English, an obvious benefit to solely or mainly English-speaking researchers.

I have been similarly fortunate, if at times somewhat overwhelmed, by the fact that there exists a wealth of relevant primary and secondary material in both Britain and Australia. This material includes labour and mainstream newspapers and journals, diaries, autobiographies and biographies, letters "back home" to Britain written by immigrants and visitors, including labour movement activists, to Australia and New Zealand, accounts of living, working and labour movement conditions in Britain by Australian visitors, the personal papers of leading labour figures in both countries and, as noted in the previous section, the reports and comments of labour movement and other trans-national radical visitors to and residents in Australia and Britain. These sources have enabled the development of both a sound understanding of the nature, changes and continuities in the perspectives of the two discrete labour movements towards empire and related issues and their connections, similarities and differences.

The second aim is to pay particular attention to the representations and evaluations of empire and imperialism developed by Australian and British labour at specific points in time, over time and in a variety of places and spaces. This process involves detailed attention to language and the common, similar, different, consensual, contested, continuous and changing *meanings* attached to the terms empire and imperialism by various individuals and parts of the respective labour movements. This is probably the most interesting, but difficult and challenging, part of this research project, involving as it does a close, *contextualized* reading of words and meanings and the detection of patterns, similarities and

---

[26] Kirk, *Comrades*, 112–16.

[27] Gavin W. Jones, "White Australia, National Identity and Population Change", in Laksiri Jayasuriya, David Walker and Jan Gothard, eds., *Legacies of White Australia: Race Culture and Nation* (Crawley: University of Western Australia Press, 2003), 8–32.

differences in the midst of contingency, complexity and nuance. My social-realist reading may be contrasted with both an idealist or self-referential approach in which the languages and representations of empire are, in my opinion, improperly detached from their contextualized determinations, especially questions of political economy, social relations, power and conflict,[28] and reductionist accounts in which language and wider systems of discourse are seen as essentially passive and non-constitutive elements in society, as being "essentially" simple reflections of an underlying material, structural base.[29]

It will be evident to the reader that my chosen approach seeks to address and *engage*, in the manner of E. P. Thompson, both the "material" and the "cultural", the "structural" and the "experiential" as being indissolubly linked in terms of social practice.[30] It will also be evident that I am challenging the picture of a simple dualism, found all too often in the historiography, that labour was either more or less uniformly and statically for or against empire and imperialism. As demonstrated in the examples provided in the following section, labour was rarely monolithic in its attitudes: different varieties and shades of empire and imperialism were perceived to exist and were subject to change over time, as were the dominant, subordinate and residual attitudes and points of emphasis within the Australian and British movements. Nuance, complexity and contextualized change over time thus took precedence over fixed uniformity of outlook and meaning.

The third goal is to correct "top down" neglect of the range of voices "from below", especially critical voices. This chapter does not, however, seek to discover and reconstruct the latter voices at the expense of the former. Rather it is to explore their natures and their shifting *engagements*. In setting into dialogue "top down" and "bottom up" voices, rather than adopting a narrow and exclusive "bottom up" approach, historians may gain valuable insights not only into labour attitudes, but also those of different and often more powerful groups whose interests and consciousness are frequently at odds with those of labour. In the process we come to observe the structures and patterns of ideology, power and social relations, involving both consensus and coercion, and the ways in which *hegemony* is made, challenged and unmade or renegotiated.

---

[28] Price, "One Big Thing".

[29] Neville Kirk, "History, Language, Ideas and Post-Modernism", *Social History* 19, no. 2 (1994), 221–40.

[30] Dorothy Thompson, ed., *The Essential E. P. Thompson* (New York: The New Press, 2001), 3–7 and part 3.

For example, part of my research project demonstrates that the hegemony of the Right and the subordination of the ALP and the British Labour Party (BLP) during the inter-war period, especially so in Australia, resulted from the ability of the former to appropriate the discourses of nation, patriotism and empire and successfully to employ them in elections and in daily life to discredit sections of the labour movement "other" as "disloyal" and "extreme". Labour contested these charges, but within the turmoil unleashed by the experiences of war, extensive industrial conflict, the Bolshevik Revolution in Russia and the birth and spread of international communism, did so with limited results. Thus Labour's undoubted rise in inter-war Britain must be set within the wider context of Conservative hegemony, while in Australia the right-wing Nationalists and their allies successfully overturned the ALP's pre-war federal domination.[31]

Finally, it will be apparent that the successful realization of my three goals necessarily involves the adoption of a comparative and trans-national approach in order to tease out and explain similarities and differences both within and between the two national labour movements in question.

Findings

Four main findings have so far developed out of my research. These may be summarized in the following way. First, setting new, neglected and in some instances forgotten questions to familiar and less familiar sources leads to the conclusion that matters of empire and imperialism figured far more prominently in labour's affairs in Australia and Britain than the conventional emphasis upon immediate "bread and butter", nationally-based issues suggests.

To be sure, this influence varied. For example, the primary reason why independent Labour parties were established in both countries at the turn of the century was in order better to represent, protect and advance the labour, and especially trade union, interest in parliament than had been the case in the 1890s when labour dissatisfaction with the mainstream parties had mushroomed. The latter were seen widely to have failed organized labour, as reflected in employer, state and judicial attacks on trade unionism and growing unemployment and falling living standards in the face of depression. The infant Labour parties in Australia and Britain set out to defend and advance the cause of labour and workers by means of

---

[31] Kirk, "'Australians for Australia'".

legislation designed to safeguard the existence and position of the unions and to improve working and living conditions.[32]

At the same time the two labour movements were motivated by more than immediate and material matters. For example, as fully recognized in parts of the literature, they shared strong desires to make their wider societies more open, democratic, fair, and just, although formal Labour commitments to socialism did not come into being until 1918 in Britain and 1921 in Australia. Furthermore, although barely mentioned, if at all, in most of the institutional party histories, these national Labour parties were formed at a time when Britain was waging, between 1899 and 1902, a major imperialist war against the Boers in South Africa. And it is my contention that both the war and the "coercive" imperialism of which it was a clear example, impinged heavily upon contemporary labour thinking.

My argument runs as follows. A striking feature of the ongoing debate, initiated by Richard Price's claim in 1972 that "indifference" towards imperialism was outweighed by "more immediate" concerns with "social reform" in British "working-class constituencies" during the "Khaki" general election of 1900,[33] is the lack of attention, by both Price and many of his critics, to the wealth of relevant material in the main socialist and labourite press organs of the time, *Labour Leader*, *Clarion*, and *Justice*. These important sources tell a very different story from that narrated by Price. Above all, they demonstrate that imperialism, "as an electoral issue", was of considerable rather than "very little force" in "working class constituencies" and figured prominently in the campaigns of the fifteen Labour Representation Committee (LRC) candidates who ran for parliamentary office. (The LRC, set up in 1900, became the Labour Party in 1906.) The three newspapers agreed that even though "jingo khaki fever", "insanity", and "hooligan" attacks on anti-war speakers and meetings had generally peaked earlier in the year, nevertheless the issues of war and imperialism were the dominant ones during the 1900 election, both in London (Price's main and limited focus of investigation) and elsewhere in the country.[34]

---

[32] Kirk, *Labour*, chap. 1.

[33] Price, *Imperial War*, pp. 96, 105, 118–19, 130–1, 237–8.

[34] *Justice*, Apr. 7; Aug. 11; Sep. 8, 22, 29; Oct. 6, 13, 1900; *Clarion*, Oct. 6, 1900; *Labour Leader*, Sep. 29; Oct. 6, 20, 27; Nov. 3, 10, 17, 1900; Paul Readman, "The Conservative Party, Patriotism and British Politics: The Case of the General Election of 1900", *Journal of British Studies* 40, no. 1 (2001), 107–45; idem, "The Liberal Party and Patriotism in Early Twentieth Century Britain", *Twentieth*

While expressing support for the "bravery" and the "hardships" endured by the British "Tommy" in South Africa, and dismissive of the charge that opposition to the war equalled "cowardice" and "treason", the LRC candidates uniformly dismissed the official explanation for the outbreak of war – the Boers' denial of the franchise to recent British immigrants – as a "deception", a "fraud", and a "lie". This was a "cover" for the "base" motives of "rapacious" capitalists, including "greedy financiers", to "annex, plunder, and rob" the goldmines and other valuable resources of South Africa, to unmercifully "smash" the Boers, "a brave and independent people" in the eyes of Robert Blatchford's *Clarion*, and to substitute "enslaved" and "cheap" "black" and probably Chinese labour for well-paid "white" labour in the mines. Although elements of racism were present in the pages of the press, the dominant view expressed was class-based and anti-racist: that the capitalists' "enslavement" of black labour and "sweating" and "pauperisation" of "free" whites were designed to whip up racism and divide workers. In the words of *Justice*, both "race" and "class domination", seen as key aspects of modern imperialism, were to be unequivocally opposed, while "class solidarity" was to be championed.[35]

The military methods employed by the British in the course of the war – martial law, concentration camps, the "butchery", the "pillage", the "English terror at Bloemfontein", the reduction of large areas of South Africa to a "charred and blackened waste" and so on – were opposed as being "barbaric" and designed to drag Britain's honour "into the dirt", "ruin" her prestige "before the whole world" and bring her Empire "to the very verge of its ruin".[36] Aggressive imperialism of the South African kind was also seen as fundamentally incompatible with the progressive causes of social reform, freedom and the further development of democracy at home.[37] Socio-economic concerns, such as poverty, unemployment, housing, old-age pensions, and the public control of monopolies did figure in the addresses of the LRC candidates and in some cases occupied pride of place. In overall terms, however, the issues of the war and imperialism, *contra* Price, were the most important.[38] Finally, despite examples to the

---

Century British History 12 (2001), 288–302; *Manchester Guardian*, Oct. 5, 9, 10, 15, 17, 1900.

[35] *Justice*, Jan. 6, 13; Mar. 24; Sep. 1, 22, 29; Oct. 27, 1900; *Clarion*, Jan. 13, 27; Feb. 10; Mar. 3, 10, 24; Aug. 4; Nov. 3, 1900; *Labour Leader*, Apr. 21, 1900.

[36] *Labour Leader*, Nov. 3, 10; Dec. 22, 1900; *Justice*, Jan. 6; July 7; Aug. 25, 1900.

[37] *Clarion*, Feb. 10; Sep. 29, 1900; *Justice*, Sep. 29, 1900; *Labour Leader*, Apr. 21, 1900.

[38] *Labour Leader*, Sep. 22; Oct. 6, 13, 27; Nov. 10, 1900; *Justice*, Sep. 29 1900.

contrary in some constituencies, "khakimania" was perceived to be the decisive factor in the Conservative victory at the election, especially in urban areas.[39]

During the next three general elections to take place before the outbreak of World War One – one in 1906 and the other two in 1910 – imperial issues were clearly of less overall significance than free trade, tariff reform, the Irish question and the position and rights of the House of Lords in relation to the Commons. In the 1906 election, however, there was, as noted by Henry Pelling, "a secondary issue of imperial significance: the issue of Chinese labour in the South African mines".[40] While some British workers undoubtedly held racialized stereotypes of the imported Chinese, the dominant response in the socialist and labour press was to oppose their employment not primarily on grounds of "race", but on account of their cheap and enforced, or "unfree" and "slave", status.[41]

In pre-1914 Australia the questions of empire, nation building and the related issue of "race" were, as noted earlier, of major political importance to both national and labour politics. Federation took place within the British imperial framework and "White Australia" was one of the pillars of the New Commonwealth in which the ALP played an important part. The Australian labour movement opposed the South African War for much the same reasons as its British counterpart, but, in the manner of the majority movement in South Africa, expressed explicit and unapologetic racism towards the Chinese in 1906.[42]

The outbreak and course of World War One raised major questions for both the British and Australian movements concerning their allegiances not only to class and nation, but also to the imperial cause. In 1914 the two movements pledged majority support for the war against "Prussianism", but the issue of conscription for overseas military service led in 1916 to an irrevocable split in the ALP. Those supporting conscription, and most strongly attached to Britain and the empire, were expelled from the party. Thereafter the ALP moved to the left, becoming increasingly critical of Britain and adopting a formal anti-war stance in 1918. Between the wars questions of loyalty to nation and empire figured very prominently in federal elections in Australia and, as we will observe below, strongly affected the declining fortunes of the ALP.

---

[39] *Labour Leader*, Sep. 22, 29; Oct. 13, 20; Nov. 3, 10, 17, 1900 *Justice*, Oct. 6, 1900.
[40] Pelling, "British Labour and British Imperialism", 96.
[41] Pelling, "British Labour and British Imperialism", 96–9; Kirk, *Comrades*, 164–5, 185–6, 190–1.
[42] Kirk, *Comrades*, 185–6, 190–1, 198–204.

In Britain, Labour's rise to a position of national importance in the 1920s – minority Labour governments were formed in 1924 and 1929 and Labour replaced the Liberals as the main alternative to the Conservatives – owed far more to "bread and butter" and domestic political issues than its stance on empire. But Labour's attempt to rid British imperial rule of its coercive character and provide support for the development of a more enlightened commonwealth, constituted an increasingly important aspect of British politics. In both countries during the 1930s specifically imperial and commonwealth matters and relations were incorporated into the wider international concern with the threat to peace and democracy posed by the rise of fascism.[43]

In sum, the subject of labour and empire has been unduly neglected in the scholarly literature. Contrary to the conventional wisdom, empire and imperialism were not incidental or peripheral to our labour movement subjects.

My second finding is that a *systemic*, structurally-based critique of imperialism formed an important part of Australian and British labour movement responses to empire. According to this critique imperialism constituted a necessary part of a modern capitalist system rooted in class rule and exploitation, and colonial competition, expansion and domination. Colonialism was seen frequently to comprise racial as well as class domination and a combination of predominantly coercive but in a minority of cases more consensual, but self-interested, aspects. This critique was articulated not only and predictably by members of Communist parties, but also, albeit to varying degrees, by socialists and labourites writing in the pages of *Labour Leader*, *Clarion*, and *Justice*.[44] It also figured routinely in three of the Australian labour movement's most important press organs, the Brisbane-based *Worker*, the Sydney-based *Australian Worker*, and Western Australia's the *Westralian Worker*. In its "new world" Australian articulation the critique was, on balance, more forceful, outspoken and extensive than in its "old world" British, or at least English, form. Close associations were drawn by colonial critics between imperialism and the "decadent" aristocracy, the "outmoded" institution of monarchy, "the robbery and murder" and the continued denial of genuine independence and self-government to "the wealth producers of the Great Empire".[45]

This systemic critique was applied with particular force to "coercive" instances of imperialism, as in the case of the South African War

---

[43] Kirk, "'Australians for Australia'".
[44] Kirk, *Comrades,* 174–90.
[45] Kirk, *Comrades,* 126–7.

highlighted above. Yet it is important to note that it was not confined to such instances. For example, it was expressed by British socialists both before and after the conflict in South Africa. It was held to have "essential", general, and structural, rather than simply "superficial", specific, and experiential application. In Australia the perceived self-interest, snobbery, incompetence and indifference to the plight of the "Diggers" displayed by British officers at Gallipoli and at other points during the Great War, the expulsion of the more moderate pro-British leaders from the ALP over the conscription issue, British suppression of the 1916 Easter Rising in Dublin, the ALP's adoption of a formal anti-war stance in 1918 when hostilities were still taking place, and the pronounced movement to the left of the labour movement as a whole in the immediate post-war years – all served to strengthen fundamental hostility to the British Empire.

During the 1920s and early 1930s systemic anti-imperialism was also a prominent feature of labour-movement thinking. This was rooted in the continued perception, notwithstanding the formal development of a more equal commonwealth, that British rule still meant metropolitan domination and colonial subordination and that British interests usually took precedence over those of Australia. In presenting itself as the "true" party of the nation, the ALP maintained that it was the only party to put the national interest "first". In contrast the Nationalists were portrayed as "plutocratic Imperialists" who were "scheming to deprive Australia of its self-governing powers…and render it subservient to a ruling class of capitalists and militarists twelve thousand miles away".[46] Highly symbolic of the latter was the "disloyal" attempt of the Nationalists to "push forward the Union Jack", "the emblem of the Empire", as "the Australian flag" during the Red Flag Riots in Sydney in 1921.[47]

British domination and Australian subordination were reflected in many ways. Among these we may list the following: Britain's denial of a loan to and subsequent "economic blockade" of Theodore's Labor administration in early 1920s Queensland; the appointment of wealthy and conservative Britons, as opposed to native-born males, to state governorships, and Game's dismissal of Lang; the months of wrangling between Labor prime minister James Scullin on the one side and king George V, supported by British Labour prime minister Ramsay MacDonald on the other, in 1930 over Scullin's determination to appoint the first Australian-born governor general (in this instance the Australians won the

---

[46] Kirk, "'Australians for Australia'", 100, 102.
[47] Kirk, "'Australians for Australia'", 102.

power battle, but only after Scullin threatened to call an election on the issue); the continuing economic dependence of Australia upon Britain and the "imposition" by the latter of a deflationary economic policy upon the former in the face of the depression – leading to the second major split in the ALP and, as in Britain, the "desertion" of prominent Labour "rats" to the 1930s National(ist) cause. There were further issues, such as the practical impossibility of Australia remaining neutral in the event of Britain declaring war, Britain's attempts during the 1920s to "dump" her own unemployed and the "cheap coloured" labour of the empire upon Australia and the lack of Australian working-class representation at the annual Imperial Conferences. It was these and other examples that led the *Australian Worker* to refer to the "utter incompatibility" between the labour movement's class-based radical nationalism and imperialism.[48]

There was also the widespread identification among 1920s and early 1930s Australian labour activists of British imperialism in general and imperialism *per se*, whether in India, the Middle East, the Far East or elsewhere in the world, as being *necessarily* "exploitative, militaristic, undemocratic, 'territory-grabbing' and intent upon 'race aggrandisement', the 'subjugation' of weaker colonial peoples and denial of their 'right of self-determination'."[49] Finally, it is interesting to note that while partly reflected in the Australian historiography, this systematic labour movement critique of imperialism has been either marginalized or overlooked in the relevant British scholarly literature. In the latter case central importance has been attached to the more limited, conditional and reformist critique of imperialism expressed by leading labour movement figures such as Ramsay MacDonald.[50]

This last point leads naturally to my third finding. While more significant than generally recognized among historians, the systemic critique of imperialism did not constitute the sole, unchallenged response. It jostled for position, effect and sometimes overlapped in quite complex ways with other predominantly critical, but often softer, more qualified and, in the longer term, more influential labour movement responses. In addition labour attitudes towards empire and imperialism were often not totally uniform and consistent. They could combine a variety of "hard" and "soft", critical, less critical and even positive and approving aspects. They could also qualify, modify and even change their positions over time

---

[48] Kirk, "'Australians for Australia'", 102–4.
[49] Kirk, "'Australians for Australia'", 104.
[50] Kirk, *Comrades*, 155–6; Stuart Macintyre, *Oxford History of Australia*, vol. 4: *The Succeeding Age, 1901–1942* (Melbourne: Oxford University Press, 1997), 132–3, 138–41, 180–2, 191.

according to prevailing and shifting circumstances. Once again, due attention must be paid to complexity, contingency, change, continuity and context as well as purely logical and consistent systems and structures.

In accordance with these general propositions, the nature and relative influence of the kinds of labour attitudes adopted towards imperialism varied according to time, place, space and experiential reality. For example, while anti-imperialism of a fundamental kind characterized large sections of Australian labour from the period of World War One to the early 1930s, this had not been the dominant case between 1900 and 1914. As noted earlier, perceptions of an increasingly beneficent imperial influence on Australian affairs in the years of federation and the infant New Commonwealth, sanctioned, of course, by Britain, led to a sharp decline in anti-British feeling. While the *Worker* continued to fulminate against Britain, the dominant attitude towards empire was articulated by prime minister Andrew Fisher. Fisher was immensely proud of leading the "new" nation, but he also retained strong ties to his native Scotland, the Scottish working class and the wider British nation as well as the British labour movement. His aim was to further develop Australia's standing and independence *within* the empire, partly by building up her own navy rather than paying a subsidy to the British government for the British navy to defend Australian waters. In 1911 Fisher declared that a powerful, mature and prosperous Australia merited admission to the "inner family circle" of the empire rather than to be kept waiting on the "veranda". In the same year he returned to a hero's welcome in his native Scotland and attended the Imperial Conference and the coronation of George V, Edward VII's successor. Fisher had described the popular Edward as "our great and peace loving sovereign". He pledged Australia's support to Britain in 1914, although he "worried" about "the exclusion of Australia from policy-making on the war". He resigned as prime minister in 1915. He subsequently became high commissioner in London, his main place of residence until his death in 1928.[51]

The most famous British labour advocate of a more "civilised", "enlightened" and reformist form of imperialism, of course, was Ramsay MacDonald, secretary, chairman and the leader of the Labour Party. MacDonald could be extremely critical of British imperialism at various points of time, especially when coercion was the dominant aspect. Yet he believed strongly in the widespread application of an "imperial" or "international" "standard", rooted in "justice being done to all subject

---

[51] Kirk, *Comrades*, 108–9, 128; D. J. Murphy, "Fisher, Andrew (1862–1928)", *Australian Dictionary of Biography*, vol. 8 (Carlton: Melbourne University Press, 1981), 502–7.

races". Moreover, "such a standard might do much to preserve native races and elevate them into the position of self-governing citizens" in the future. MacDonald's view was highly paternalistic in character. While the dominions had already demonstrated their "maturity" and hence their rightful claims to more independence and autonomy within the empire, India and other dependencies were to be "nurtured" towards independence on a gradual basis.[52] This attitude, widespread in British labour movement circles, was also to be found in the thinking of Keir Hardie. Fiercely critical of British rule in India, Hardie nevertheless also adopted a gradualist approach to the questions of British withdrawal from India and Indian progression to self-government.[53] Following the departure of Macdonald, Snowden and other moderate "renegades" from the Labour Party in 1931, systemic anti-imperialism did enjoy a renewed period of popularity within the party. In the longer term, however, MacDonald's reformist attitude to imperialism became the dominant force. Thus the "transformation of the old British Empire into the first inter-racial Commonwealth of free nations" was described in the Labour Party's 1959 manifesto as "the supreme achievement" of the 1945 Labour government.[54]

Australian labour movement attitudes towards Britain and the infant Commonwealth also shifted significantly during the 1930s and 1940s. Notwithstanding its imperfections, the Commonwealth was increasingly seen to be more receptive to Australia's needs than the old empire. In addition "the gradual rise of Labor to governmental control in various parts of the Empire" made possible the establishment of "a loftier conception of Imperial destiny", the "ending of 'jingo' and 'plutocratic' control and 'aggression' and the triumph of peace, democracy and freedom".[55]

Most significantly, the changing pattern and balance of international affairs, in which imperial and commonwealth relations were overshadowed by the "Rise of the Dictators" and the threat of war, ensured that Australia, including Australian labour, would, despite the latter's deep divisions about involvement in another war overseas, move to an alliance with Britain in defence of democracy and freedom against the threat of worldwide totalitarian dictatorship. There is no more telling example of this transformation than the career of socialist and internationalist, John Curtin. For most of the inter-war period Curtin was highly critical of the

---

[52] Kirk, *Comrades*, 173; Howe, *Anti-Colonialism*, 45–6.
[53] Morgan, *Keir Hardie*, 190–5; Kirk, *Comrades*, 156, 172.
[54] Caroline Knowles, *Race Discourse and Labourism* (London: Routledge, 1992), 95–6.
[55] Kirk, "'Australians for Australia'", 102–3.

British empire and a strong advocate of peace and reconciliation in international affairs. In 1941 he became the new prime minister and successfully guided Australia through the war as a firm ally of Britain and the United States against the Nazis. As a result of his wartime experiences Curtin came to the belief that the empire/commonwealth "was more of a potential force for good in the post-war world than he had believed".[56]

The expression of a complex and at times seemingly contradictory combination of attitudes towards imperialism may be seen in the case of British socialists between the South African War and World War One. In the midst of the former and while condemning "greedy financiers" intent upon "wars of annexation, plunder and robbery for their own profit", Robert Blatchford's *Clarion*, much in the manner of Macdonald, nevertheless looked forward to a time when the British empire would be transformed into one which preached and practised "international brotherhood, honesty and fair dealing and recognition of the rights of others" as opposed to "brute force" and "arrogance".[57] Even the Marxist *Justice* declared that it did not wish to see England "defeated and humbled", but "triumph" by "the justification of her rule and the freedom and prosperity of her peoples".[58] Despite their common opposition to the further expansion of empire, neither Blatchford, Hyndman nor Hardie, the three main ideological influences upon the *Clarion*, *Justice*, and *Labour Leader* respectively, advocated its immediate dismemberment. This was because they perceived British imperial rule generally to be more enlightened than that practiced by routinely "aggressive" and "autocratic" Russians and Germans. It was opposition to German "authoritarianism" that led many British socialists, including the "patriot" Blatchford and the Marxist Hyndman, to support World War One.[59]

My fourth and final finding is that attitudes to imperialism were simultaneously strongly informed by questions of race, class, nation and gender. As such their characteristic expressions and historical articulations

---

[56] For Curtin see *Australian Worker*, Apr. 11, 1951; Geoffrey Serle, "Curtin John (1885–1945)", *Australian Dictionary of Biography*, vol. 13 (Carlton: Melbourne University Press, 1993), 550–8.

[57] *Clarion*, Jan. 13, 27; Feb. 10; Mar. 3, 10, 24; Aug. 4; Sep. 29, 1900.

[58] *Justice*, Apr. 7, 1900.

[59] *Clarion*, Jan. 27; Mar. 3, 10; Apr. 28; Sep. 29, 1900; Kirk, *Comrades,* 166–7; Judith Fincher Laird and John Saville, "Blatchford, Robert Peel Glanville (1851–1943)", in Joyce M. Bellamy and John Saville, eds., *Dictionary of Labour Biography*, vol. 4 (London: Macmillan, 1977), 34–42; Graham Johnson, "Hyndman, Henry Mayers (1842–1921)", in Bellamy and Saville, *Dictionary*, vol. 10 (London: Macmillan, 2000), 101–11.

and interactions constitute an obvious, but much neglected, area of study for trans-national and comparative historians. The Australian and British labour-movement attitudes explored in this paper were predominantly those of male spokespersons. "Whiteness" was often equated with "manliness" by Australian labour-movement activists, who also often dismissed upper-class Britons, and especially British officers during World War One, as effeminate, self-interested and incompetent snobs.[60] As seen at various points above, class and race widely and repeatedly informed the character of imperialism and labour attitudes towards it. Labour activists in both Britain and Australia presented highly "classed" notions of empire whereby imperialism was seen as an essential part of capitalism and class rule and its eventual transformation as necessarily involving the ending of "plutocratic" power, control and exploitation. "Race" manifested itself, for example, in the "mixed race" character of the British empire and the "whiteness" strongly informing Australian attitudes to both empire and nation. Within the labour movements of both countries "coercive" imperialism was widely seen as being fundamentally incompatible with "true" nationalism and patriotism.

Throughout the period under review, but especially at the time of nation building between 1901 and 1914, the fledgling ALP saw labour's cause as inseparable from the creation of the progressive "new" nation. In contrast, the "Imperialists" who "worshipped" at the feet of the British empire were claimed to be "disloyal to Australia".[61] The view was often expressed in the pages of Clarion, the Labour Leader, and Justice that there was an urgent need to "rescue" Britain's national honour and reputation from the "cesspit" into which the war had cast them. "We had lost the respect of the common peoples of Europe", declared Hardie, as a result of the government's policies of "brutality" and "annihilation" in South Africa. He urged the LRC candidates to expend "restless, untiring effort" to see the country "rescued from the clutches of the Mammon-inspired war fiend".[62] Will Thorne, the LRC candidate in South West Ham, in London, believed that as a result of the war, public opinion "all over the world" had become "bitterly anti-English".[63] "Nunquam"

---

[60] Marilyn Lake and Henry Reynolds, *Drawing the Global Colour Line: White Men's Countries and the Question of Racial Equality* (Carlton: Melbourne University Press, 2008), 6–12, 27–32; Bill Gammage, *The Broken Years: Australian Soldiers in the Great War* (Canberra: Australian National University Press, 1974), 269; Macintyre, *Oxford History of Australia*, 180–1.

[61] *Worker*, Aug. 6, 1904; Jan. 29, 1910.

[62] *Labour Leader*, Sep. 22, 29; Nov. 3, 10; Dec. 22, 1900.

[63] *Justice*, Sep. 29, 1900.

(Blatchford) in the *Clarion* and John E. Ellam in *Justice* exhorted the radical "people" to re-possess patriotism, in the words of "Nunquam" to, "take it out of the hands of the heartless bullies who would squander its heart and blood and prostitute its honour to serve their greed and avarice".[64] For Ellam the "ideal of England" had become that of "the race-course welcher and the hooligan", "an insensate lust for gold" and the "destruction" of "all sense of honour, all morality and all religion": if not checked, if would destroy "civilisation".[65] For many British, as well as Australian socialists and labourites, the labour movement had a special duty to appropriate, restore and develop the "true" patriotism of "the education and uplifting of England herself as a nation", of democratic advance, of "a love of freedom", of social justice, of fairness and toleration, of working-class advancement and "social emancipation".[66] Thus nation, like empire, was a highly "classed" construction.

Conclusion

My specific concern with Australia and Britain carries a number of implications for the wider study of the subject matter of labour and empire. It suggests the importance of paying due attention to methodological and conceptual as well as the historian's, or at least the British historian's, usual and overriding concern with substantive matters. It invites scholars to reject "core-periphery" and "top-down" approaches in favour of more nuanced attention to both the encounters and mutual influences and exchanges among people, their ideas, cultures and institutions within the complex circuits of empire, and the nature and outcomes of the dialogue between "top down" and "bottom up" voices and influences. It advocates close attention to language in order to describe and explain the various labour movement representations of empire and imperialism. At the same time, however, it highlights the importance of firmly contextualizing language in terms of time, place and space in order to tease out the complexities, contradictions, continuities, changes and variable influences of representations of empire in history. It also highlights the importance of engaging both the structural and cultural aspects of empire and imperialism, of questions of contextualized political economy as well as discourse. Finally, my limited focus would be greatly

[64] *Clarion*, Jan. 13, 27; Mar. 3, 1900.
[65] *Justice*, Jan. 6; Oct. 27, 1900.
[66] *Justice*, Jan. 13, 20, 1900; *Labour Leader*, Nov. 3, 1900; *Clarion*, Jan. 13, 27; Mar. 3, 1900; Robert Blatchford, *Merrie England* (London: Clarion Press, 1908); Kirk, "'Australians for Australia'", 97–104.

enriched and challenged by the adoption of a wider framework of reference – of the study of labour movements and empire in many other locations of both the British and other modern empires. In turn this would stimulate the collaborative international research which is so urgently required if we are to successfully develop the study of comparative, transnational and global labour history.

WEAVING TALES OF EMPIRE:
GANDHI'S VISIT TO LANCASHIRE, 1931[1]

HESTER BARRON

In the autumn of 1931, Gandhi was one of a number of Indian delegates who journeyed to London to meet Ramsay MacDonald and other politicians for the Second Round Table Conference. Taking a weekend off at the end of September, and upon the invitation of the Joint Committee of Cotton Trade Organizations, he travelled north to the cotton towns around Blackburn. It was a private visit and he accepted no public engagements, instead spending the weekend meeting deputations of cotton workers and employers, and talking with local notables.

His visit was set against a backdrop of national political and economic upheaval. A month earlier, on August 24, the Labour government had collapsed following a crisis over unemployment benefits, having already endured almost two years of the "economic blizzard" (as Ramsay MacDonald characterized it) occasioned by the Wall Street Crash. Amidst cries of betrayal from most of his previous Labour colleagues, MacDonald had taken his place at the head of a National government. Despite a raft of economy measures, the new government faced a sterling crisis and, on September 21, a few days before Gandhi's visit, the Bank of England had reluctantly abandoned the gold standard.

If the British political and economic situation was in turmoil in the closing months of 1931, the structure of the empire was also in flux. The Second Round Table Conference, which Gandhi was in England to attend, had been called to discuss possible dominion status for India. Meanwhile, British legislators were busy drawing up the Statute of Westminster, which would be signed in December of that year, and would recognize the constitutional autonomy of the white dominions. And on the other side of

[1] At the "The British Labour Movement and Imperialism" conference at UCLan in June 2008, I shared a stimulating panel on this subject with Irina Spector-Marks; thanks also to those who made comments in the discussion that followed. I am also grateful to Saul Dubow, Vinita Damodaran and Chris Prior for their suggestions and advice.

the world – although with implications that could not yet be known – on 19 September, the Japanese had begun their invasion of Manchuria. Against such a heady political and international backdrop, Gandhi's reception raises important questions about the wider experience of empire on British society.

The workers of Lancashire cannot, of course, be taken as representative of working-class attitudes throughout Britain in the inter-war years. Compared to other industrial areas of Britain, the greater number of women in employment created a different gender dynamic; a significant Irish presence disrupted ethnic and religious homogeneity; and paternalistic involvement in leisure and cultural activities reduced the ability of cotton and mining unions to create a unitary discourse. Writing about the years before World War One, Peter Clarke has described the Lancastrian working class as "characterised by Conservative politics and aggressive Churchmanship."[2] The politics of Protestantism were fading by the inter-war years, and "Tory Lancashire" was becoming more receptive to a different type of progressive politics, but the Labour Party failed to make the inroads that it did in other industrial areas. In the county constituency of Darwen, where Gandhi was to spend the first twenty-four hours of his stay, the Labour Party trailed in third in every general election between the wars. Even when the country swung leftwards en masse in 1945, the Labour candidate in Darwen could still only manage second place, ahead of his Liberal rival. In the neighbouring two-member constituency of Blackburn, the first and only Labour members of the inter-war years were elected in 1929. Both lost their seats two years later.[3] In his recent study of the Lancashire working classes, Trevor Griffiths documented the religious, ethnic and occupational divisions that cut across the social worlds of miners and cotton workers. He concluded that "at several points in working-class life, from the workplace to the ballot box, class, as an influence affecting the choices made, appears to have been secondary, at best."[4]

But this is not to suggest that class was unimportant. If the economic crisis was international in its causes and its impact, its immediate consequences could be felt within working-class homes throughout Lancashire. Although not specifically designated a "special area" by the

---

[2] P. Clarke, *Lancashire and the New Liberalism* (Cambridge: Cambridge University Press, 1971), 74.
[3] F. W. S. Craig, *British Parliamentary Election Results, 1918–49* (Glasgow: Political Reference Publications, 1969), 92, 394.
[4] T. Griffiths, *The Lancashire Working Classes, c.1880–1930* (Oxford: Oxford University Press, 2001), 331.

government,[5] the North West's dependence on both coal and textiles made it particularly vulnerable to the economic downturn. The cotton industry was in a devastated state in 1931: in Lancashire as a whole, government figures counted 44.6 percent of spinners and weavers unemployed on September 21, 1931.[6] The suffering was particularly acute in the weaving sector, which was geographically concentrated in the north and north-east of the county: in Blackburn, eighty mills were reported as idle in the week preceding Gandhi's visit.[7] Amidst such economic privation, class remained an important reference point. The Amalgamated Weavers' Association (AWA) was one of the largest trade unions in Britain. In 1931 it could congratulate itself on maintaining a membership of over 150,000, despite the travails of the industry: "a truly magnificent achievement," in the words of its annual report.[8]

A study of Lancashire cotton workers and their attitudes to the visit of the Indian leader is therefore interesting as a case study of what was – at least in some ways – a "traditional" working-class industrial community. However, Lancashire is of further importance because of the fact that the county's economic situation was intimately associated with imperial concerns. Although the causes of the economic downturn in textiles were diverse, resulting from a general decline in exports on top of structural problems at home, the state of the Indian market was a major factor. Indian imports had begun to decline after World War One, following the development of indigenous Indian industry and an increase in Japanese competition, but they had been further cut by the imposition of protective tariffs by the government of India, and, more recently, by the boycott of foreign cloth initiated by the Indian National Congress (INC) as part of the civil disobedience movement. Indeed, Lancashire cotton was the symbolic enemy of the nationalist campaign in India, and Gandhi's anti-Lancashire rhetoric was a recurring motif in his speeches.

The effects of the boycott were tempered following the Gandhi-Irwin talks of March 1931, after which the boycott was recast as anti-foreign rather than anti-British, in line with Gandhi's emphasis on self-sufficiency and *swadeshi*. However, although the position in the cotton trade was beginning to show signs of a revival in the later months of 1931, the boycott continued to have a significant effect on cotton exports. Imports of

---

[5] The 1934 Special Areas Act singled out Durham and Tyneside, West Cumberland, West-Central Scotland and South Wales as such.
[6] The National Archives [TNA], BT56/36. Memorandum on the Cotton Industry.
[7] *Cotton Factory Times*, Sep. 18, 1931.
[8] Working Class Movement Library [WCML], F03/06. AWA report and statement of accounts for year ending Apr. 2, 1932.

cotton piece-goods into Bombay fell from over 300 million square yards in 1930 to 230 million in 1931; into Madras from 76 million to 59 million; into Calcutta from 345 million to 71 million.[9] In May 1931, the AWA acknowledged the gravity of the situation, noting that the raising of import duties, the boycott and "the intimidation that is being exercised" was "unquestionably ... having very serious effects upon certain specific manufacturing districts which produce primarily for the Indian markets."[10]

When Gandhi arrived in Lancashire on September 25, these were facts and figures that were placed before him. J. W. Sunderland, the secretary of the Great Harwood Weavers' Association, for example, used one meeting to call the Indian leader's attention to the extent of unemployment in the district, which he estimated at around 60 percent and which he believed to be very closely connected to the boycott.[11] At times Gandhi's rejoinders verged on the hostile. "Prior to and during the intensity of the boycott," Gandhi pointed out to one deputation, the Indian people were virtually at war with Britain: his listeners "should realise that it was quite impossible for people at war with another country to trade with that enemy country."[12]

Responses to Gandhi's Visit

Given such an economic backdrop, Gandhi's impending visit was viewed with some alarm by politicians and government officials. One civil service memorandum worried that those involved in the textile industry were men "whose horizon does not extend far beyond Lancashire and whose views are strongly coloured by the troubles of the cotton trade ... Mutual understanding might in these circumstances be difficult."[13] The government of India was also uneasy, writing to the British government to ask that every step be taken to protect Gandhi's safety while in England. It anticipated that the greatest threat would probably come from his many Indian enemies, but it also feared that he might be roughly treated if he visited Lancashire.[14] Extra police were therefore drafted in for the visit, in

---

[9] S. R. B. Leadbeater, *The Politics of Textiles: The Indian Cotton-Mill Industry and the Legacy of Swadeshi, 1900–1985* (London; New Delhi: Sage, 1993), 34–6.
[10] TNA, BT56/36. Memorandum from the AWA, May 6, 1931.
[11] *Blackburn Times*, Oct. 3, 1931.
[12] Ibid.
[13] TNA, BT56/36. Undated memo, unsigned.
[14] British Library [hereafter, BL], IOR/L/PO/1/30 (iii). Telegram from Home Department, government of India, to secretary of state for India, Sep. 1, 1931.

addition to a bodyguard of Scotland Yard men who accompanied Gandhi from London.[15]

Perhaps Gandhi shared such concerns, for he himself was surprised by his reception. "I have never expected anything but courteous treatment from the working people of Lancashire," he announced on the final day of his visit, "but I was unprepared for the manifestation of deep affection that the crowds of people that lined the streets yesterday spontaneously showed to me. I shall ever treasure that affection as one of the pleasing recollections of my life."[16] He expressed similar sentiments in private, claiming to one Board of Trade official on his return to London that he had been made to feel like "a member of their family."[17] Nor was this simply Gandhi's optimistic assessment. The American journalist and historian William Shirer documented the visit and later described how "the bluff Lancashire cotton-mill hands ... knew a man who was devoting his life to helping the poor when they saw one. They gave him a tumultuous welcome."[18] Local press reporters described the crowds and the applause that met the Indian leader wherever he went, while their papers carried the famous picture of Gandhi surrounded by cheering female millhands.[19] The *Cotton Factory Times*, the operatives' newspaper, also spoke of the vociferous welcome given to the Indian leader.[20] And so the fears of the authorities turned out to have been groundless. In fact the only untoward incident involving the police occurred when the assistant chief constable of Lancashire fell over while getting into his car and dislocated his shoulder.[21]

There were some moments of discord. The *Darwen News* reported overhearing one woman rebuking those who were clapping. "What do you want to clap him for?", she was quoted as saying, "He's the biggest enemy you've got!"[22] A reporter for *Time* magazine noted that as well as cheers of "Good old Gandhi!", boos could also be heard amongst the crowds, and cries of "tear his eyes out."[23] Furthermore, the large numbers of people

---

[15] *Blackburn Times*, Sep. 19, 1931.

[16] *Manchester Guardian*, Sep. 26, 1931.

[17] TNA, BT56/36. Letter from G. G. Barnes to Sir Horace Hamilton, Sep. 29, 1931.

[18] W. L. Shirer, *Gandhi: A Memoir* (New York: Simon and Schuster, 1979), 180.

[19] See, for example, the *Blackburn Times*, Sep. 26, 1931, Oct. 3, 1931; *Northern Daily Telegraph*, Sep. 28, 1931.

[20] *Cotton Factory Times*, Oct. 2, 1931.

[21] *Darwen News*, Sep. 30, 1931.

[22] Ibid., Oct. 3, 1931.

[23] *Time*, Oct. 5, 1931.

who lined the streets to catch a glimpse of the Indian leader were not necessarily a straightforward indication of his popularity, as curiosity also drew the crowds. Gandhi's manner of dress naturally excited a great deal of comment. One old man, born in Darwen in 1901, was later asked about the visit by an oral history interviewer: "Well, I've nothing to tell about it. He was a man who just had a loincloth, that was all."[24] Another respondent gave a different reason for Gandhi's novelty: "In those days it was very rare to see a black man."[25]

Such curiosity was encouraged by the press. Even the *Manchester Guardian* succumbed, revelling in the (inaccurate) reportage of curious tit-bits. "Rarely can a liner have carried such a remarkable assortment of luggage," it commented in early September, describing the ship bearing Gandhi and his entourage to England. One of Gandhi's followers had been denied permission to bring his own cow with him, it stated, but had instead brought 120 quarts of ritualistic pasteurised milk for consumption on the journey. The newspaper also claimed that another had brought a consignment of nearly half a ton of mud from the Ganges, to be converted into miniature gods for worshipping purposes.[26] Speculation on the Mahatma's living style continued after his arrival in Britain. As Gandhi travelled up to Lancashire, one local reporter interviewed Mrs J. P. Davies, with whom he was to stay, and asked her what she had planned for his supper. She wasn't sure. "But you have got a goat," he asked? She reassured him that although she possessed no goat, she had managed to procure a good supply of goat's milk.[27]

Stories about both Gandhi and his ideology would remain long after he had left, and were often exaggerated. One cotton worker was born in 1934 but had heard all about the visit of the Indian leader to his home county. Years later, he described how Gandhi had encouraged people to spin their own cotton. But, he said, Gandhi had made the Indian people do it the whole time: "every person had to walk around the streets doing their daily business with a spinning spindle and they'd have to spin the yarn no matter what they were doing, [if] they were walking down the street, they were all spinning yarns."[28] Another oral history interviewee had been fifteen years old at the time of the visit. She had not seen the Mahatma herself, but she had known about his arrival. Gandhi had come to Salford, so she claimed, and sat "in a shop window for everybody to see. I don't

---

[24] North West Sound Archive [NWSA], GK 2022.0188.
[25] NWSA, Ryders 11B.
[26] *Manchester Guardian*, Sep. 4, 1931.
[27] *Blackburn Times*, Sep. 26, 1931.
[28] British Library Sound Archive, 1CDR0024051. Vincent Newton.

know how long for, but as kids we sort of heard about it, and he sat there, you know, cross legged with his loincloth. And it was like, well it was a peepshow kind of thing because nobody had ever seen anything like that."[29] In fact, Gandhi did not visit Salford in 1931, but the respondent persisted with her story despite the interviewer's gentle questioning of it. Perhaps it originated though the presence of a mimic, which itself says something about the extent of his notoriety.

But, curious as Lancashire was likely to be, many of its inhabitants would have also known at least something about Gandhi's role as a politician and an Indian leader. Lancashire's cotton workers would have learnt about empire in the same way as the working classes elsewhere in the country. Visits to the cinema or to sporting fixtures, or simply the glimpse of advertisements in the local press, all had the potential to spread knowledge and pride in empire, while the school classroom could also act as a powerful propagator of imperial ideas. It is, of course, difficult to ascertain the sentiments engendered by such contact, if indeed any were engendered at all.[30] As workers in an industry dependent on exports, however, Lancashire weavers were perhaps likely to possess a greater awareness of imperial and global issues than workers in other industries. In May 1931, the monthly journal of the Darwen Weavers, Warpers and Winders' Association commented that whatever position a worker took on the situation in India, most held some view on the matter. "Societies pro-Indian and pro-Anglo are flooding the country with meetings and literature," it explained, "while public meetings are being held to protest against the boycott of Lancashire goods."[31] Four months earlier, B. Shiva Rao, of the All-India Trade Union Federation, had visited the county. "A splendid meeting was held, which did much to stimulate sympathy with Indian aspirations," reported the Great Harwood Weavers' Association.[32] A wider attempt was also made by those sympathetic to the Indian cause to acquaint men and women with aspects of Gandhi's ideology. In June

---

[29] NWSA, PH 2005.0017.

[30] This debate has spawned much historical discussion, particularly following the publication of John MacKenzie's *Propaganda and Empire: The Manipulation of British Public Opinion, 1880–1960* (Manchester: Manchester University Press, 1984). For contrasting views see also B. Porter, *The Absent-Minded Imperialists: Empire, Society and Culture in Britain* (Oxford: Oxford University Press, 2004) and A. Thompson, *The Empire Strikes Back? The Impact of Imperialism on Britain from the Mid-Nineteenth Century* (Harlow: Pearson Longman, 2005).

[31] Lancashire Record Office [LRO], DDX1078/2/24. Darwen Weavers, Warpers and Winders' Association. Monthly journal, May 1931.

[32] *Blackburn Times*, Sep. 19, 1931.

1931, two addresses on Gandhi and his ideas were given in Manchester by Horace Alexander, a supporter of Gandhi and a lecturer at the Woodbrooke Settlement in Birmingham. He spoke about Gandhi's background in South Africa, his economic outlook and the philosophy behind *satyagraha* and *ahimsa*. There is no way of knowing the size of his audience, but both lectures received lengthy write-ups, including summaries, in the local press.[33]

To some extent, such an interest and awareness was inevitable given the interdependence of the Lancashire and Indian industries. The *Blackburn Times*, for example, commented that it was a direct consequence of the industrial situation that Gandhi had become "a man whose name is known to every cotton operative."[34] J. B. Priestley made a similar observation when he completed his English journey in 1933. Once, he said, there had been this

> rum little chap called Gandhi, who provided the most promising raw material for music-hall jokes … What had his antics to do with the stout cotton men, grinning in their clubs, the weavers roaring in the music hall gallery? Nowt at all, it seemed. And then all manner of unpleasant things began to happen in India. The peasants were poorer than they had been, owing to bad harvests. Then there was strong local competition in the cotton trade. Then heavy import duties on Lancashire cotton. And then a boycott of English goods. The whole Indian trade, which had taken millions and millions of yards of the cheap grey stuff woven in Blackburn and district, was crumbling away; and the next thing they knew, firms went out of business, mills were idle, then empty, and folk by the street and by the town were thrown out of work.[35]

The economic crisis had further stimulated debates about the Empire due to the vigour with which Conservative politicians renewed their calls for protection. By the end of September 1931 specifically, interest in wider political issues was at a peak as rumours spread that a general election was imminent.[36] In the county constituency of Darwen in particular, the impending election brought discussion of the economic role of the dominions and colonies to the fore. There, the Liberal Sir Herbert Samuel campaigned hard to keep his seat, for despite running under the "National" banner, and despite a private appeal to Baldwin, he was opposed by a Conservative protectionist candidate. Samuel, initially reluctant to focus

---

[33] *Darwen News*, June 27, 1931.
[34] *Blackburn Times*, Sep. 26, 1931.
[35] J. B. Priestley, *English Journey* (Harmondsworth: Penguin, 1977 edn.), 261.
[36] MacDonald formally announced the dissolution of parliament on Oct. 2, 1931.

on the issue of free trade, was drawn into it by the aggressive attacks of his opponent; his biographer, Bernard Wasserstein, has commented that "even by the low standard of 1931 the campaign in Darwen was exceptionally abrasive."[37] Samuel would keep his seat with a huge turnout of 92.2 percent, although elsewhere across the county the Conservatives made substantial gains.

Attitudes to India

If most cotton workers were likely to have had some awareness of who Gandhi was and what he stood for, the question remains as to how far any support given to him was a consequence of wider sympathy with Indian aspirations. Studies have demonstrated that sympathy amongst the British labour movement for Indian self-government – let alone full independence – was often lukewarm at best.[38] Annual Labour Party conferences were keen to nod to Indian affairs and pass resolutions of support: a resolution affirming a belief in the Indian people's claim to "full self-government and self-determination, including the right to independence" was carried by an overwhelming majority at the Labour Party conference in October 1930, for example, although the debate also saw a number of delegates express concern.[39] However, Stephen Howe has suggested that the Labour Party was dominated by two broad currents of opinion in the inter-war years. Some (including MacDonald) adhered to "constructive imperialism", and advocated the gradual progress towards self-government (even then probably within the empire itself); others advocated a more active preparation for self-government and a more positive commitment to the rights of colonial subjects. Howe argues that while there were some within the Labour Party who vigorously advocated anti-colonialism, and some who were just as vigorous in their affirmation of imperialism, such beliefs were absent from mainstream Labour Party debates and policy-making and had little influence on the Labour leaders.[40] The record of the 1929–31

---

[37] B. Wasserstein, *Herbert Samuel: A Political Life* (Oxford: Clarendon, 1992), 331. For details of the campaign, see 330–3.
[38] See, for example, M. Ahmed, *The British Labour Party and the Indian Independence Movement* (London: Oriental University Press, 1987); P. Gupta, *Imperialism and the British Labour Movement, 1914–64* (London: Macmillan, 1975); S. Howe, *Anticolonialism in British Politics: The Left and the End of Empire, 1918–64* (Oxford: Clarendon, 1993).
[39] Labour Party, *Report of the 30th Annual Conference, Oct. 1930* (London, 1931), 216–20.
[40] Howe, *Anticolonialism*, 47–8.

Labour government was therefore viewed with disappointment by the nationalist movement: the Labour Party's involvement with the Simon Commission in particular did much to alienate it from Indian nationalists.[41]

Howe points out, however, that the Labour Party did at least take a degree of interest in colonial issues. In contrast, "the focus of attention of British trade unionism was almost wholly parochial."[42] Even when trade union leaders did look to imperial concerns, it was not always with sympathy. Nicholas Owen has argued that many within the trade unions were sceptical of the effectiveness of the INC and were mistrustful of its links with the Indian middle classes.[43] Relations between the British trade union movement and its Indian counterpart were also strained because of the communist influences within the latter, especially after the split of the All-India Trade Union Congress in December 1929. Suspicions of Comintern subterfuge similarly dogged the attempts of the League Against Imperialism, founded in 1927, to garner widespread support amongst the British labour movement. Tensions were often visible, and sometimes surfaced within the most amicable of settings. In November 1930, B. Shiva Rao of the All-India Trade Union Federation addressed the Trades Union Congress (TUC) as one of that year's fraternal delegates. His speech made reference to the Simon Commission and criticized the tendency of some amongst the British labour movement to doubt the future of the Indian people under self-government. It was greeted with cheers from most of his audience, but he was interrupted at several points and hecklers had to be removed from the room.[44]

However, once again, the cotton trade unions were perhaps more likely than others to be receptive to affairs relating to the subcontinent, due to the interrelationship of the two textile industries. The International Federation of Textile Workers' Associations had been founded in Manchester in 1894, and Lancashire men made up by far the most numerous of its representatives, with the Labour MP for Preston, Tom Shaw, as one of its central figures. Its annual congress was held in August 1931, a month before Gandhi's visit, and seven delegates of the AWA attended. "Contact with other nationals makes us realise the particular and peculiar aspects of our industry," they concluded in their report, "The depression we are suffering from is common to all our colleagues; if there be any difference,

---

[41] Ahmed, *British Labour Party*, 106.

[42] Howe, *Anticolonialism*, 77.

[43] N. Owen, *The British Left and India* (Oxford: Oxford University Press, 2007), 11.

[44] TUC, *Report of Proceedings at the 62nd Annual Trades Union Congress, September 1930* (London, 1931), 316–9.

it is only in degree."[45] Such attitudes amongst the union leaders were not necessarily shared by their rank and file, but there is some evidence that such sentiments were more widely diffused throughout the industry. Andrew Thompson has noted that the Bolton Operative Spinners' Association supported a resolution calling for Indian self-government as early as 1924.[46]

Lancashire also had a history of political sympathy with international struggles. Recent historiography on the American Civil War has demonstrated that the folk memory of support given to the Union by unselfish Lancastrian cotton workers was in reality rather more complicated and varied; nevertheless the memory remains.[47] In fact, in 1931 the references made to the earlier conflict were remarkably few, at least as preserved in the historical record. Indeed, when such mention was made, it was a record that could just as easily be turned on its head by *opponents* of Indian self-government. In October 1931, for example, a local justice of the peace, Henry Smalley, addressed a meeting at the Bright Reform Club in Darwen:

> So far as he could make out [he declared], all that he [Gandhi] said of importance was that if the people of Lancashire were prepared to concede independence to India he was prepared to advocate as far as he could that India should buy Lancashire's goods. In other words, we are to sell the Empire for a mess of pottage. He evidently was not aware of the fact that during the American Civil War, when ... Lancashire was starving, Lancashire remained solid for the North, and I don't believe now that Lancashire is prepared to sell the British Empire for the sake of doing a little more trade with India.[48]

Perhaps more significant were memories of the help given by Lancashire in times past in response to Indian hunger crises. During the famine of 1897, for example, almost £160,000 was raised following an appeal to the cotton industry. Charles Macara had been the president of the Federation of Master Cotton Spinners' Associations at the time, and in his memoirs he later praised the goodwill of the Lancashire working classes, to whom he believed a great part of the credit had been due.[49] It was a

---

[45] WCML, F03/06. AWA report and statement of accounts for year ending Apr. 2, 1932.
[46] Thompson, *Empire*, 77.
[47] See, for example, R. J. M. Blackett, *Divided Hearts: Britain and the American Civil War* (Baton Rouge, LA: Louisiana State University Press, 2001).
[48] *Blackburn Times*, Oct. 3, 1931.
[49] C. Macara, *Recollections* (London: Cassell and Co., 1921), 152–5.

historical record that was to be called upon by the cotton union leaders in their talks with Gandhi over thirty years later. J. W. Sunderland, the secretary of the Great Harwood Weavers' Association, told a reporter that he had reminded the Indian leader of Lancashire's past kindnesses in times of famine, and suggested that such kindness was not being reciprocated.[50]

As far as Gandhi was concerned, an attempt to build on this sympathy for the poor Indian worker was one of the purposes of his visit. He had long been an astute player of the international media, and was aware of the influence that successful coverage could have on British policy-makers and the added momentum that it could give his campaign back in India. Judith Brown has argued that one of the reasons for Gandhi's journey to Britain in the first place was precisely to allow him to appeal to British public opinion over the heads of the Indian and British governments, and that he believed that his most important task in Britain lay outside the formal parameters of conference work. After all, Lancashire was only one of various trips he made during his stay in England: he also gave addresses at a number of universities; accepted invitations to some major public schools; and met with various Christian groups and prominent churchmen.[51]

In Lancashire (as elsewhere) therefore, Gandhi chose to focus his speeches on the poverty of the Indian worker. To deputation after deputation, he informed cotton workers, employers and journalists that India did not speak of standards of living but of standards of poverty; that Britain's problem of three million unemployed was insignificant compared to India's hundreds of millions unemployed; that compared to the starving millions of India, the poverty of Lancashire dwindled into insignificance.[52] This message made a stronger impression on one old weaver than the political implications of the visit. Born in Burnley in 1913, he was asked years later why Gandhi had come to Britain in 1931. "I think he came to explain the difficulties of India and various countries and how they were suffering, and that sort of thing," he replied.[53]

As well as stressing the suffering of the poor Indian peasant, Gandhi also presented an image of himself as one of the people, and this was enhanced by the details given in the local press. The operatives' *Cotton Factory Times* ran sympathetic coverage before his visit, informing its readers that Gandhi only ever travelled in third-class rail compartments

---

[50] *Blackburn Times*, Oct. 3, 1931.
[51] J. M. Brown, *Gandhi and Civil Disobedience: The Mahatma in Indian Politics, 1928–34* (Cambridge: Cambridge University Press, 1977), 257–9.
[52] LRO, DDX1078/2/24. Darwen Weavers, Warpers and Winders Association, monthly journal, Nov. 1931; *Blackburn Times*, Oct. 3, 1931.
[53] NWSA, JH 1998.0030.

and that he would be staying in "an ordinary working man's cottage."[54] The *Darwen News* noted with approval that "our Indian visitor will be received with simple Lancashire hospitality, he will, presumably, use the same kind of dishes and plates as are used in thousands of working-class Lancashire homes, and he will warm himself before a fire of Lancashire coal."[55] Comments such as these complemented the saintly image already cultivated by the Mahatma. Earlier in the month, the *Cotton Factory Times* had described his "Spartan mode of living, which involves the renunciation of almost all the amenities which the civilised world looks upon as making life worthwhile, his fearlessness and fatalistic willingness to suffer imprisonment and ignominy in order to achieve his purpose – these are the traits of the true martyr."[56] Such sentiments were echoed by at least some of its readers. The union leader Alice Foley, later to be secretary of the Bolton and District Weavers and Winders' Union, noted in her memoirs that having seen Gandhi, she had come away with the impression "that a saint had mingled with us for a brief moment in time."[57]

Not all were convinced. If Gandhi's image won Alice Foley to his cause, she admitted that her opinions were contradicted by "a few of our hard-headed folks [who] considered him to be a 'bit of a fraud.'"[58] Union officials might also be sceptical. J. W. Sunderland spoke to a local newspaper after one meeting, and reported that he had

> expressed the hope to Mr Gandhi ... that in considering the question of poverty he would remember that suffering and hardship was really a relative matter. For instance, if one makes a bald comparison between the poor person in Lancashire and the poor person in India, the latter will appear far the worst. But if one examines the respective positions of both and the loss that each has sustained in a relative way, it is quite easy to conceive that the moral and mental suffering of the Lancashire person is quite as great as that experienced by the Indian.[59]

In an attempt to foster international labour solidarity, Gandhi was keen to emphasize his links with the British working classes further. At one meeting he told a group of union leaders about his leadership of a strike

---

[54] *Cotton Factory Times*, Sep. 25, 1931.

[55] *Darwen News*, Sep. 26, 1931.

[56] *Cotton Factory Times*, Sep. 4, 1931.

[57] A. Foley, *A Bolton Childhood* (Manchester: Manchester University Extra Mural Department/North Western District of the Workers' Educational Association, 1973), 90.

[58] Ibid., p. 90.

[59] *Blackburn Times*, Oct. 3, 1931.

against the cotton-mill owners in Ahmedabad in 1918, which had been resolved in favour of better wages and conditions for the workers. "They had scarcely imagined Gandhi as a strike leader," William Shirer later recalled, "When he revealed it, they burst into applause."[60] In fact, regular readers of the *Cotton Factory Times* might already have had some awareness of the struggles of the Indian working classes, if not of Gandhi's part in them. Such news frequently found its way into its columns: in early September, for example, it reported in some detail on a strike by textile workers in Sholapur; towards the end of September it reported on a strike amongst silk and cotton workers in Benares.[61]

However, appeals to international labour solidarity could also be used by those hostile to Gandhi, for the Congress-imposed boycott could easily be represented as a tool of the Indian employer class. When one of the Manchester MPs, the Conservative Sir Gerald Hurst, denounced the boycott in the House of Commons, he used a description of the terrible conditions in Indian textile factories to support his argument: "it cannot be said that this system of boycotting British goods serves the true interests of the working people employed in the mills in Bombay ... The truth is that the mill-owning classes in India are exploiting the idealism which animates Mr Gandhi's group of nationalists."[62] But even if weavers agreed, and expressed reservations about Gandhi's methods, this did not prohibit them from maintaining a sympathetic stance towards his political aspirations. Addressing a meeting on September 23, the general secretary of the AWA, Andrew Naesmith, argued that it was the economic effect of the nationalist movement rather than its aims that was causing dissatisfaction in Lancashire. He suggested that the cotton workers would "welcome a large measure of Dominion status, or even self-government ... but I am satisfied that the Indian Question is not being assisted by the policy that is being exercised upon us."[63]

Opinions such as these were not confined to the union leaders but could also be found amongst the rank and file. In July, "A. B.", a cotton operative from Accrington, wrote to Muriel Lester, a settlement leader in the East End and the woman with whom Gandhi would stay while in London. The operative reassured Lester of his or her "profound admiration" for Gandhi, and continued:

---

[60] Shirer, *Gandhi*, 183.
[61] *Cotton Factory Times*, Sep. 4, 1931, Sep. 25, 1931.
[62] *Hansard Parliamentary Debates* (Commons), 5th. ser., 250, cols. 406–7.
[63] *Blackburn Times*, Sep. 26, 1931.

a great many of my fellow workers in Lancashire share that spirit of admiration ... We are very anxious to see our fellow Indian workers raised upon a higher economic plane of life, and we would only be too pleased if we could assist them by whatever means in our power to enable them to achieve their laudable object. But I believe it is in the realm of practicable possibility to assist our Indian fellow workers to a higher standard of living and at the same time for our friend Mr Gandhi and his Indian colleagues to modify their views upon the Economic Boycott of Lancashire cotton goods.[64]

Such a separation of economic and imperial objectives was encouraged at the highest political level. It was another reason why many at Westminster had harboured reservations about the visit. One civil servant at the India Office pointed out that "the discussion about the proposed visit to Lancashire would naturally lead into a discussion of the more general question of bringing the tariff relations between Great Britain and India into the scope of the Round Table Conference discussions."[65] He then wondered what Gandhi's purpose in going to Lancashire might be. "Is it to be a bargain? Will Lancs. offer to support Dominion status if a market for Lancs. goods is assured? ... I needn't develop the objections. The future constitution of India is not to be bought and sold as part of a trade bargain."[66]

In fact, this particular official's fears were realized, as this was indeed something that the Indian leader had in mind. To various deputations of both employers and operatives, Gandhi suggested that Lancashire had the potential to benefit substantially if the British government were to grant India her independence. He promised that in the aftermath of such a development he would propose a ban on the importation into India of all foreign cloth except that from Lancashire. "You see," Gandhi reportedly explained, "it would just be a case of friendly business relations between two equal partners. We would not like to discriminate against Japan, the United States and Western Europe. But naturally two happy equal partners like India and Great Britain could not be blamed for making an arrangement to their mutual interests and benefit."[67] Further such statements were reported in the local press.[68]

Even discounting such a suggestion, it was likely that trading interests would best be served by friendly relationships between the two countries;

---

[64] Lester, *Entertaining Gandhi*, 36–7.
[65] TNA, BT56/36. Letter from W. D. Croft to W. B. Brown, Sep. 8, 1931.
[66] BL, IOR/L/PO/1/30 (iii). Unsigned letter to Croft, Aug. 15, 1931.
[67] Shirer, *Gandhi*, 182.
[68] *Blackburn Times*, Oct. 3, 1931.

after all, the result of hostility had been the boycott. For purely pragmatic reasons, therefore, it made sense for the weavers to support Indian aspirations, or at the very least to support good relations between Britain and India. In August 1931, the monthly journal of the Darwen Weavers, Warpers and Winders Association welcomed the news of a possible visit of Gandhi to Lancashire:

> Good results are certain to ensure [sic] from personal contact between representatives of the Lancashire Cotton Trade and the peoples of India. We need tea, rubber, rice, spices, ivory and other commodities which India can supply. Our main service in payment for those goods it to take the raw cotton and assemble it into cloth by our processes of spinning and weaving, which the Indian people can wear.[69]

During Gandhi's visit itself, Shirer noted that "at one silent mill in Darwen he [Gandhi] had beamed with pleasure at a large notice of greeting plastered on the wall. 'We welcome Gandhi in all friendliness because we realise the future of Lancashire and India depends on reconciliation and cooperation.'"[70]

It was also argued that the granting of independence to India would actually improve Lancashire's position as a trading partner, with or without Gandhi's promises of preference. One Liberal MP for a Manchester seat, P. M. Oliver, railed against government policy in the House of Commons. At present, he suggested, Britain was in the position of a trustee, with certain obligations to India. With a free constitution, however, India would become an equal, with whom the British government could bargain and have only the interests of Lancashire at heart: "Now the predominant consideration of the Secretary of State must be, I suppose, the interests of India; then the predominating consideration will be the interests of Lancashire."[71]

The Traditional Concerns of Labour

The goodwill shown towards the Indian leader was therefore a result of both a degree of political sympathy and a measure of economic pragmatism. However, if the hostility he encountered was limited, this was also because many did not necessarily feel that he was the man to blame

---

[69] LRO, DDX1078/2/24. Darwen Weavers, Warpers and Winders Association, monthly journal, Aug. 1931.
[70] Shirer, *Gandhi*, 181.
[71] *Hansard*, 254, cols. 2387–8.

for the industry's troubles. This view was encouraged by Gandhi, who argued both at private meetings and to the press that the economic problems of the textile trade had been caused by world trade conditions rather than by any action on his part. "If there had never been a boycott in India," he told journalists on the final day of his visit, "the progress of indigenous manufacture in India would nevertheless be irresistible."[72]

This argument was also made by other commentators. The inter-war years saw a number of investigations into the cotton industry on both sides of the political divide, and all agreed that the depression had a number of causes. Those written from a labour perspective tended to place responsibility on the capitalist system. The United Textile Factory Workers' Association, for example, blamed the depression on a decline in consumption owing to wage cuts both in Britain and abroad.[73] An ILP publication argued that the public flotations of 1919–20, the multitude of sinecure directorships, the "toll levied on the industry by parasites and middlemen" and the stranglehold of high finance on the industry were responsible.[74] William Rust, the district organizer of the Communist Party in Lancashire, suggested that while some "learned Lancastrians" were satisfied to explain everything by the loss of foreign markets, the truth was that Lancashire's problems could be solved if only "the workers in Britain could buy back what they had produced; if the huge sums swallowed up by rent, interest and profit were available for work schemes ... of social value."[75] Such conclusions were echoed by the weavers themselves. In May 1931, for example, the AWA delivered a memorandum to the Board of Trade calling for a reorganization of the industry and the elimination of duplicated charges and numerous middlemen.[76]

This was partly due to the desire of the Labour government and its supporters to play down the importance of the boycott, and Indian civil disobedience generally, which had flared up on its watch. A joint Labour Party and TUC document of May 1931 which collated advice for Labour speakers therefore advised that although many people might assume that the *sole* cause of the loss of trade with India was the political situation in that country and the boycott, in fact the exports of British cotton cloths to

---

[72] M. Dupree, ed., *Lancashire and Whitehall: The Diary of Sir Raymond Streat,* vol. 1: *1931–39* (Manchester: Manchester University Press, 1987), 98.
[73] United Textile Factory Workers' Association, "Memorandum on the Cotton Industry", 1928.
[74] T. Myers, *Real Facts about the Cotton Trade Industry, etc* (London: ILP Publications Dept., 1929), 16.
[75] W. Rust, *What's Wrong with Lancashire?* (Manchester: 1936), 3.
[76] TNA, BT56/36. Memorandum from AWA, May 6, 1931.

all markets had fallen greatly since the war, due also to a fall in agricultural prices (meaning a loss in purchasing power) and to Japanese competition.[77] By stressing longer term causes for the state of the industry, such arguments also shifted the blame onto the Conservatives. William Tout, a Labour MP in the West Riding and previously a weaver himself, commented in the House of Commons that:

> What has surprised me most is the evident concern of Members of the Opposition for the condition of the industry and for the tremendous amount of unemployment that exists in the industry now. One would think that this was a development of the last year or so, but we have been suffering since 1920... It sounds to me very strange that these heartrending appeals should now be made. They ought to have been made in the earlier days of the depression, when something might have been done ... We on the operative side now say that if the same concern had been shown by the Conservatives, when in office, for the depression in the cotton trade, something might have been done.[78]

The result was that it tended to be the employers – or at least the capitalist class – who were blamed for the state that Lancashire was in, serving to diminish Gandhi's responsibility. "The conditions are simply heartbreaking," lamented the Darwen weavers' journal, "but it is clear that we ... [cannot] depend upon ordinary individual capitalists for ... change to be effected."[79] And in fact those ordinary individual capitalists frequently proved just as keen to use the same analytical framework in their search for explanations. When G. W. Armitage, the managing director of a spinning firm, listed what he believed to be the most important causes of the decline in Lancashire trade, he placed "heightened race consciousness seeking to keep out foreign goods simply because they are foreign, and expressing itself in boycotts, Swadeshi mvts, &c." thirteenth out of thirteen factors. Above it in the list he included problems such as higher wages, high rates and social service charges, and shorter hours, as well as the return to gold standard, the increase of tariff barriers and foreign competition.[80]

---

[77] BL, IOR/L/PO/1/51(ii). "Notes for speakers", published by the Labour Party and TUC, May 1931.

[78] *Hansard*, 250, col. 397.

[79] LRO, DDX1078/2/24. Darwen Weavers, Warpers and Winders Association, monthly journal, Aug. 1931.

[80] G. W. Armitage, *The Problem of the Cotton Trade* (Repr. from the *Manchester Guardian*, 1929), 2–3.

It was not just the British employer class who bore the brunt of the blame from the cotton operatives, but the Indian employer class could also be held responsible. In March 1931, Commander J. M. Kenworthy, the Labour (though formerly Liberal) MP for Central Hull, argued in the House of Commons that the nationalist agenda was being manipulated by the Indian mill owners for their own ends:

> a certain ring of mill-owners in Bombay and elsewhere ... have undoubtedly started this boycott, not for any altruistic reasons at all, or because they believe in nationalism, but because they are the worst type of blood-suckers and sweaters. The conditions of labour in their mills are appalling and have been condemned again and again on these benches. I hope that they will not be able to profit by exploiting the perfectly natural feeling of nationalism and patriotism of Young India.[81]

For some, blame simply lay with the international capitalist system as a whole. A couple of days before the visit, the *Cotton Factory Times* ran a sympathetic leader on its front page, explaining Gandhi's suggestion that one reason for Lancashire's loss of trade was the declining capacity of the Indian people to buy goods:

> We think his argument is sound ... The falling off in consuming capacity will be among those who are forced to spend what little they have on the common necessities that make for trade. The wealth of the world is in too few hands at the present time. It is controlled, hoarded and greedily held by a few. When the wealth of the world is in too few hands it becomes poisonous; when it is free and flowing, widely distributed and spent on necessaries week by week by the common people, it gives life to trade.[82]

A few days after the visit it continued its defence, suggesting that:

> It was, indeed, surprising and significant that the Indian leader should have met with such a reception from people who have been asked to believe that the loss of our trade in India was due in no small measure to the activities of him and his like, and it is some proof of the fact that the workers are no longer giving credence to everything which is served up to them in the columns of the Press.[83]

If the troubles of the cotton industry continued to be interpreted in the main within the standard parameters of labour versus capitalism, it was also these concerns that dominated the thinking of the cotton operatives.

---

[81] *Hansard*, 250, cols. 385–6.
[82] *Cotton Factory Times*, Sep. 25, 1931.
[83] Ibid., Oct. 2, 1931.

The inter-war period saw an increasing intensification of work within the industry and the simultaneous reduction of wages. Cuts were imposed in the spinning and weaving sectors in 1921, 1922, 1929 and 1932, and in weaving in 1935; some individual employers then pressed further reductions on their employees. The result was an increase in industrial tension and disputes. Arthur McIvor has spoken of "a phase of direct brinkmanship" in the 1920s culminating in the period of militancy at the end of the decade: he has calculated that in 1931–32, a total of around 32 million working days were lost due to disputes in the textile sector.[84]

At the end of September 1931 the area was in the midst of the "more looms" disputes of 1931–2, which had seen a county-wide lockout at the beginning of that year. On September 18, a few days before Gandhi arrived in the area, around 1,000 unemployed Great Harwood operatives gathered to condemn the decision of a local mill to implement wage cuts.[85] In the same week, a meeting of operatives in Darwen collapsed in disorder over the proposal to establish a six-loom system at five of its mills: "It was evident from the temper of the meeting that there will be a large number of the firm's operatives, who have been unemployed for twelve months, giving in their names for re-engagement."[86] The flurry of interest in the days immediately surrounding Gandhi's visit aside, therefore, it was such labour concerns that dominated the local news throughout the period. Most of the surviving union logbooks of 1931 failed to record the visit of the Indian leader, instead detailing the more pressing economic and industrial issues at the forefront of operative concerns: the union benefits distributed that month, grievances against employers, and other similar issues.[87] The minute book of the Darwen Weavers, Warpers and Winders' Association was unusual in noting that Gandhi was coming and that a deputation to meet him had been arranged, but this made up only a small item in a meeting which also was taken up with the discussion of other matters such

---

[84] A. McIvor, "Cotton Employers' Organisations and Labour Relations, 1890–1939", in J. A. Jowitt and A. J. McIvor, eds., *Employers and Labour in the English Textile Industries, 1850–1939* (London: Routledge, 1988), 14–15.

[85] *Blackburn Times*, Sep. 19, 1931.

[86] Ibid.

[87] See for example the minutes of the Accrington, and Church and Oswaldtwistle branches of the AWA in LRO, DDX 1138/1/; DDX1138/2/6; minutes of the Burnley and district textile workers' union, LRO, DDX 1274/2/18; minutes of the Blackburn and district weavers, warpers and winders association, LRO, DDX 1078/1/7. Admittedly union logbooks are a problematic source for the historian: minutes of meetings can provide only a flavour – and sometimes a misrepresentative one – of the discussions that went on at any given meeting.

as the political levy, the Labour Party agenda and the upcoming union social event.[88]

Conclusion

At the beginning of the twenty-first century, the empire and its impact on British society continues to interest historians.[89] The debate which came under sustained focus following the publication of John MacKenzie's seminal work in 1984 has shown little sign of easing, and in fact has been reignited in recent years, most controversially with the work of Bernard Porter.[90] Meanwhile, amongst the wider population, notions of Britishness continue to draw the attention of politicians, journalists and social commentators.

Gandhi's visit to Lancashire provides an interesting case study of imperial attitudes amongst the British working class at a time when the depression of the inter-war years was nearing its worst. The men and women with whom he met were not representative of all workers of those years, but they were men and women living in communities in which a local identity was strong and in which class remained an important (although by no means the only) determinant of social and political values. The popular memory of a warm welcome given to Gandhi by the people of Lancashire, encouraged by press reports and photographs, has much substance to it. The sympathetic response of the cotton workers was recorded by government officials, press reporters, union leaders and by Gandhi himself. In the main, these were men and women who were neither "steeped" in imperial discourse, nor in sympathy with anti-colonial rhetoric. Writing about working-class attitudes to empire, Andrew Thompson has suggested that "workers in Britain were [often] torn between their instincts of self-protection, their humanitarian sympathy for

---

[88] LRO, DDX 1078/2/13. Minutes of the Darwen Weavers, Warpers and Winders' Association, Sep. 23, 1931.

[89] For a discussion of recent literature, see R. Price, "One Big Thing: Britain, its Empire, and their Imperial Culture", *Journal of British Studies* 45 (2006), 602–27.

[90] MacKenzie, *Propaganda and Empire*; Porter, *Absent-Minded Imperialists*. The MacKenzie/Porter debate continues in recent issues of *Journal of Imperial and Commonwealth History*. See B. Porter, "Further Thoughts on Imperial Absent-Mindedness", *Journal of Imperial and Commonwealth History* 36, no. 1 (2008), 101–17; J. MacKenzie, "'Comfort' and Conviction: A Response to Bernard Porter", *Journal of Imperial and Commonwealth History* 36, no. 4 (2008), 659–68.

the poor and their class identification with the oppressed."[91] However, at least in Lancashire in 1931, many did not find themselves so torn: sympathy for the Indian people could be presented as something that need not necessarily conflict with their own well-being. Certainly some degree of international solidarity can be detected amongst the workers with the political aspirations of their Indian counterparts, encouraged by the self-sacrificing image of the Mahatma. However, support for India's demands could also be presented as economically convenient. Moreover, many cotton workers and their leaders sought both an explanation and a solution for cotton's decline from within the industry itself, and so failed to see Gandhi as a key figure of blame.

For others, the excitement was purely the fleeting attraction of a visiting celebrity, and a particularly exotic one at that; and ultimately, the visit had little effect on either Gandhi's or the INC's policy towards cotton (nor would it have any effect on the British government's policy towards India). Andrew Naesmith, asked afterwards what he thought the visit might have achieved, believed that little of benefit would come from the meetings: "I do not think that Gandhi will vary his purposes because of what he has seen in Lancashire and learnt from us."[92] A fellow official of the Weavers' Association, J. Hindle, who had himself visited India in 1927, suggested that it had at least brought enlightenment, "but it is enlightenment without hope."[93] Representatives from the employers' associations were similarly pessimistic. T. Ashurst of the Cotton Spinners and Manufacturers' Association simply told the press that "I do not think we have progressed very much."[94]

But amongst Naesmith, Hindle, Ashurst, and others, there had been no expectation that a visit from the Indian leader would provide the answer to Lancashire's suffering anyway. For the union leaders, Gandhi was of less relevance to the cotton industry and its troubles than the negligence of the previous government and the machinations of the employers; as far as Ashurst was concerned, the responsibility of the Indian leader paled beside the negligence of the current government and the stubbornness of the union. One local newspaper summed it up. "Lancashire gave Mr Gandhi a

---

[91] Thompson, *Empire Strikes Back*, 82. This is Thompson's general conclusion to his chapter on "The Working Class at Work", but he spends a couple of pages specifically addressing Gandhi's visit to Lancashire, and here he does note that workers might separate out fiscal and constitutional concerns in their response to Indian nationalism. See 77–8.

[92] *Blackburn Times*, Oct. 3, 1931.

[93] Ibid.

[94] Ibid.

courteous and orderly reception as being the guest of His Majesty's Government; what he may do for 'the suffering operatives' will, to our mind, neither start a solitary loom nor sell a single piece of cloth," it reported. "Mr Gandhi has seen Lancashire, and Lancashire has seen Mr Gandhi, and there is the end of it."[95]

---

[95] *Darwen News*, Oct. 3, 1931.

LABOUR, RACE AND EMPIRE:
THE TRADES UNION CONGRESS
AND COLONIAL POLICY, 1945–51

MARY DAVIS

Until the 1920s, the labour movement's attitude to the empire was supportive but not pro-active. Thereafter the leadership actively developed a colonial policy. This chapter will examine the reasons for this as well as analyzing the policy especially in relation to colonial independence movements and post-independence governments. This will entail an assessment of the evolution of policy in the years of preparation and the ways in which the Trades Union Congress (TUC) acted as the conduit of Labour Party colonial policy, as well as assisting in the implementation of that policy during the Labour governments of 1945–51. This will also necessitate a consideration of the labour movement's anti-communist ideology and the way this shaped its attitude to colonial independence movements. In policy terms, the extent to which TUC-inspired trade unionism in the colonies was intended as a buffer against independence movements and provided a bulwark against anti-western post-independence outcomes will also be considered.

Imperial Consensus: The Years of Policy Formulation, 1918–39

The Versailles settlement divided German colonies between France and Britain. The British empire was territorially at its largest in the inter-war years. This was accompanied by "empire-strengthening" strategies.[1] Cultural imperialism found new outlets in film and radio and it can be argued that, despite Britain's post-war economic difficulties, the inter-war years witnessed a truly hegemonic triumph of already well entrenched imperial and racial ideology. The inter-war years saw the beginnings of

---

[1] Barbara Bush, *Imperialism, Race and Resistance* (London: Routledge, 1999).

greater labour-movement interest in colonial issues. This did not betoken a more enlightened attitude to race as the silence of the labour movement on the racial attacks suffered by black Britons (especially seamen) in the 1920s showed. Interest in the colonies in this period was in the main motivated by two concerns. Firstly, the fear that the British empire (now hugely expanded as a result of the World War One peace treaties) might be lost due to the rise of national liberation movements in many of the colonies. Secondly, the perceived threat of Bolshevism in the form of the Comintern, especially given the latter's involvement in the anti-imperialist struggle. The Comintern provided the alternative model of a form of internationalism which provoked fear and dread in the West, especially among the colonizing powers. Such fears were not without foundation. In 1920 the second Comintern Congress conducted an in-depth discussion on the "national and colonial question". In the same year, under the auspices of the Comintern, the first congress of Peoples of the East was held. (The term "East" was not used in its geographical sense; it was a generic term for non-white colonized people.) This was strongly anti-imperialist; concentrating particular invective towards British imperialism against which Zinoviev called the delegates to mount "a holy war, above all against English imperialism".

In the late 1920s black anti-imperialists were welcomed in Moscow as students of the Communist University of the Toilers of the East. This attracted many existing and would-be leaders of national liberation movements. The security service showed great interest in many of the key figures in the Pan-African Movement due to their actual or suspected links to communist organizations or to the Soviet Union, rather than because of their pro-independence or pan-African activities. For example, Jomo Kenyatta came to the security service's attention in 1929 when he arrived in Britain and was kept under surveillance by the Metropolitan Police Special Branch because of his suspected links to the International Committee of Negro Workers. The same was true of George Padmore and others who were active Pan-Africanists. Padmore lived in Moscow from 1929 to 1935 and was head of the Negro Bureau of the Red International of Labour Unions (RILU). The first file on Kenyatta follows his activities in this period through Special Branch reports, and from 1934 through intercepted mail.[2] The warrant for intercepting his correspondence states that Kenyatta was "believed to be succeeding George Padmore as principal

---

[2] The National Archives, Security Service (MI5) files, KV 2/1787 (1930–40).

Soviet propaganda agent for the British colonies".[3] This activity post-dates his visit in 1932–3 to the Lenin school in Moscow.

In the light of the perceived threat from the Soviet Union and the alignment of black activists with the Comintern's anti-imperialist stance, it was necessary for the Labour Party (and especially because it was a party of government in 1924) to pay more attention to colonial policy which thereafter slowly evolved.

Labour Party Colonial Policy

In 1918 the Labour Party published its manifesto *Labour and the New Social Order,* written by Sidney Webb (later Lord Passfield). It said that the empire was of special concern due to Britain's responsibility to "non adult races" (redolent of the "white man's burden" theme). It called for greater democracy in the empire where there was a demand for independence, but it did not advocate the abandonment of the empire, rather its strengthening through a newly created Britannic Alliance. Thus it was that, for the first time, Labour sought to develop its colonial policy. The main mechanism for so doing was via the establishment in 1924 of the Imperial Affairs Sub-Committee (later Imperial Advisory Committee); its secretary was Leonard Woolf. However, despite a more pro-active policy, as manifested by the 1925 first British Commonwealth and Labour conference, the tide of anti-British feeling was apparent in the colonies. The Labour Party clearly recognized this. It explains the publication in 1933 of its policy statement *The Colonial Empire.* This *recognized* the fact of independence struggles, but made distinction between India (and south-east Asia), Africa and the Caribbean.

This distinction was to persist in Labour thinking – India was written off as a colony because of the strength of its independence movement and the strong communist influence there. But it was hoped to delay independence at best or at worst retain influence post-independence by ensuring that as far as possible the British constitutional model was adopted. South-east Asia was also regarded as very prone to communist influence. The Caribbean was viewed by Labour as a very promising area (for imperialism) since despite the fact that trade unionism was stirring, it was thought that the communist influence was weak. Labour's strategic "line" on Africa was more fully expressed in its 1943 pamphlet *The Colonies.* It took the traditional racist line that Britain's African colonies were inhabited by "backward peoples" of "primitive culture", whose

---

[3] Ibid., at ser. 23.

economic and political systems were so backward that they were "not yet able to stand by themselves". The conclusion drawn from this was that British rule had to be maintained "as a trust for the native inhabitants"[4] until such time as the natives could be trained to govern themselves. This was, of course little different from the classic nineteenth-century "white man's burden" justification for the maintenance of empire.

TUC Colonial Policy

It was not until the 1930s that the TUC began to develop its colonial policy and even then this was not a product of democratic discussion within the trade union movement, rather, as Marjorie Nicholson observes, "all TUC colonial work was done on the initiative of a few men at the top".[5] It was obviously greatly influenced by government policy. During Labour's minority government, the Passfield Memorandum of 1930 urged colonial administrations to legalize trade unions. Sir George Foggon, who served in the Colonial Office from 1949 and was overseas Labour advisor at the Foreign and Commonwealth Office, noted that the Passfield Memorandum gave "the first impetus to colonial trade unions".[6] However it is thought that this policy was not purely altruistic and that it was initiated as a consequence of a three-week strike in 1929 in the Gambia.[7]

In 1937 the TUC established a new committee – the Colonial Advisory Committee (CAC). Its secretary W. B. Kemmis was the TUC's first colonial specialist. Preliminary preparation of data for the committee's work was "greatly facilitated by the courtesy of the Colonial Office". The purpose of the committee's work was defined by the General Council as:

> an investigation into the conditions of the principal races of the colonial empire, the principal object being to see how far the TUC can contribute

---

[4] "The Colonies", 1943, Marjorie Nicholson Collection [hereafter, MNC], TUC Library Collections, Box 19.

[5] Marjorie Nicholson, *The TUC Overseas* (London: Allen and Unwin, 1986). Nicholson worked in the International Department of the TUC, 1955–72. Before that she worked for the Fabian Colonial Society and was the editor of its journal *Venture*.

[6] G. Foggon, "Trade Unionism in the Colonies", TUC Library Collections, Colonial Office Memorandum, 1950, MNC, 932.5/3.

[7] See A. Hughes and D. Perfect, "Trade Unionism in the Gambia", *African Affairs* 88 (1989), 549–72. Hughes and Perfect credit Drummond Shiels, Passfield's under-secretary, as being the prime mover of this initiative.

towards raising their standard of life and generally improving their conditions.[8]

Two policy aims were outlined. The first was to consider best means of remedying immediate grievances and the second was to extend trade unionism among native workers. The latter was to be accomplished "having regard to local conditions and differences ... or, where as in Africa, trade unionism is still largely unrealisable, to safeguard the interests of indigenous workers, pending their transition to industrial organisation, by the appointment of qualified labour commissioners".[9]

The CAC dealt with all British colonies excluding India. (India was the purview of the TUC's International Committee.) Because at first their detailed knowledge of the colonies was so scant, the CAC sought advice from the International African Service Bureau (IASB), an organization formed in 1937 from a remarkable group of Pan-Africanists resident as exiles in London. These included Ras Makonnen, C. L. R. James, Jomo Kenyatta, I. T. A. Wallace Johnson, and George Padmore. The IASB itself was a product of the Ethiopian solidarity movement, being an outgrowth of International African Friends of Abyssinia group. The IASB lasted for seven years until 1944. It was the longest-surviving of all the Pan-African associations formed during this period. It merged in 1944 with the Pan-African Federation, the organization which was largely responsible for the convening of the 1945 Pan-African Congress. The motto of the IASB was "educate, co-operate, emancipate – neutral in nothing affecting the African people". These men were revolutionary Marxists, and after being warned off by the Labour Party, which regarded the IASB as a suspect organization, the TUC dropped the contact. This in effect meant that both the TUC and the Labour Party were determined to hold anti-imperialist activists at arm's length. The fact that the CAC included Labour Party "specialist" advisors like Arthur Creech Jones (later to become colonial secretary) meant that from the outset the policies of the two organizations would be harmonized.

In 1938 the TUC formulated its demand for the appointment of "labour advisors" to be sent to British colonies in order to assist the development of trade unionism on the British model. The impetus for this arose from government enquiries into the struggles of trade unionists (operating in conditions of illegality) in the Caribbean which resulted, in the 1930s, in a wave of labour unrest "far more widespread and intense than anything that

---

[8] M. Nicholson, "Note On TUC Committees & Departments Dealing With International & Imperial Affairs, 1916–26", Jan. 25, 1974, MNC.
[9] Ibid.

had preceded".[10] The publication in 1938 of the Forster report, *Labour Disturbances in Trinidad*, led to CAC's main demand for trade union advisors, while the appointment of Walter Citrine (TUC General Secretary, 1926–46) as a member of West Indies Royal Commission (Moyne Commission) undoubtedly stimulated greater TUC awareness of colonial issues. However a record of a conversation between Citrine and Major Orde-Browne in 1937 on native questions suggests that the idea arose as a result of shared concern on the part of both the Colonial Office and the TUC.[11]

Labour in Power, 1940–51: The Years of Influence

The Western attitude to race and empire changed from racial confidence in the hey-day of imperialism, to racial fear in the period of decolonization.[12] World War Two was the catalyst for change – thereafter an apparently more tolerant attitude to race was perceptible. This was due to the cold-war fears of the USSR and its support of liberation struggles – in other words a factor which provided a continuum with pre-war anti-communism. Poor conditions, lack of democracy, and racism in the colonies could be perceived as a weak point in the liberal democratic armoury. Race was now identified as a potentially de-stabilizing element in both the international order,[13] and in the domestic order for those countries like the United States with large black populations. This was also becoming a factor in Britain due to the 1948 wave of immigration, and because no restrictions were placed on immigration until 1962 with the Commonwealth Immigrants' Act. Despite the small scale of the "wave", this period witnessed, nonetheless, the beginnings (or possibly the continuation) of a very racialized debate which focussed on supposed social problems of having too many blacks with an alien culture settling in Britain.[14] Trade unions, as in the 1920s, were part of this "racialized debate" in that they attempted to restrict immigrant labour even during periods of full employment.[15] Although the full debate on black immigration

---

[10] Richard Hart, "British Policies in Relation to Labour in the Colonies of the Caribbean", *Communist Review* 30 (1999), 16.
[11] Memorandum of interview, Oct. 12, 1937, MNC, Box 16, 932.5.
[12] Frank Furedi, *The Silent War* (London: Pluto, 1998).
[13] Ibid.
[14] John Solomos, *Race and Racism in Britain* (Basingstoke: Macmillan, 2004), esp. his chap. "The Politics of Race and Immigration since 1945", 48–75.
[15] A. Phizacklea and R. Miles, *Labour and Racism* (London: Routledge, Kegan & Paul, 1980).

into Britain did not surface until the mid 1960s, Solomos rejects the notion that 1945–62 was an "age of innocence" on race and immigration.[16] In terms of colonial policy, however, whilst still opposing independence movements, this period witnessed a move to reform in which trade unions were scripted to play a key role.

By 1940 the entry of the Labour Party into the coalition government meant that TUC influence on official thinking on colonial (and other) matters was much greater and that the mutual interaction between the TUC and the government was more pronounced. The 1940 Colonial Development and Welfare Act encouraged the spread of trade unionism in the colonies by legalizing trade unions and encouraging their development, and by appointing colonial trade union advisors to ensure that such unions were established on the "right" lines. TUC policy, it would seem, had come of age, especially after 1945 when the first majority Labour government was elected (1945–51). Now as a government, Labour was forced to accept the fact that it ruled a vast colonial empire and the absence of an anti-imperialist policy inevitably implied the opposite. The Fabians filled the breach and in 1940 the Fabian Colonial Research Bureau was established. As Billy Frank explains in his chapter, leading figures Creech Jones and Rita Hinden argued against negative anti-imperialism and in favour of a "positive" colonial policy. This was grist to the mill of Clement Attlee, Ernest Bevin (foreign secretary), and Herbert Morrison (Lord President) who warmed as to the manor born as guardians of Britain's imperial role. Indeed Bevin fully acknowledged the social imperialist argument as justification for labour imperialism. In 1946 he proclaimed to an unshocked House of Commons:

> I am not prepared to sacrifice the British empire [because] I know that if the British empire fell ... it would mean that the standard of life of our constituents would fall considerably.[17]

On this argument it is possible to view the great achievements of the welfare state as the ultimate expression of the social imperialist ideal. The racist attitudes informing this were never far from the surface. Hugh Dalton referred to the colonies as "pullulating poverty stricken, diseased nigger communities", but, echoing the theme of the "white man's burden", he did not advocate relinquishing them. In the case of South Africa, a prized part of the "white" commonwealth, Labour, perceiving its strategic

---

[16] Solomos, *Race and Racism in Britain*.
[17] Quoted in Ron Ramdin, *The Making of the Black Working Class in Britain* (Aldershot: Gower Publishing, 1987), 63.

and economic importance, was content to condone the vicious racism in the form of the apartheid system established by the Nationalist government under Malan after its election victory in 1948. The fact that Malan was an open supporter of the Nazis during the war did nothing to deflect Labour support.

Colonial Independence

1945–51 witnessed a high point in the struggle for colonial independence, particularly in the African continent where the trade union movement, contrary to the prevailing Colonial Office orthodoxy, was vibrant and militant. There were general strikes in Nigeria in 1945, in Kenya and Ghana in 1950, and many other industry-wide strikes in other colonial territories. The Fairfield Commission, established to look into the "disorders" in Nigeria expressed the view that trade unionism as experienced in the civilized world was a product of considerable struggle and thus "the Nigerian worker … [should] consider himself very fortunate that he is not faced with a similar struggle and that those hard won rights are available to him."[18] Such views prompted Jack Woodis (head of the Communist Party of Great Britain's International Department) to declare that:

> The Colonial Office and the Fabians have combined to foster the myth that trade unionism in Africa was not the result of African effort but the fruit of British generosity.[19]

Although the domestic policy of the first majority Labour government is considered to be radical, this has led to the presumption that its foreign and colonial policy was also progressive. The achievement of Indian independence in 1947 is often cited as representing the triumph of an anti-colonial policy. However, Labour was not anti-imperialist – apart from India, only Israel, Burma and Ceylon won their independence during the life of the Labour government. ("Won" being the operative word, and in all cases since independence was the product of a sustained and often bitter struggle.) Labour did as much as it could to preserve the empire and if it could not it concentrated all its effort on ensuring the post-colonial world was still safe for British capital investments. In general the policy

---

[18] "Report of a Commission of Enquiry into the Disorders in the Eastern Provinces of Nigeria", Nov. 1949, quoted in J. Woodis, *Africa: The Lion Awakes* (London: Lawrence & Wishart, 1961), 42.
[19] Ibid., 48.

was to head off the independence movements in the colonies by granting reform – in this sense Labour is regarded as being enlightened, but in fact the roots of this policy were laid before World War Two. After the war, Labour adopted a policy of attempting to kill colonial independence by kindness. Labour colonial policy from 1945 to 1951 was primarily motivated by fear that grievances among colonial peoples could be "exploited" by communists. Hence, whilst not motivated by anti-imperialist sentiment, Labour policy recognized that reform was necessary. One of the key features of the reform programme was to permit the development of non-militant trade unionism. This, together with labour legislation, was regarded as both vital in its own right and a measure of social control. This was particularly so during the cold war in the years following the establishment of the International Confederation of Free Trade Unions (ICFTU), which, with the TUC, was regarded as a vital means of safeguarding British colonial investments, whether direct British rule survived or not.

The TUC, Anti-Communism, and the Split in the International Trade Union Movement

It has already been noted that the USSR and communism generally were regarded by the British government as a threat to the existence of the empire. Now, in a period when it was clear some form of colonial independence was at worst inevitable, or at best deferred, the most important issue was to ensure that emerging governments remained friendly to western capitalism. This meant that communist influence in colonial liberation movements had to be identified and opposed. The TUC was firmly committed to an anti-communist line anyway. Citrine had pronounced much earlier (in 1928) that communists were different from Liberals or Tories because "they have sold their birthright to revolutionary dictators and have tried to corrupt the unions they profess to support".[20]

In 1948 the General Council urged all affiliates "to counteract every manifestation of communist influence within their trade unions". It published three pamphlets on the subject. Two of these were written in 1949: *Defend Democracy* and *Tactics of Disruption*, and the third in 1953, *The TUC and Communism*. The TUC argued that the Communist Party of Great Britain (CPGB) was not a party in the normal sense, in that it was allegedly controlled by Moscow and that Communist Party factions, which

---

[20] Walter Citrine, *Democracy or Disruption: An Examination of Communist Influences in the Trade Unions* (London: TUC Publicity Dept, 1928), 28.

were in widespread operation in trade union branches, were directed by the
industrial organizer at King Street (headquarters of the CPGB). According
to the TUC, the CPGB posed not only a great danger to the British trade
union movement but also presented an equal threat to colonial trade
unionists. This line of argument emerged when the issue of trade union
education was discussed and a difference of opinion emerged as to
whether it was better to bring colonial trade union students to Britain (to
Ruskin) or to educate them in their own countries. Eventually it was
decided to pursue the latter course on the grounds that, while in Britain,
students "are exposed to communist contacts and even a single experience
of colour discrimination can have the most adverse affect on a student's
outlook".[21] However the decision to educate colonial trade unionists in
their own countries also raised the vexed question of the content of syllabi.
In particular, the TUC was concerned by the inclusion of the period 1780–
1850 in the compulsory British trade union history course on the grounds
that much of it (that is, the early period):

> makes unhappy reading [due to its] emphasis of the militant phase of
> British trade unionism – a not altogether wholesome influence on young
> and inexperienced trade unionists who are in some cases already too prone
> to regard a strike as the only worthwhile effort in the trade union
> armoury.[22]

The World Federation of Trade Unions (WFTU) was, the TUC argued,
the main vehicle for communist infiltration internationally. Hence the
TUC disaffiliated from it in 1949 in favour of the American-backed
ICFTU which had "forged ahead in constructive service to workers in five
continents" while the WFTU "has become an integral part of the
machinery of international communism and includes virtually no
organization which is not communist dominated".[23] However the TUC
argued that its own constructive approach to the colonies was wilfully
misunderstood by many colonial political leaders inspired by the "negative
anti-imperialism … a feature of communist propaganda propagated
through the WFTU".[24]

This line also induced vehement opposition to the Movement for
Colonial Freedom, founded in 1954 to campaign for Asian and African

---

[21] "Trade Unionism in the Colonies", Colonial Labour Advisory Committee
[hereafter, CAC], 1950 (G. Foggon), Box 14 MNC, 932.
[22] Ibid., 13.
[23] "The TUC and Communism", 1953, 7, TUC Library Collections.
[24] "Reassessment of the Situation in British Africa", CAC, Feb. 4, 1959, TUC
Library Collections.

independence. It also meant that the TUC's apparently benign influence in aiding the development of trade unions in the colonies had an overt anti-communist purpose.

The TUC and the Implementation of Colonial Policy

The agency for the delivery of the government's colonial strategy during this period was to be the TUC and the legalization of colonial trade unions, but under controlled conditions. The TUC, at the time and later, justified its interest in the colonies on what it considered to be purely altruistic grounds. Trade unions according to the TUC line "can contribute to economic stability", and are also "a nursery of democratic practice".[25] The mechanism for establishing and controlling colonial trade unions was three-fold:

Legalizing Trade Unions in the Colonies

There is some confusion over the process of legalization of trade unions. The Fabians and the TUC suggested there had been rapid progress even by 1942,[26] but even so they admitted that progress was patchy, with the West Indies being the most "promising" and Africa lagging far behind. This, according to the government, the Fabians and the TUC, was because Africa was less developed. The Fabian Walter Bowen argued that for the African workers:

> trade unions are as strange to them as industrial employment, and the very fact of organising together with workers from other tribes is foreign to their culture.[27]

Nonetheless, throughout the war and beyond, legislation was introduced to ensure that "authorised unions" were formed, especially in Asia and Africa, for fear that alternative political, and therefore non-authorized, unions were established. Hence, the legalization of authorized trade unions went together with their compulsory registration.

---

[25] Ibid.
[26] See "Labour in the Colonies: Some Current Problems", in *Reports Submitted to the Labour Committee of the Fabian Colonial Bureau*, Research ser., 61 (1942), 6.
[27] Walter Bowen, *Colonial Trade Unionism* (London: The Fabian Society, 1954), 8.

The Compulsory Registration of Colonial Trade Unions

The Fabian Society argued that although compulsory registration might at first sight seem to be interference, it was necessary because colonial trade unions were inexperienced and this measure was essential to safeguard their "financial integrity" and "democratic control".[28] The TUC wholeheartedly concurred and even went a step further. Its Colonial Advisory Committee argued that the powers of the registrars should be extended to root out political troublemakers:

> that the existing powers to refuse or cancel registration might not enable the registrars to ... prevent irresponsible individuals or groups from forming unions for political or non-industrial objects.[29]

Kenya provides a good example of the purposes to which the British government, supported by the TUC, used compulsory registration. In 1950 Makhan Singh and Fred Kubai, president and general secretary of the East African Trades Union Confederation (EATUC) respectively, were arrested on the grounds that they were the leaders of an illegal organization. They had fallen foul of the rule that only individual unions, rather than federations, could register, despite the fact that the EATUC was a federation composed of individual unions! The real purpose was a political one; this was a militant trade union and Makhan Singh was a communist and hence not to be tolerated. In fact, Makhan Singh was imprisoned for eleven and a half years on a trumped-up charge by the British Court in Kenya, and the EATUC banned.

Trade Union Advisors

The practice of sending trade union advisors to the colonies from the British TUC with the full support of the Colonial Office gained momentum during and after World War Two. Their function was to influence the development of orderly industrial relations via compliant trade unions built on the British model.

The first two colonial trade union advisors had been appointed by 1941 – one for Trinidad and one for the Gold Coast – and many more were planned, but the war intervened. However, the practice was resumed and, according to Woodis, by 1954 they operated in fifteen colonies with a total

---

[28] Ibid.
[29] Minute of TUC Colonial Advisory Committee, Apr. 21, 1949, TUC Library Collections.

staff of 400.[30] Again, TUC influence was in evidence in the Colonial Labour Advisory Committee (CLAC), established in 1942. This was a government body containing TUC nominees (they were not regarded as representatives of the TUC; official TUC views continued to be made direct to the Colonial Office). Its chief importance, according to Marjorie Nicholson, was that "its existence gave the final stamp of authority to the policies of using TUC advice and positively encouraging the growth of trade unions".[31] Thus it was that before, during and after the war, TUC policy and practice were encouraged by governments which saw trade unionism as central to their colonial policy. The Colonial Office expressed it thus: "It is clear that the British TUC is capable of exercising an important and formative influence on the trade unions of the colonies."[32] The same memorandum went on to say that because of suspicion of government bodies by the indigenous population in the colonies, the TUC's role would be particularly important because "more than any official body, [it] can build up understanding and faith in this country's aims".[33]

The newly established ICFTU, which the TUC had joined in 1949,[34] was regarded warmly by the Colonial Office because it would "play a more direct part in combating communism than the TUC".[35] Interestingly, however, the TUC did not share this view and clearly regarded the ICFTU and especially the Americans as interlopers in the long-standing TUC project of building an ordered civil society in colonial territories through the encouragement of the kind of trade unions that were the "nursery of democratic practice".[36] The TUC view was that the ICFTU and the Americans fostered the myth that colonialism and the British government were the enemy, ignoring the fact that the government had fostered the development of trade unionism and that the TUC "know[s] more about the

---

[30] Jack Woodis, *The Mask is Off* (Ilford: Thames Publications, 1954).

[31] Nicholson, *The TUC Overseas,* 213.

[32] "Trade Unionism in the British Colonies", Colonial Office Memorandum, Oct. 14, 1950, MNC, 932, box 14.

[33] Ibid.

[34] The TUC had initially affiliated to the World Federation of Trade Unions when it was established in 1945, but, inspired by cold-war anti-communism, it left four years later to join the US-backed alternative.

[35] "Trade Unionism in the British Colonies", Colonial Office Memorandum, Oct. 14, 1950, MNC, 932, box 14.

[36] "Re-assessment of Situation in British Africa", CAC, Feb. 4, 1959, 2.

sound development of African trade unions than either the ICFTU or the Americans".[37]

The TUC went ahead, pursuing what in practice turned out to be a somewhat contradictory policy. On the one hand, with government backing, it was busily encouraging the development of trade unions via its colonial labour advisors (and as the Fabian Walter Bowen said, doing what no other government in Europe had ever done[38]), but on the other hand it lamented the capability of the native worker ever to truly comprehend the principles of trade unionism. Reports of the trade union advisors frequently criticized the home-grown colonial trade unions, accusing their leaders of being venal, inexperienced, corrupt or too political. Handbooks and guides were frequently issued by labour advisors to show the colonials the error of their ways and suggest alternatives.

The Kenya guide *What is a Trade Union?* offered this:

> Trade Unions are formed so that strikes can be avoided. Trade unions try to make sure that workers and employers understand one another. [...] The value of a worker to his employer depends on the kind of work he does ... good, hard work is of more value than bad, lazy work.[39]

The Gold Coast guide *Your Trade Union* took a similar line:

> Trade Unions are really formed to avoid strikes. Experience shows that strikes are not of any benefit either to the worker or to the employer. Trade unions are formed to try to make sure that workers and employers understand one another.

In the case of Burma, the minutes of the TUC's International Committee reported that the secretary of state for India had expressed concern about "the present unsatisfactory state and mushroom growth of trade unions in Burma".[40] The government thus asked the TUC to nominate an expert trade unionist to go to Burma "under TUC auspices and at the invitation of the government in order to give guidance to the trade union movement there".[41] Andrew Dalgleish was accordingly sent, and he submitted his report a year later.[42] In it he noted that, of the two trade union

---

[37] Ibid., 4.

[38] Bowen, *Colonial Trade Unionism*, 4.

[39] Apparently the Kenyans were not clever enough to take this advice; the East African TUC was banned in 1950.

[40] Minutes of TUC International Committee, Jan. 15, 1946.

[41] Ibid.

[42] Minutes of TUC International Committee, Jan. 16, 1947, "Report of Mr. Andrew Dalgleish on Mission of Enquiry into Trade Union Situation in Burma".

confederations, one was communist-controlled and was behind the big strike wave of 1946. In dismissing such politically motivated antics he noted that it was an indication of the need for help and guidance for trade unions and that he found "employers favourable to the establishment of unions in their works providing they were not influenced by communists".[43]

In Malaya, John Brazier, colonial labour advisor with effect from 1945, was clear that his aim was to set up tame trade unions free of communist influence. Clearly this failed, with the result that in 1948 the British commenced hostilities against the Malayan Federation. Woodis noted that Brazier's main function, however, was to act as a government informer. He quoted from a government directive issued to Brazier which instructed him:

> to keep government constantly informed of all developments within the trade union movement ... to bring immediately to the notice of the government of any events or activities ... which are considered prejudicial to the development of sound trade unionism. [...] To inform the government of any behaviour on the part of members or officials of trade unions ... which may give rise to suspicion that their activities may be prejudicial to the government or the welfare of country.[44]

The End of TUC Influence, 1951–65

It is clear that TUC policy mirrored and supported that of the government, especially Labour governments, or those with labour ministers (as during World War Two). But what of the period after 1951, one of uninterrupted Tory rule until 1964? The Colonial Office, under a Conservative administration, now pursued a different line on trade union matters for two major policy reasons. Firstly, "the wind of change" pursued by Macmillan, that is to say, a recognition that some form of colonial independence was inevitable and unstoppable, and that the British empire as it had existed was no longer viable. His government's policy was that the empire must be replaced with a much smaller British Commonwealth and that as far as possible, British interests and investments should be safeguarded in a neo-colonial world. Secondly, the Conservatives now recognized, albeit reluctantly, that Britain was forced to face the reality of, and submission to, United States post-war worldwide hegemony – a fact which the TUC was clearly reluctant to accept. Naturally, such a transformation of

---

[43] Ibid., 7.
[44] Woodis, *The Mask is Off*, 16.

government policy had a concomitant impact on their attitude to the
TUC's colonial role.

The change was clearly spelled out in the conclusion of the 1955
Report of the East Africa Royal Commission. This stated that:

> the attempt to encourage the growth of trade unions on the British model is
> likely, for some time to come, to represent an expenditure of effort which
> might be employed more effectively in other directions.

The TUC could not accept this conclusion.[45]

By 1956 it was clear that the influence of the Colonial Office was
contracting. It no longer wished to employ colonial labour advisors, and
suggested that the TUC might wish to carry out this function alone.[46] The
situation was summed up neatly by the TUC in 1956:

> Believing that the British Trade Union movement has a continuing
> contribution to make in assisting Trade Unions abroad, especially in the
> developing areas of the commonwealth, Congress invites the General
> Council to consider creating within the TUC a Commonwealth secretariat.
> This secretariat to be not only a training centre for personnel sent for
> periods from the commonwealth but also a focal point and spur to
> encourage development and growth of democratic trade unionism.[47]

The CLAC was disbanded in early 1960s "in consequence of its shrinking
area of interest" and the fact that contact with government had been
"intermittent" since then because "the necessary Whitehall machinery has
been lacking".[48]

The TUC sadly noted that the Foreign and Commonwealth Office was
not interested in labour questions any more. The TUC had some contact
with the Ministry of Overseas Development, but the terms of reference of
the latter precluded it from direct interest in trade unions. Meanwhile the
United States had moved in, especially to Latin America and the
Caribbean. Hence the TUC concluded that the most useful policy would be
for it to develop more fruitful relations with the government on
commonwealth matters.

---

[45] CAC, Oct. 19, 1955, MNC, 932.9.
[46] Letter from Sir Hilton Poynton, Secretary of State for the Colonies, reported to
TUC CAC, July 16, 1956.
[47] Finance and General Purpose Committee minute, Dec. 20, 1965, MNC, 24.1.
[48] Ibid.

Conclusions

TUC colonial policy was a very late development, and in common with the Labour Party, was never anti-imperialist. Whatever the rhetoric about the desire for colonial self-government, very little was forthcoming during the period of the third Labour government. Implicit racist thinking, overtly nurtured in the previous seventy or so years, continued to influence the labour movement's views. The use of trade unionism to discourage the development of a pro-communist political movement, which might take advantage of the much delayed voting rights granted in most colonies after 1945, was partially successful. Where it did not deliver compliance, the movement was crushed, as in the Malayan Federation and in Kenya. But for the most part, British-inspired trade unionism, working with the Colonial Office and through trade union labour advisors, began to take hold. Supplemented by a major programme of government-funded trade union education and later by the resources of the ICFTU, the colonial world was left safe for neo-colonialism once independence had been won. The groundwork had been thoroughly prepared in this period.

LABOUR'S "NEW IMPERIALIST ATTITUDE":[1]
STATE-SPONSORED COLONIAL
DEVELOPMENT IN AFRICA, 1940–51[2]

BILLY FRANK

Britain's post-war drive to develop the colonies as economic assets, which could help promote British economic recovery, was complicated by major changes in the composition of the empire. Independence for India, Pakistan and Burma meant that the remaining colonies, especially Africa, acquired a new importance in the field of colonial economic development policy. This, along with the economic crisis of 1947, significantly altered Labour's African policy.

The British government put pressure on colonial administrations to favour the production of dollar-earning and dollar-saving commodities. Sir Stafford Cripps, the minister for economic affairs, was careful to emphasize that the development of African colonial resources was just as important to the recovery of Western Europe as the restoration of European productive power was to the future progress and prosperity of Africa.[3] This complementary relationship between colonial development and European recovery was a common theme among commentators of the left during this period. It was an attempt to allay criticisms levelled at the government that Britain was moving into a new phase of colonial exploitation. Sir Norman Brook, Cabinet Secretary, warned Attlee that criticism of this kind would come about due to the new focus on colonial development in Africa. Brook argued that if policy statements were

---

[1] Rita Hinden uses this term in the introduction to her book *Plan for Africa* (London: George Allen and Unwin, 1941), 24.

[2] My thanks to Murray Steele and Tony Webster for earlier comments on this chapter; also to David Stewart and Craig Horner as well as my co-panel members at the "British Labour Movement and Imperialism" conference held at UCLan, 2008.

[3] Cited by P. J. Cain and A. G. Hopkins, *British Imperialism, 1688–2000* (London: Longman, 2002), 629.

disclosed "incautiously or incidentally, without proper justification and explanation", it could come as a shock to many of Labour's supporters.[4] Rita Hinden of the Fabian Colonial Bureau believed that the economic needs of the colonies were compatible with the requirements of the British economy.[5] Hinden, and other Labour colonialists, argued that the emphasis upon development and welfare under Labour represented a shift away from colonial exploitation for the benefit of the metropolitan economy.[6] The colonial development policy which emerged after the war was couched in a language of progress and fairness, and most official statements stressed the role of welfare services, education and training, and the concomitant benefits these brought to the colonies. Behind the rhetoric the British government's priorities were dictated by the needs of the British economy, particularly the urgent necessity of supplying scarce raw materials and foodstuffs, and earning precious dollars. Although there were those who passionately believed in development to suit the needs of the colonial peoples, the stark realities of the post-war economic difficulties meant that Labour's "new imperialist attitude", as Hinden had put it, began to look more like a traditional exploitative colonial policy, especially after the sterling convertibility crisis of 1947.

The inspiration for Britain's colonial development policy had changed in the years immediately prior to the war as Fabian ideals became more popular. Traditional trusteeship, where development of social provision in the colonies was left mostly to the whim of the colonial government concerned, gave way to a far more positive emphasis on welfare provision. This new emphasis was perhaps most evident in the Colonial Development and Welfare Act (CDWA) of 1940. War-time conditions called a halt to many schemes to be funded with CDWA money, but the Fabian ideals

---

[4] Minute by Sir Norman Brook (Cabinet Secretary) to Mr. Attlee, Jan. 14, 1948: PREM 8/923 in *British Documents on the End of Empire: The Labour Government and the End of Empire, 1945–51*. Part 2: *Economics and International Relations* (London: HMSO, 1992), 257 [Hereafter, BDEE2].
[5] The Fabian Colonial Bureau was formed in 1940. An offshoot of the Fabian Society, it comprised socialist and social democrat thinkers interested in colonial affairs. The Bureau became an influential "think-tank" with many of its members coming from within the Labour Party. Many of its most prominent members would be involved in formulating Labour's colonial policy during its term of office after the war. One of the dominant themes running through Fabian colonial thought was the need to end the one-sided economic relationship between colony and metropole. See for example, Hinden, *Plan for Africa*, esp. chaps. 2 and 3.
[6] Stephen Brooke, *Reform and Reconstruction: Britain after the War, 1945–51(Documents in Contemporary History)* (Manchester: Manchester University Press, 1995), 90.

enshrined in the Act remained high on the Colonial Office agenda and were firmly restated in the 1945 Act.

Fabian efforts to influence colonial development policy continued after the war.[7] Within the Colonial Office, the Colonial Development and Economic Council (CEDC) was established in 1946 to examine the ten-year development plans submitted by the colonial governments under the CDWA scheme. Rita Hinden, a founder member of the Fabian Colonial Bureau, was invited to sit on the CEDC by Arthur Creech Jones, who wanted a strong ally to help promote the welfarist agenda. Hinden believed that colonial governments were unwilling to invest in public works because of their high costs and limited immediate returns in production levels or other commercially orientated dividends.[8] She argued that the high cost of colonial administration also militated against such investment, since it absorbed a high proportion of the scarce funds available for all aspects of colonial governance.

For the Fabian colonialists, the Labour Party's election victory was their opportunity to put their version of development policy into practice. They believed that the Chamberlainite approach, which had dominated development policy in the early part of the century, had been discredited.[9] Fabians favoured a version of trusteeship in which the African was to be protected from the "evils" of a colonial system that favoured expatriate producers and commercial interests. The Fabian critics of colonial policy saw the Chamberlainite doctrine as a great failure in Africa. In colonies such as Kenya and the Rhodesias, with their strong settler presence, it was argued that the African had become poorer as a result of the rise of white-owned private estates in which Africans were coerced into wage labour by colonial government taxation.[10] This was seen as a betrayal of trusteeship as the Chamberlainite desire to "develop the great estate" had become a reality in many southern and central African colonies to the detriment of indigenous peoples.

Soon after the convertibility crisis the United Kingdom government looked at the possibility of expanding the production of valuable

---

[7] For an excellent and fuller account of the ideological debates within the Labour Party at this time see Paul Keleman, "Planning for Africa: The British Labour Party's Colonial Development Policy, 1920–1964", *Journal of Agrarian Change* 7, no. 1 (2007), 76–98.

[8] Hinden, *Plan for Africa*, 24.

[9] Michael Cowen and Robert Shenton, "The Origins and Course of Fabian Colonialism in Africa", *Journal of Historical Sociology* 4, no. 2 (1991), 146.

[10] Michael Cowen and Robert Shenton, *Doctrines of Development* (London: Routledge, 1996), 295.

commodities in Africa. New government agencies established under the Overseas Resources Development Act of February 1948 played an important part in this new drive. The Overseas Food Corporation (OFC), charged with increasing food production for the domestic market, embarked on the extensive East African Groundnut Scheme. The Colonial Development Corporation (CDC) promoted the majority of its schemes in Africa. The sense of urgency was infectious and doomed a number of schemes to failure, as effective planning and investigation were circumvented in the haste to get production under way. It was a problem compounded by the lack of reliable intelligence about local conditions in many parts of the continent.

In an attempt to address this lack of knowledge, a number of high level visits to Africa took place in 1947 and 1948. In 1947 Field Marshall Lord Montgomery toured British Africa. Montgomery believed that Africa could prove the solution to Britain's economic woes, but lamented the lack of any "grand design" for economic development.[11] In particular Montgomery argued that there were too many authorities involved which made policy "patchy and disjointed". He compared the task of African development to the Normandy landings of 1944 arguing that, "in the development of Africa we must adventure courageously, as did Cecil Rhodes".[12] Montgomery's report was staunchly rejected by Creech Jones, Labour's secretary of state for the colonies, who highlighted the recent requirement for African territories to prepare ten-year development programmes under the CDWA.[13] Creech Jones argued that "Africa is not an undiscovered Eldorado. It is a poor continent which can only be

---

[11] Memorandum by Field-Marshall Lord Montgomery, "Tour of Africa, November–December 1947", Dec. 19, 1947, DO35/2380 [BDEE2], 189. Montgomery suggested that the British territories of Africa should be divided into three economic federations: Central Africa (Southern Rhodesia, Northern Rhodesia, Nyasaland and Bechuanaland); East Africa (Kenya, Uganda, Tanganyika, Mauritius, Seychelles, Zanzibar and Somalia); and West Africa (Nigeria, Gold Coast, Sierra Leone and Gambia).
[12] Ibid., [BDEE2], 191.
[13] "Development in Africa": Memorandum by Creech Jones, Jan. 6, 1948, DO35/2380 [BDEE2], 196. The 1945 Colonial Development and Welfare Act (CDWA) made £120 million available to colonies over a ten-year period to 1956. Colonies were expected to prepare development plans for the ten years of the Act and submit these to the CEDC for approval. The development plans received by the CEDC demonstrated the woeful lack of economic expertise among many serving colonial officers. Many plans were poorly conceived, being little more than "shopping lists" for capital equipment and steel, with no overarching plan for their effective use.

developed at great expense of money and effort".[14] However, the timing of Montgomery's report coincided with the government's desire to force the pace of colonial development in order to aid the balance of payments situation and helped to precipitate the rapid expansion of government machinery focussed on increasing economic activity in the empire. The elevation of colonial development policy in the wake of the 1947 crisis necessitated a thorough reorganization of the economic planning apparatus within government. The old arrangements for devising colonial economic policy, which were largely the province of the Colonial Office, were no longer deemed to be adequate, now heavyweight departments like the Treasury wanted closer control. Cabinet ministers concluded that the economic situation made it necessary to review policy and the adequacy and suitability of government machinery to promote it.[15]

In this respect, January 1948 proved to be a watershed in the planning of colonial development. In the previous September Stafford Cripps had moved from the Board of Trade to become minister of economic affairs in a newly created Ministry of Economic Planning.[16] Although this ministry lasted only a few months before it was absorbed into the Treasury, it established the Central Economic Planning Staff (CEPS) in January 1948. This was staffed by Treasury officials and government ministers, and operated from within the Treasury.[17] The CEPS was created to co-ordinate economic policy throughout the colonial empire. Its aim was "to keep in touch with major developments affecting United Kingdom economic policy and, ensuring that colonial implications of such developments were not overlooked, either by the rest of the United Kingdom or by the Colonial Office and the colonial governments".[18]

Nine specialist committees were also set up in January 1948 which reported directly to the CEPS. Six of these were primarily concerned with colonial affairs. Paramount among them was the Colonial Development Working Party (CDWP), an interdepartmental body dominated by the

---

[14] Ibid., 199.

[15] "Report by CIGS on his visit to Africa": minutes of a committee of cabinet ministers to discuss the memorandum by Field-Marshall Montgomery, Jan. 9, 1948, PREM 8/923, GEN 210/1 [BDEE2], 205–6.

[16] See "Economic Planning", *The Times*, Sep. 30, 1947.

[17] Although no attempt was made to co-ordinate its work with that of the Economic Section of the Cabinet Office; this came later with the establishment of the Cabinet Committee on Colonial Development, see below. B. W. E. Alford, *British Economic Performance, 1945–1975* (Basingstoke: Macmillan, 1988), 29.

[18] Allister Hinds, *Britain's Sterling Colonial Policy and Decolonization, 1939–1958* (London: Greenwood Press, 2001), 159.

Treasury and charged with examining all aspects of colonial development. The other committees included the Colonial Dollar Drain Committee (CDDC), charged with reducing as far as possible the money spent by the colonies on expensive imports from the dollar-area by way of setting so-called "dollar ceilings" on individual territories. The Colonial Primary Products Committee (CPPC) was created to assess which areas of the empire were best suited to producing commodities scarce in the United Kingdom. The Review of Programmes and of Colonial Capital Investment Requirements Committee was responsible for allocating capital equipment from British manufactures for colonial development schemes.[19] The Colonial Aspects of the Economic Activities of the United Nations Committee was charged with identifying and evaluating UN funds available for reconstruction and development.[20] The new CEPS committee structure also incorporated existing bodies involved in the formation of colonial economic policy; the CEDC was the most prominent of these. After its incorporation into the CEPS committee structure, Creech Jones expanded the CEDC's remit to include the examination of all aspects of colonial development policy. This seems to have been motivated partly by a desire to maintain the Colonial Office's role in administering the new policies in the face of increasing Treasury influence.[21]

Other CEPS committees, not directly or solely concerned with colonial economic policy nonetheless also exerted a powerful influence in this field. The Sterling Area Development Working Party (SADWP) drew its membership from the Cabinet Office, Treasury, CEPS, Commonwealth Relations Office (CRO), Ministry of Food, and Ministry of Supply, and inevitably its attention was drawn to development schemes in the dominions. At the first meeting of the SADWP in February 1948, its chair Edward Roll alluded directly to the importance of colonial development within the sterling area, as a way of earning dollars and minimizing dependence on imports from the dollar area.[22] The SADWP looked to the Board of Trade and Ministries of Supply and Food to identify the main commodities and foodstuffs which would be valuable currency earners.

---

[19] This was a short-lived committee whose work was submerged into the CDWP by the start of 1948.

[20] Hinds, *Britain's Sterling Colonial Policy,* 168.

[21] See Colonial Development Committee System diagram which demonstrates the complex planning apparatus established under the CEPS and the inter-relation between Treasury and Colonial Office.

[22] Sterling Area Development Working Party, Minutes of Meetings. Minutes of first meeting, Feb. 18, 1948, TNA: CO/537/3081.

Colonial Development Committee System, 1945–51

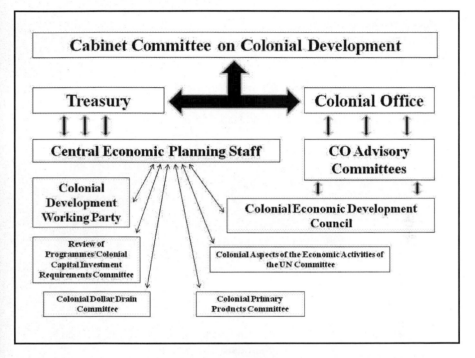

The Attlee government's planning apparatus for colonial development was typically over-bureaucratic[23] and also provided an arena in which the welfarist agenda came into conflict with the short-term economic imperatives of the Treasury.[24] In order to make sense of the sometimes confusing and complex web of committees and bureaucracies, in December 1948 the Government created a Cabinet Committee on Colonial Development (CCCD) to oversee their work, and ensure a clear and consistent direction for policy. The CCCD met for the first time in late December 1948. It was manned by top officials and politicians from most of the major departments like Dalton (Chancellor of the Duchy of

---

[23] For a wider exploration of the Attlee government's planning structures that includes the domestic arena, see Kenneth O. Morgan, *Labour in Power, 1945–1951* (Oxford: Clarendon Press, 1984), 130–6, 366–9.

[24] "The Formation of British Colonial Development Policy in the Trans-World War Two Period, 1942–1953: With special reference to Central and Southern Africa" (PhD diss., Lancaster University, 2005), by author.

Lancaster), and was chaired by E. A. Hitchman, the Government's Deputy Chief Planning Officer responsible for United Kingdom economic development, and a member of the CEPS. Representatives from the Treasury, Colonial Office, Foreign Office, Board of Trade, and Ministry of Food also sat on CCCD.

The Perils of the African Periphery

Despite the huge increase in the metropolitan desire to organize and drive forward its state-sponsored colonial development programme, especially in Africa, the periphery would test this policy, at times to breaking point. The examples of Tanganyika (Tanzania), Nyasaland (Malawi) and Northern Rhodesia (Zambia), amply demonstrate this fact.

In April 1948, the Paymaster General, H. Marquand, who subsequently wrote an extensive report, also undertook an official fact-finding visit to Africa. The Marquand report is a catalogue of the problems facing colonial administrations trying to promote economic development.[25] Labour shortages, poor farming methods, insufficient investment in infrastructure, poor education policies, bottlenecks in supply routes, huge areas of bush controlled by tsetse fly, and the lack of effective research – were all cited in the report as factors impeding the pace of development.[26] It was recognized that the expansion of colonial export production would not come cheaply. The example of Tanganyika, doomed to be the home of Labour's worst colonial development disaster, illustrates many of the practical problems involved in turning development plans into reality.

The colonial officials who produced Tanganyika's ten-year development plan under the CDWA scheme believed that it would require a high level of expenditure.[27] The plan required CDWA finance for railway construction, replacement of government motor vehicles, replacement of port machinery, township water supplies, and investment in the sugar, coffee, and cotton industries.[28] It was estimated that the total funds required for 1948 alone would be £24.8 million, by far the largest for any African territory. Originally mandated to Britain after World War One, Tanganyika's economic development had then required the official

---

[25] Report by the Paymaster-General on his visit to Africa, Jan. 16 to Mar. 9, 1948. Hand-marked copy by Paymaster-General for the attention of Gorell-Barnes (Colonial Office), Apr. 2, 1948, TNA: CO537/3159.
[26] Ibid., para. 9, p. 4.
[27] See Tanganyika's ten-year development plan, Jan. 13, 1947, TNA: CO852/872/1.
[28] Ibid., 3–5.

sanction of the League of Nations. While Article 9 of the mandate permitted the creation of state monopolies for the development of natural resources in the interest of the local population, such arrangements were not supposed to benefit the mandatory power.[29] In practice, however, there was ample opportunity to develop Tanganyika's resources in ways which suited British interests, so long as such schemes could be defended as being primarily designed to meet local needs.

In April 1948 the chairman of the CEDC Rees-Williams reported to his colleagues on the Council that there was huge potential in Tanganyika for all types of development. But he found that few of the development schemes outlined in the Territory's Ten-Year Development Plan had moved beyond the initial stages. As elsewhere, this was in part due to problems of supply, transport and manpower, but it was also due to particularly ineffective colonial administration. Tanganyika's governor, Sir William Battershill, had been ill for most of his time in office and had spent most of 1948 in Britain. This had a detrimental effect on the colonial officials who had produced the development plan that had been well received by the CEDC in 1947.[30] Without Battershill's leadership, his subordinates proved unable to turn their ambitious ideas on development into reality. To get things moving, in 1949 Creech Jones replaced Battershill with Sir Edward Twining (a member of the famous tea-merchant family), who was at the time governor of North Borneo.[31]

Twining was set two objectives. First, he was instructed to prepare the territory for self-government; and second to begin the implementation of Tanganyika's economic development plan. But although Twining's appointment gave the colonial government new direction, conditions in the territory were very poor, especially in agriculture, underlining the daunting scale of Twining's second task. The twelve-million cattle owned by Africans were "useful neither for meat nor for milk".[32] This was because locally Africans used cattle as a form of savings account and to "buy wives". Another major problem which blighted all of sub-Saharan Africa since the first imperial incursions was the predominance of the tsetse fly which spread disease among cattle herds.

---

[29] UN Mandate cited by B. T. G. Chidzero, *Tanganyika and International Trusteeship* (Oxford: Oxford University Press, 1961), app. 1. The UK assumed the Mandate in 1920 after World War One.

[30] Tanganyika's plan had received much praise by the CEDC when it came up for discussion in Jan. 1947: CEDC Minutes, Jan. 13, 1947, TNA: CO852/866/6.

[31] Correspondence and minutes between Sydney Caine and Creech Jones, May–July 1949, TNA: CO967/66.

[32] CEDC Meetings, minutes for May 21, 1948, TNA: CO852/868/1.

To tackle such problems and to generate growth, Rees-Williams had suggested a number of development objectives for the territory. The untapped mineral wealth of the country was identified as one area of potential. Rees-Williams applauded a hydro-electric project under consideration at Jinja, which could facilitate the industrial development of the deposits of copper and iron ore. A second, urgent, priority was the promotion of better land use and farming methods by local farmers, to reverse a growing problem of soil erosion in parts of the territory. Rees-Williams had advocated evictions of uncooperative farmers, but the conflict likely to arise from such draconian measures ensured that the proposal was never implemented. The main barrier to new agricultural development, however, was the tsetse fly. To open up new areas for cultivation it was necessary to clear the land and use insecticides to kill off the insect. Rees-Williams then wanted the land to be settled quickly through the establishment of state-owned farms. Local farmers would then be compelled to abandon their traditional farming methods in favour of modern techniques as well as providing labour and therefore tax revenue. To bring about this planned increased production in Tanganyika the British government looked to European entrepreneurs to achieve the fastest results.

African agriculture was held in low esteem by colonial administrations. It was believed that African land-tenure practices led to impersonal attitudes to land which resulted in very little desire for improvement because local farmers did not have a "western" sense of land ownership.[33] Previous colonial administrations had been unwilling to impose changes to land-tenure practices as this would threaten social stability. However the Colonial Office believed that attitudes were changing in the field as many local officials now believed that their territories could ill-afford to sit back and wait for social change to work itself out over generations.[34] Mechanized production and the modern techniques associated with

---

[33] See "Development in Africa", address by Mr Marquand to a press conference, Mar. 18, 1948, CAB124/1089 [BDEE2], 208. See also B. D. Bowles, "The Political Economy of Colonial Tanganyika 1939–61", in M. H. Y. Kaniki, ed., *Tanzania under Colonial Rule* (London: Longman, 1979), 171–3. Vernon Porritt has shown how the colonial administration in Sarawak encouraged a diversified system of agriculture for "native" producers. C. W. Dawson, Sarawak's acting governor, believed that diversification away from rubber could help the territory become self-sufficient in food production, moving away from the land-intensive production of rubber: Vernon L. Porritt, *British Colonial Rule in Sarawak, 1946–1963* (Oxford: Oxford University Press, 1997), 182.
[34] S Cain to A B Cohen, 23 April 1946. CO852/1003/3 [BDEE2], 233.

European producers were generally favoured. It was for this reason that the East Africa Groundnut Scheme rejected the notion of African farmers leading the efforts to increase production. Echoing the earlier Marquand Report, Rees-Williams argued that for his development programme to be successful, plentiful supplies of steel and consumer goods would be necessary, together with improved teaching and education of Africans by European technicians.[35] To promote these, Twining tried to publicize opportunities for new business ventures in Tanganyika. During his visits to London he often entertained potential customers and investors in an attempt to encourage new business.[36]

Of all the colonial development projects initiated in Africa after World War Two, Tanganyika was home to perhaps the most infamous, the East Africa Groundnut Scheme. The scheme was administered by the OFC and was one of the most notorious colonial development disasters. The initial impetus for the scheme came from the privately owned United Africa Company (UAC), which first identified the possibility of large-scale plantation style production in Tanganyika.[37] In 1947 the British government despatched an official mission led by A. J. Wakefield to Tanganyika to assess the potential of the scheme. The Wakefield Commission took only nine weeks to complete its investigations in the vast Kongwa region, the area selected for the scheme. Kongwa was relatively sparsely populated, but Wakefield portrayed this as an advantage, because the scheme could use machinery for land clearance and planting, without having to provide much local employment. The indigenous Africans who did inhabit the Kongwa area referred to it as *Yisis Yanghwanu* – "the country of perpetual dryness".[38] The initial management of the scheme was undertaken by the UAC (part of Unilever) from 1946 until the Overseas Resources Development Act created the OFC (and CDC) in 1948.[39]

---

[35] See "Visit to East and Central Africa" by Rees Williams (undated draft), TNA: CO822/119/6.

[36] See Julian Crossley, General Manager of Barclays Bank (Dominions, Colonies and Overseas), unpub. diaries, Mar. 7, 1951, Barclays Group Archives [BGA].

[37] The UAC was already a large-scale producer in British West Africa. The oil pressed from groundnuts was used to increase the fat ration in the UK; most of the oil produced went into the production of margarine.

[38] Cyril Ehrlich, *The Poor Country: The Tanganyika Economy from 1945 to Independence*, in D. A. Low and Alison Smith, eds., *History of East Africa*, Vol. 3 (Oxford: Oxford University Press), 310.

[39] *Tanganyika: A Review of its Resources and Their Development* (Government of Tanganyika Publication, 1955), 542.

This type of scheme was greatly favoured by planners within the British government immediately after the war. Creech Jones was a particularly ardent supporter. The short-term benefits of the groundnut scheme were expected to be very good as groundnuts grew quickly in the right conditions. The British government was so optimistic about the scheme's prospects that it estimated an expected £10-million annual dollar-saving and extended the size of the project.[40] The Treasury had argued from an early stage that the Ministry of Food and not the Colonial Office should administer the scheme. One Treasury official argued that the scheme would be a financial disaster if left to the Colonial Office because it would regard it "not as a commercial venture in which H. M. Government have invested money which they expect to see returned, but as a scheme for the betterment of the colonies concerned."[41] The plantations were expected to cover 5,000 square miles and the OFC was advanced £25 million to begin the land-clearance operation. John Strachey, a former extreme leftist who had been appointed as minister of food by Attlee, sang the loudest praises of the scheme. In July 1948 he asserted that he had "perfect confidence that in a very few years the groundnut scheme will be one of the acknowledged glories of the British Commonwealth".[42] Strachey's continued willingness to "play up" the scheme's potential, even when he became painfully aware of its flaws, contributed to the scheme's notoriety as a monumental failure in state-sponsored colonial development.

Strachey appointed Leslie Plummer as the chairman of the OFC, a man with no African experience, although he was a part-time farmer.[43] The OFC took over the East African Groundnut Scheme on April 1, 1948 – hardly an auspicious date. The OFC was granted £50 million to administer the scheme and it aimed to plant 2,355 acres between 1948 and 1958. However, poor planning and investigation meant that the initial estimates produced by the Wakefield Commission were totally inaccurate. In

---

[40] See paper CP(47)176, "East Africa Groundnuts Scheme": Cabinet memorandum by John Strachey, June 8, 1947, CAB129/19 [BDEE2], 255–7.
[41] See Treasury brief, "Groundnuts in East and Central Africa", by J. I. C. Crombie (third secretary to the Treasury), Oct. 28, 1946, T161/1371/553997/1 [BDEE2], 242.
[42] Quoted in Amanke Okafor, *Nigeria: Why we Fight for Independence* (Privately published, 1949) 26. Also cited in Robert Clough, *Labour: A Party Fit for Imperialism* (London: Larkin, 1992), 93.
[43] Plummer was an old friend of Strachey from their Independent Labour Party days in the 1920s: Michael Newman, *John Strachey* (Manchester: Manchester University Press, 1989), 113.

addition, land clearance proved far harder than originally expected as the equipment was unsuitable to African conditions. The scheme was further hampered by low rainfall, 1948 being especially poor. A further problem was the lack of interest among local Africans, in spite of promises of better social and educational services in conjunction with the scheme.[44] By March 1949, Strachey and Plummer knew that the scheme was in serious difficulties, but kept a brave public face. Strachey strongly defended the scheme in the House of Commons, stating "the revenues of the scheme ... may well add up to anything up to twice the original estimate".[45]

By late 1949 the groundnut scheme had only brought 26,000 acres under cultivation. The scheme cost the British taxpayer £36.5 million, a spectacular failure even by modern standards.[46] John Blandford has pointed out that the only real benefit derived from the scheme was to local farmers who were sold machinery from the scheme at a strongly discounted rate.[47] If we examine the growth in imports into Tanganyika after 1947 it is clear that increases in supplies were being obtained. But the effects of the groundnut scheme hugely distorted the scale of colonial development investment in the colony. Between 1947 and 1950 the OFC procured much agricultural machinery for the scheme, but as Blandford points out, most was inappropriate for the country's needs.[48]

In terms of Britain's mandate over the colony, the scheme obviously did constitute a "monopoly of the natural resources for the benefit of the Mandatory". When the suggestion for the groundnut scheme was put forward, without any consultation with the UN, Creech Jones gave his consent for 3,250,000 acres of "native land" to be handed over to the newly created OFC to administer the scheme. The Wakefield Commission report overflowed with the apparent benefits of the scheme for Tanganyika. It argued that the scheme would be "a great catalyst for development" with large "unused" areas being opened up and brought under cultivation. Secondly, it was claimed that the scheme would require improved communications in the shape of new port facilities in the Southern Province and a new railway line to connect it to the scheme.

---

[44] Ibid.

[45] Ibid., 114.

[46] See Michael Havinden and David Meredith, *Colonialism and Development: Britain and its Tropical Colonies, 1850–1960* (London: Routledge, 1993), 281.

[47] Blandford points out that it would have proved much too expensive to ship machinery back out of East Africa so the decision was taken to sell it locally for whatever the market would support. Author's interview with John Blandford, former Barclays employee in East Africa, Aug. 19, 1999.

[48] Ibid.

Wakefield believed these infrastructural improvements would "kick-start" other development schemes in the region. Even a UN Visiting Mission which visited Tanganyika in 1948 believed the scheme "a bold undertaking which may in the long run be of great benefit to the inhabitants of Tanganyika".[49] But in truth, the whole project was conceived entirely for the benefit of the imperial government and had little to do with the advancement of economic or political development in Tanganyika. The scheme is the best example of colonial development policy emanating from the metropole and failing on the periphery. The driving force behind the scheme came from London's desire to increase output of a commodity scarce in the world market.[50]

The failure of the groundnut scheme demonstrates several weaknesses which characterized the state-led colonial development approach. Although the initial idea for the scheme came from Unilever in the private sector, which did not want to pursue the scheme itself as it was expected that huge associated investment in infrastructure was the responsibility of government, it was the short-term urgency of the 1947 crisis which prompted the British government to take it up under the auspices of the newly created OFC. As with so many projects prepared in such politically-driven haste, serious mistakes were almost inevitable. Strachey and Creech Jones were convinced it would be a success, but metropolitan dreams soon became nightmares on the periphery.

The possible dangers and risks associated with the scheme *were* known within the Colonial Office. But as shown, the plan proceeded on the

---

[49] Chidzero, *Tanganyika and International Trusteeship,* 235. The Wakefield Report also reported that new townships would be built with schools, hospitals, and community centres.

[50] Another disastrous project that brought much criticism for the Attlee government was the Gambia Poultry Scheme, this time planned and administered by the CDC. Chosen for its relative proximity to Britain, the scheme was intended to generate a profitable export trade in poultry and eggs for the British market, but ultimately it made a loss of over £800,000. Amidst the public furore following the failure of the scheme Herbert Morrison, the Lord President of the Privy Council, lamented the lack of initial research into local ecological conditions, which would have revealed their unsuitability for the scheme. See Morrison to Gaitskell, Mar. 2, 1961: TNA, T/220/1255. The CDC had expected the farm to produce twenty million eggs and just one million pounds of dressed poultry for the domestic market within a few years. Only three weeks after Attlee's government was forced to write off £36 million lost due to the East Africa Groundnut Scheme, Lennox Boyd, shadow spokesman for colonial affairs, was able to gleefully report that only 38,000 eggs had been delivered to Britain, most of which were deemed unfit for human consumption. See extracts from *Hansard*, contained in TNA, T/220/1255.

strength of the flawed Wakefield Commission report. As a member of the Ministry of Food later argued, the groundnut plan proceeded despite these "explicit warnings" because those charged with reviewing the scheme "were the objects of ministerial pressure of the severest kind."[51] Clearly the political drive in favour of colonial development saw the advice of experts within the civil service ignored in favour of large-scale state-led development. The difficulty of local conditions, the poor quality of staff on the periphery, and the inadequacies of the plan, demonstrated clearly the inability of the metropolitan government to create a coherent policy. There was a general confusion about the purpose of the scheme, and Creech Jones saw it as a project to aid the East Africa economy and prepare the colony for independence. However, others within the government, and especially the Treasury, saw it as a commercial venture for the benefit of the British economy.[52] For the Attlee government the failure of the scheme was politically damaging and this was certainly exacerbated by the Colonial Office's desire to maintain confidence in the scheme within southern Africa. Rushed planning, short-term (and short-lived) political motivation, confused and conflicting objectives, inadequate communication and intelligence networks – all of these shortcomings tended to typify the state-led approach to development.

The Problems of Regional Infrastructure

Another area of colonial development also illustrates the problems of trying to adapt plans conceived in the metropole to the conditions on the periphery. In the immediate post-war years Northern Rhodesia was one of the world's largest sources of copper ore. Production in the territory stood at 138,000 tons in 1936 and had increased to 183,000 tons by 1946.[53] As one of the most valuable commodities produced in the region, copper was very important to Britain's dollar earning/saving policy, and it determined British policy in the region. In 1949 the Colonial Office informed the CCCD that poor availability of coal in the region was a barrier to the

---

[51] See "Note on the latest paper on the East African Groundnuts Scheme", memorandum by Dr E. E. Bailey (Ministry of Food), Oct. 6, 1949, MAF 85/589 [BDEE2], 284.
[52] See "Groundnuts in East and Central Africa", Treasury minute by J. I. C. Crombie, Oct. 28, 1946, T161/1371/553997/1 [BDEE2], 242.
[53] Colonial Economic Development Council papers and minutes, Draft Interim Report of the CDWP, 1948, TNA: CO852/868/1.

expansion of copper production.[54] The only coal supply came from the
Wankie (Hwange) Colliery in Southern Rhodesia, over 600 miles away.
The main problem was the slow production of coal at the colliery and the
poor rail link between the two areas.[55] Inadequate coal supplies were also
hindering production of chrome in Southern Rhodesia, and the Colonial
Office argued for improvements as both chrome and copper were "dollar
earners and dollar savers".[56] The Colonial Office demonstrated that the
demand for chrome in the United States was growing, pointing out that
Southern Rhodesia produced 22,000 tons of chrome per month and the US
market was said to be able to absorb 48,000.[57] In its 1948 survey of
Rhodesia's economic potential, the CDWP recommended a regional
approach to the development of the colony.[58] This emphasized the need to
make local development more dependent on local resources. For example,
a proposed scheme for the production of nitrogenous fertilizers was based
on the assumption that the Wankie colliery would supply fuel.[59] Barclays
Bank (Dominions, Colonies and Overseas) was invited to open a branch at
the colliery in 1951, and this helped to provide financial security for the
local workforce.[60]

In 1949 copper ore was worth more than chrome due to expanding
demand from the electrical industry. Northern Rhodesia produced 213,000
tons of copper in 1948 and 250,000 tons in 1949, but supply commitments
to the Union of South Africa, India, Australia, and Sweden, meant that the
balance available was far short of British requirements. The Colonial
Office argued that any shortfall in British imports of Rhodesian copper
would necessitate imports from hard-currency areas.[61] Clearly, Rhodesian

---

[54] Colonial Office Memo to CCCD, "Coal for the Copperbelt in Northern
Rhodesia", Sep. 17, 1949, TNA: CAB/134/66.
[55] On a visit to the Rhodesias in 1950, Julian Crossley noted that the dramatic rise
in white immigration to Southern Rhodesia since the war had seen the population
double since 1939. He believed this was a contributory factor to the colonies' slow
economic progress due to the increased demand on resources. This was
demonstrated by the principal municipal power station which regularly had only 24
hours' supply of fuel on hand. See "Chairman's notes on Rhodesian visit
February/March 1950" in Accession 80/3671 (BGA).
[56] Colonial Office memorandum to CCCD, "Coal for the Copperbelt in Northern
Rhodesia", Sep. 17, 1949, TNA: CAB/134/66.
[57] Ibid.
[58] Paper CDWP (48) 7, "Possible Development Projects in British Colonies", Feb.
14, 1948, TNA: CO852/875/1.
[59] Ibid.
[60] J. Crossley, unpub. Diaries, Feb. 22, 1951 (BGA).
[61] See minutes of CCCD Meeting, Jan. 13, 1950, TNA: CAB/134/66.

copper output needed to be increased, and this depended upon a larger supply of local coal. In February 1950 Sir Edwin Plowden, chairman of the CDWP, and D. B. Pitblado, of the Treasury, met with Sir John Chancellor, chairman of the board of the Wankie colliery. Chancellor claimed that although the company was doing its best to increase production, new equipment ordered by the firm was being held up at the port of Beira in Mozambique. The government officials agreed to make representations to the relevant department (in this case the Board of Trade) to try and speed up the procurement and delivery of the necessary equipment.[62] Many development schemes in the region depended upon adequate fuel supplies from Wankie.[63] This was particularly true of the joint CDC and Northern Rhodesian government cement project at Chilanga. The cement scheme was very important to Northern Rhodesia, as post-war development schemes had seen cement imports rise steeply since 1945. But for the scale of production envisaged by the CDC and the Northern Rhodesian authorities to be reached, they needed far more power than would be available from coal generators. This was why hydro-electric power became so important for the development of these territories.

Transport difficulties had huge implications for the development of these territories. Delays in unloading cargo at the port of Beira plagued the British territories of the region throughout the 1947–51 period. Poor facilities meant that cargo ships often had to wait off shore – sometimes for over a month – before they could unload. The Conference shipping line suffered heavy losses through "enforced idleness" of its ships at the port. Between September 1949 and February 1950 Conference estimated their losses at £300,000 and the company subsequently imposed a 60-percent surcharge on all its freight rates to Beira.[64] Other shipping companies talked of ending deliveries to the troubled port. So even when the supply of equipment was improving by 1950, local conditions and problems continued to cast doubt on the future. But if the poor facilities at Beira halted the supply of equipment it also hampered the efforts of those in landlocked Northern Rhodesia and Nyasaland who needed access to valuable export markets. Copper exports from Northern Rhodesia were

---

[62] Ibid.

[63] Coal from Wankie was also vital to the railways of Nyasaland. In Oct. 1948 Sir Geoffrey Colby, Nyasaland's recently appointed governor, wrote to Creech Jones to highlight the problems of coal supply for the railways; he reported that stocks of coal were down to less than a month. Colby to Creech Jones, Oct. 12, 1949, TNA: CO525/210/3.

[64] Commonwealth Relations Office memorandum to CCCD, June 30, 1950, TNA: CAB/134/66.

delayed to such an extent that in the later months of 1949 the Northern Rhodesian government was forced to transport copper overland to the Union of South Africa at great extra cost.[65]

Transport problems within the territories of southern Africa were generally severe in the 1945–51 period. Nyasaland and Tanganyika suffered from very poor rail networks. The new importance attached to colonial development after 1947 prompted the British government to try to alleviate these difficulties. Material shortages meant, however, that in Tanganyika no rail improvements were started until 1949. The existing rail network ran from the east to west, from the coast to the interior. The territory had no north-to-south railway lines capable of connection with the central African railways of Northern and Southern Rhodesia. In 1948, the CEDC had at least identified the need for such a link.[66] It stressed that the production of food and other commodities would be unable to grow rapidly without it.[67] But a serious obstacle to the proposal was the fact that the Rhodesian and South African railways operated on a different gauge to that of Tanganyika.[68] The CEDC wanted an investigation into the financial viability of the proposed link, but had to approach the United States for technical support as a British survey team was not available due to the scarcity of technical staff. The American survey team began work in March 1949, but no progress was made in building such a line until 1954.

Metropolitan Limits on Colonial Imports

For many African colonies, "dollar ceilings" imposed on import spending were rigidly enforced by the Treasury. When Nysasland applied for an amendment to its dollar ceiling for 1950 in order to purchase additional agricultural machinery the request was refused on the basis that "minor amendments" to dollar ceilings would open the door to many such requests from other colonies.[69] In early 1950 Sir Geoffrey Colby, Nyasaland's governor, applied for a licence to import wheat from Canada, in part to alleviate famine conditions, but was only allowed to do so by reducing planned expenditure on other imported commodities.[70] Escalating

---

[65] Ibid.

[66] Minutes of CEDC meeting, Dec. 20, 1948, TNA: CO852/866/7.

[67] Ibid., 3.

[68] Rhodesia railways operated on the three-feet-six-inches gauge while the Tanganyikan system operated on a one-metre gauge.

[69] J. L. Croome (CEPS) to Cargill (CO), Feb. 10, 1950, TNA: CO852/1133/11.

[70] Telegram from Secretary of State for Colonies to Sir Geoffrey Colby, Oct. 4, 1950, TNA: CO852/1133/11.

costs saw many proposed developments abandoned. A good example was the proposed 44-mile stretch of road to connect Monkey Bay at the Southern end of Lake Nyasa to the rail network. The scheme was granted CDW funds in 1946 to the tune of £88,000. Construction was delayed for the usual reasons of scarce resources and manpower and the colonial government cancelled the scheme in 1949 as the estimated cost had risen to £200,000, an increase of 127 percent.[71]

Colby was a "development minded" governor whose personal determination tied in perfectly with the UK government drive for colonial development.[72] But the best laid plans of colonial developers could not always cope with the vagaries of African conditions and Colby's administration was beset with problems from the day he took office. In 1948 an island of water vegetation released from the Elephant Marsh by heavy rains surged down the Shire River and washed away the Chiromo Bridge. This ill-timed disaster severely damaged export trade for the following year, and a ferry service, even more vulnerable to the vagaries of African conditions, was brought back into operation.[73] Colby found that the safety of the Chiromo Bridge had been in doubt for many years and no plan had been made by previous administrations to replace it. One member of Nyasaland's Legislative Council complained that 250 tons of tea grown in the territory for export was awaiting rail transport but due to the Chiromo disaster the rail companies did not expect to move the crop for many months by which time the new crop would also be ready for export.[74] In April 1948 Nyasaland's transport problems were further compounded. A head-on collision between two goods trains on the Beira railway killed a railway driver and irreparably damaged one of the territory's new locomotives and rolling stock.[75] Throughout 1949 a new railway bridge was constructed, but this combination of an under-developed transport infrastructure and the misfortunes of the African

---

[71] Nyasaland general correspondence, Jan. 1949, TNA: CO525/198/1.
[72] Colin Baker, *Development Governor: A Biography of Sir Geoffrey Colby* (London: British Academic Press, 1994).
[73] Colby later commented that the 52 days it took to establish a rudimentary ferry service cost the territory dearly in export revenue. Minutes of Nyasaland Legislative Council, July 19, 1948, TNA: CO525/210/3.
[74] Speech by Rt. Hon M. P. Barrow CBE at Legislative Council, July 19, 1948, TNA: CO525/210/3.
[75] Ironically this locomotive had been ordered before the outbreak of war. Codrington (Chairman of Nyasaland Railways) to Cohen (CO), July 29, 1948. See also *Nyasaland Times*, Apr. 29, 1948, "Railway accident – Goods trains collide near Beira", TNA: CO525/210/3.

environment seriously frustrated British hopes for the territory's export performance.

The dollar policy of the sterling area had a dramatic effect on development planning at the local level. The reduction of colonial dollar ceilings by the British government between 1948 and 1951 saw the dollar ceilings for Tanganyika, Northern Rhodesia, and Nyasaland significantly reduced. This forced these territories to rely mainly on British manufactured supplies of machinery and other scarce commodities. The supplies which were available were subject to the severe delays in transportation previously outlined. Consequently, the much hoped-for increase in local production was stymied by the enforced reduction in dollar spending. In addition, commodity production in the British territories of southern African still lagged far behind pre-war levels. For example, in 1936 Tanganyika produced 25-million pounds of cotton, but during the war many areas under cotton had been given over to food production because of war-time disruption of food imports. As late as 1948, cotton production had yet to recover to pre-war levels. In contrast, Northern Rhodesia saw profound advances in production. Cash crops like tobacco were also beginning to become more significant. In 1930, Nyasaland had produced 1.2 million pounds, increasing to 3.8 million by 1936. In 1946, output was expected to rise to 14 million per year by 1953.[76]

Inevitably, the looming question of the future governance of central and southern Africa held important implications for economic development strategy. Southern Rhodesia enjoyed close political and social links with Northern Rhodesia, and the white-settler regimes in both territories thought and acted alike on many local issues. Southern Rhodesia had gained autonomy over local policies in 1923 when the British government granted the colony "self-government" status. The territory had been heavily settled, with the majority of immigrants coming from Britain. Because of the close integration between the economies of Northern and Southern Rhodesia, the British government, through the CDWP, also examined the development objectives set by the Legislative Council of Southern Rhodesia.[77] But Britain's relationship with its African settler communities was changing. Before the war, British policy towards political development in the colonies was generally cautious and conservative. The defence of "native interests" was usually regarded as

---

[76] CDWP report, app. C, ibid.

[77] It was the Commonwealth Relations Office (CRO) that was legally responsible for policy relating to Southern Rhodesia and it was primarily for this reason that CRO officials were invited on to the CDWP.

paramount. But after the war this policy changed, especially in the multiracial societies of Kenya, Tanganyika, and the Rhodesias. Emphasis was now laid upon the notion of "partnership" between the races, with the rights of indigenous people receiving the same recognition as those of settlers. James Griffiths, Labour's secretary of state for the colonies in 1950, stressed that this would "safeguard the proper rights and interests of all the different communities".[78] However, white settlers in southern and central Africa rejected this shift in imperial policy because it would erode their privileged status.[79] Settlers believed such policies were formulated in London by men with no knowledge and understanding of local conditions. In addition, such policies were seen as misguided because settlers believed they knew "their Africans" and had a better understanding of what was best for them.

This change in imperial policy would have dramatic effects on the central African region after 1951. The idea for the Federation of Rhodesia and Nyasaland had originated before the war, but gained growing support from the colonial governments concerned after 1947. The federal scheme was deemed "essential" to the development of economic resources.[80] In essence, the federal scheme was designed to promote a complementary relationship between the three central African territories. It was thought that workers from Nyasaland could be recruited to the secondary industries of Southern Rhodesia and the mining industry in Northern Rhodesia. Under an appointed governor-general, the federal government would handle external affairs, defence, currency, inter-colonial relations, and federal taxes for its constituent members, which would retain most of their former legislative structures. The plan was supported by Britain on the grounds that only a white dominion in the region would keep it within the

---

[78] Chidzero, *Tanganyika and International Trusteeship*, 136.

[79] Most white settlers were drawn to the Rhodesias because they expected a lifestyle high above that which they enjoyed in Europe. When Creech Jones visited Northern Rhodesia in Feb. 1949 he enjoyed a very cold reception due to his "disproportionate racial views". See "Visit of Secretary of State to Northern Rhodesia", Apr. 5, 1949, CO822/120/3 (PRO).

[80] *Southern Rhodesia, Northern Rhodesia and Nyasaland: Report by the Conference on Federation held in London in January 1953* (London: HMSO, 1953), 5. Colonial Office officials also looked to the formation of closer political union in East Africa, bringing together Tanganyika, Kenya and Uganda – but this was seen as a long term strategy. See "Closer Association in East Africa" by P. Rogers, to A. B. Cohen, Dec. 3, 1951, CO822/338, No. 4. British Documents on the End of Empire: *The Conservative Government and the End of Empire*. Part 2: *Politics and Administration* (London: HMSO, 1994), 216–77.

empire.[81] Some in the British government saw the scheme as a way to improve local conditions. Patrick Gordon Walker toured Southern Rhodesia informing Africans that the scheme would involve a great increase in social services like education and healthcare.[82] But federation hastened the growth of African nationalism in all three territories, as Landeg White has argued.[83]

Before federation the nationalists did not know what their aims were – the anti-federation movement gave them focus. For the new Conservative administration after 1951, the growth of African nationalism was seen as partly due to a lack of leadership by the previous Labour government who had allowed the scheme's opponents to misinterpret the proposal.[84] The federal government did take economic planning and development very seriously and commissioned a number of detailed reports about schemes in progress and the predicted economic growth of each territory.[85]

Conclusions

The welfarist agenda much championed by figures such as Hinden and Creech Jones was inevitably sidelined after 1947 when short-term economic development was seen as a major factor in Britain's economic stability. At the heart of this was the high priority given to promoting dollar earnings from exports, especially from the primary producing economies of the colonies. As a result, colonial development policy now became the United Kingdom's favoured method of promoting economic recovery, the creation of the CCCD being the ultimate testament to this fact. Strategies to promote colonial development were no longer simply a moral question to be left to philosophers, socialists, or enlightened colonial officials in the field.

Many of the general problems which inhibited the promotion of effective colonial development can be amply displayed in the British colonies of Nyasaland, Northern Rhodesia and Tanganyika. Poor supply of materials, labour shortages, and inadequate research all hampered the

---

[81] Colin Leys and Cranford Pratt, eds., *A New Deal in Central Africa* (London: Heinemann, 1960), 47.

[82] Ibid., 49.

[83] Landeg White, "Was Federation Doomed?", Centre for Southern African Studies paper, University of York, Feb. 23, 1995, 4.

[84] See joint-cabinet memorandum entitled "Closer Association in Central Africa" by Lord Ismay and Oliver Lyttleton, Nov. 9, 1951, CAB129/48 [BDEE3], 282–3.

[85] See, for example, "Central African Federation Development Plan 1954–7" (also known as the Strachan Report), TNA: T220/280.

impetus for economic development. In addition, an earlier lack of investment in infrastructure left severe problems for central and southern Africa. The colonial administrations had displayed little coherent planning in the development of the regional rail network. The port of Beira in neighbouring Mozambique was so badly equipped that essential supplies could wait months before being transported to the interior. In addition, enforced reductions in dollar expenditure after the convertibility crisis meant that the southern and central African territories were forced to look only to Britain for machinery and other essential supplies. All of these problems converged to frustrate British efforts to formulate a coherent development policy in this period. At the same time that colonial development was being trumpeted as the cure for Britain's economic woes, the British government was limiting southern Africa's ability to buy available and essential equipment from dollar areas.[86] Colonial development planning in the metropole also displayed a lack of understanding about local conditions. The failures of large-scale development schemes due to poor investigation and planning were compounded by the British panic in the face of financial crisis. The crisis also spurred the Labour government into abandoning its traditional caution in a desperate gamble for quick results through such flawed schemes as East African groundnuts and Gambian poultry.

Clearly, the colonial governments struggled until the early 1950s to make a success of development strategies. The doomed federal scheme in central Africa was aimed at surmounting some of these difficulties, but growing political unrest, in part prompted by federation, saw its demise after only a few years. African nationalist groups in the region had been a disparate group before the war, but they soon found common ground in the campaign against the federal scheme. Britain's colonial development policy floundered at the periphery for a number of reasons, but ultimately it was an inability to "understand Africa" which was the greatest of these.

---

[86] Writing in 1953, the general manager of the East African Railways and Harbours Company looked back at the lack of progress to develop the territory's infrastructure. T. Baker argued that the secretary of state's stern dictates to keep capital requirements to an absolute minimum were totally contradictory to the equally stern dictates to increase colonial production. Baker's comments are reproduced in a Board of Trade file, "Tanganyika and Kenya", TNA: BT193/42.

LABOUR AND THE CENTRAL
AFRICAN FEDERATION:
PATERNALISM, PARTNERSHIP AND BLACK
NATIONALISM, 1951–60[1]

MURRAY STEELE

John Darwin has termed the establishment of the Central African Federation (now Malawi, Zambia and Zimbabwe) an "extraordinary and baffling inconsistency" in British post-war colonial policy, running counter to the prevailing current of decolonization.[2] Labour's agreement in principle with the federal concept seems an even more baffling inconsistency, given its pre-war attitude to white settlers in tropical Africa. This chapter explores the reasons why Labour, which had facilitated the first proposals for closer association while in office, continued to support the principle of federation when the final scheme was drawn up by the new Conservative administration in 1952, albeit with the proviso that a final effort be made to persuade Africans of its economic advantages – a stance taken despite a strong campaign against federation in Britain as well as central Africa, and within the party itself.

Based on archival work carried out on Labour Party records, and Fabian Colonial (later, Commonwealth) Bureau (FCB) and related materials at Rhodes House and elsewhere, this chapter contextualizes the analysis of Labour policy set out in the classic works of Howe and Goldsworthy within the framework of central African history.[3] While not

---

[1] My thanks to Billy Frank, who suggested this enquiry; to Lucy McCann and her predecessors at Rhodes House, Oxford; Darren Treadwell and Jo Robson of the People's History Museum for helping to make it possible; and participants at the June 2008 "British Labour Movement and Imperialism" conference at UCLan for their comments on an earlier draft.
[2] J. Darwin, "British Decolonisation since 1945: A Pattern or a Puzzle?", *Journal of Commonwealth and Imperial History* 12, no. 2 (1984), 190.
[3] S. Howe, *Anti-Colonialism in British Politics: the Left and the End of Empire, 1918–1964* (Oxford: Clarendon Press, 1993); D. Goldsworthy, *Colonial Issues in*

disagreeing with their verdict that the party played a small part in the eventual demise of the Federation as compared to that of its Tory architects and black nationalists themselves, it advances as a defence Clement Attlee's commitment of his party to make the Federation work once the federal scheme received parliamentary approval. This was by advocating the development of social and educational provision for the underprivileged black majority, fostering black trade unions and political organizations, and campaigning for the end of the colour bar and other forms of racial discrimination – in short, to translate pious declarations about racial partnership into reality. As a corollary to this constructive approach, the party encouraged more amenable black politicians to stand for the federal parliament, to keep out "stooges". Yet only a year into the Federation, an attempt by one of these figures, Dauti Yamba, to introduce a motion to end racial discrimination in certain public places had been heckled out of existence by white members of the legislative assembly and answered with taunts from the federal prime minister Godfrey Huggins.[4]

The snail-like progress towards racial partnership that ensued led to a sense of mounting disillusionment amongst Labour MPs and inevitably created tensions between the party's black clients and their sponsors. Expectations were created that Labour, in opposition throughout this period, were powerless to fulfil. One of these was over the continued existence of the Federation. As the incumbent administration, the Macmillan government eventually found ways of dissolving it when it was no longer expedient to keep it in being. And this was after years when Labour – and black nationalists – had been told that all four governments had to agree to its dissolution, and in any case would not be put on the agenda of the future review conference. The other corresponding anxiety, about the prospect of a Federal Unilateral Declaration of Independence from Britain, first reared its head in 1956, but, ironically, it was Labour that faced the reality when the successor (Southern) Rhodesian government declared independence unilaterally in 1965.

Labour and the Federal Project

So, how and why had Labour come to be involved in the federal project? Before the war, it had been committed to the principle of African

---

British Politics, 1945–1961: From "Colonial Development" to "Winds of Change" (Oxford: Clarendon Press, 1971).
[4] J. R. T. Wood, *The Welensky Papers: A History of the Federation of Rhodesia and Nyasaland* (Durban: Graham Publishing, 1983), 418. A sanitized version of this debate appears in *The Times*, July 31, 1954.

paramountcy as re-stated by its colonial secretary Sydney Webb in 1930; and at the outbreak of war, Attlee had roundly declared that there had to be an "abandonment of Imperialism".[5] However, once Labour assumed power in 1945, priorities changed: the need to develop African colonies economically as well as politically in preparation for eventual majority rule and independence; and, as Holland and others have suggested, the belief in the value of Africa as a "bankable asset" that could assist Britain's post-war recovery and lessen its dependence on the United States.[6] For white-settler colonies in Africa, this meant a recognition of the role of immigrant communities as agencies for material progress, which resulted in Labour ministers awarding them a permanent status there.[7] In a similar vein, it was felt that the evolution of black politics in these colonies was, in comparison with British West Africa, at a very initial stage indeed. In 1951, the year when the Gold Coast won internal self-government, Arthur Creech Jones commented: "As yet the issues of majority rule or of ultimate independence [in East and Central Africa] are almost irrelevant".[8] Hence the shift from "paramountcy" to "partnership", encapsulating post-war imperial transformation, and attempting also to harmonize what were in reality increasingly discordant elements in the local situation.

In central Africa, this shift served to create a more favourable environment for the realization of a long-standing white-settler objective, the closer association of the two Rhodesias, Northern (now Zambia) and Southern (now Zimbabwe).[9] Hitherto, the River Zambezi had been seen as

---

[5] As reported in *East Africa and Rhodesia*, Nov. 16, 1939: cited in E. Clegg, *Race and Politics: Partnership in the Federation of Rhodesia and Nyasaland* (London: Oxford University Press, 1960), 108.

[6] R. F. Holland, "The Imperial Factor in British Strategies from Attlee to Macmillan, 1945–63", *Journal of Imperial and Commonwealth History* 12, no. 2 (1984), 165–86, See also: R. F. Holland, *European Decolonization, 1918–81* (London: Palgrave Macmillan, 1985); P. J. Cain and A. Hopkins, *British Imperialism*, vol. 1: *Crisis and Deconstruction, 1914–1990* (London: Longman, 1993); and J. Darwin, *Britain and Decolonisation: Retreat from Empire in the Post-war World* (London: Palgrave Macmillan, 1988).

[7] As reported in *The Times*, May 3 and 4, 1949. See also Lord Listowel's reply in *Hansard Parliamentary Debates* (Lords), 165 (Nov. 30, 1949), cols. 1115–8.

[8] A. Creech Jones, "British Colonial Policy with Reference to Africa", *International Affairs* 27 (1951), 180.

[9] An extensive literature on the history of closer association appeared in the 1960s. Apart from Clegg, *Race and Politics*, see: T. R. M. Creighton, *The Anatomy of Partnership: Southern Rhodesia and the Central African Federation* (Westport, CT: Greenwood Press, 1976); C. Dunn, *Central African Witness* (London: Victor Gollancz, 1959); H. Franklin, *Unholy Wedlock: The Failure of the Central African*

the traditional boundary between the white-ruled south, in the shape of the internally self-governing colony of Southern Rhodesia, and the Colonial Office (CO)-dominated north. Before 1939, the general belief was that their so-called "native policies" affecting the black majority were at that stage too diverse to allow amalgamation of the two Rhodesias.[10] But after 1945, ways were found to get round this obstacle with a device nurtured by Labour's colonial secretary Arthur Creech Jones and influential civil servants such as Andrew Cohen (CO) and G. H. Baxter (Commonwealth Relations Office [CRO]), responsible for Southern Rhodesia. The outcome was the compromise[11] proposal of federation, leaving "native policy" and affairs affecting the daily lives of Africans in the hands of the territorial governments.[12] The scheme would be infused with the new spirit of "partnership", a middle way between South African apartheid and exclusive black nationalism.[13]

However, none of these considerations explain the urgency with which Labour proceeded with the project at the start of the 1950s. Other factors bearing down on ministers include anxiety about Afrikaner influence in the two Rhodesias, the start of the cold war, and the array of economic arguments put forward in support of closer association. The first, the South African dimension, has largely been discounted: as Harry Franklin has asked, would the Malan government have wanted additional black

---

Federation (London: George Allen and Unwin, 1963); P. Keatley, *The Politics of Partnership* (Harmondsworth: Penguin, 1963); and C. Sanger, *Central Africa Emergency* (London: Heinemann, 1960). J. R. T. Wood, *Welensky Papers* provides a magisterial if lengthy overview of the period as a whole.

[10] See HMSO, *Cmd 5949: Rhodesia-Nyasaland Royal Commission Report* [Bledisloe Report].

[11] See G. Ross, "European Support for and against, and Opposition to Closer Union of the Rhodesias and Nyasaland, with Special Reference to the Period from 1945–1953 (M Litt diss., University of Edinburgh, 1988), 366–70, which makes the valid point that this compromise satisfied neither the white Rhodesians, who wanted amalgamation, nor black nationalists, who wanted rapid progress to majority rule. I am grateful to Billy Frank for this reference.

[12] One ironic and presumably unintended effect of this safeguard was that it limited any would-be progressive federal government to reforms that the territories (notably self-governing Southern Rhodesia) found consonant with their "African policy". This, apart from the general shortcomings of the federal scheme, which would require another chapter to cover.

[13] The key document out of many is HMSO, *Cmd 8235, Comparative Survey of Native Policies*, which glossed over many of the objectives as well as existing differences between respective policies.

people?[14] Possibly not, but ever since the late 1930s, Afrikaner immigrants had arrived to work in the Northern Rhodesian copperbelt and now amounted to about half of the territory's white population, while there were clusters of Afrikaner farmers in both Rhodesias. Whatever the view of their home government, some of these settlers were keen to extend Afrikaner control northwards. A letter from an unnamed Fabian Colonial Bureau correspondent spelled it out: "'Nothing can stop us', said one young [Afrikaner] man, 'We have the will, the ideals, and we know how to handle the native'".[15] Labour ministers, like the left in Britain as a whole, saw South Africa, now ruled by a government some of whose ministers had dallied with Nazism and fascism during the war[16], as a threat to British interests which could only be met by strengthening the bonds between British territories in central Africa and stemming the tide of Afrikaner immigration. In addition, from 1949 the cold war underlined the importance of closer association, with the two Rhodesias now major suppliers of the strategic metals copper and chromium.[17]

The economic case for federation was sedulously cultivated by Labour ministers, to be endorsed even more wholeheartedly when Oliver Lyttelton (later, Lord Chandos) and his colleagues took over in the autumn of 1951. The junction of Northern Rhodesian copper and Southern Rhodesia coal would be an advantage to both territories, while the inclusion of the economically-backward Nyasaland protectorate (modern Malawi) – at Creech Jones's insistence – would help that territory and facilitate the flow of black labour supplies to the Rhodesias. The notion grew of three essentially complementary economies cushioning each other in difficult times. A few doubted its claims, such as the former Labour colonial minister John Dugdale, when the scheme was debated at Westminster, while the Northern Rhodesia African National Congress (NRANC) asked

---

[14] H. Franklin, *Unholy Wedlock* (London: George Allen and Unwin, 1964), 7.

[15] Letter (n. A.) dated Jan. 14, 1951, to Fabian Colonial Bureau: Fabian Colonial Bureau papers, Rhodes House, Oxford, MSS Brit Emp s365 [hereafter, FCB], Box 101/1: N[orthern] R[hodesia]: Social Welfare and Development. I heard similar remarks from Afrikaner schoolmates in Zambia during the mid 1950s. See also J. Griffiths, *Pages from Memory* (London: J. M. Dent and Co, 1969), 113.

[16] See P. Furlong, *Between Cross and Swastika: the Impact of the Radical Right on the Afrikaner Nationalist Movement in the Fascist Era* (Hanover, NH: Wesleyan University Press, 1991).

[17] P. S. Gupta, *Imperialism and the British Labour Movement, 1914–1964* (London: Macmillan, 1975), 340. L. J. Butler's recent article, "The Central African Federation and Britain's Post-War Nuclear Programme", *Journal of Imperial and Commonwealth History* 36, no. 3 (2008), 509–25, suggests the addition of uranium to the list.

the pertinent question: how could federation prevent an economic slump, which would affect all three territories?[18]

While it took some time for the financial and other shortcoming of the scheme, which in practice advantaged Southern Rhodesia and the white minority at the expense of others, to become evident,[19] the value of the safeguards put in place to protect the African majority received criticism from many quarters during the planning stage, most notably the FCB. Similar safeguards in Southern Rhodesia's constitution, giving Britain the right to disallow legislation that discriminated against non-whites, had never been invoked, though as Claire Palley suggested, they may have deterred the authorities in Salisbury (modern Harare) from proceeding with legislation likely to upset British public opinion.[20] The protective device in the federal scheme,[21] a committee of the Federal Assembly, to be termed "The African Affairs Board" which would scrutinize and refer potentially racially discriminatory legislation to London, suffered from the same defects as its predecessor, falling at the first hurdle when, despite Labour pressure, the Macmillan government approved legislation surrounding amendments to the Federal constitution in 1957. In reality, the African Affairs Board was yet another wholly negative device: as some critics pointed out at the time, it could not recommend measures that would actively foster racial partnership.[22] In any case, the use of "disallowance", as earlier precedents in British imperial history had shown,[23] had not been regarded by successive colonial ministers as a practical way of dealing with white-settler governments. Significantly, even a Labour government had acknowledged this in the later 1940s when

---

[18] *House of Commons Debates, 513*, Mar. 24, 1953, col. 699; N. R. ANC, "Case against the Federal proposals ... Presented to the Secretary of State on 11 September, 1951": FCB Box 101/3: NR: Corresp. and related papers: Political and Constitutional, 1940–55, ff 97–101. The 1957/8 recession illustrated the fallacy of the "complementary economies" assumption.

[19] See A. Hazlewood, "The Economics of Federation and Dissolution in Central Africa", in A. Hazlewood, ed., *African Integration and Disintegration* (London: Oxford University Press, 1967), 183–250; and HMSO, *Cmd 1148, Advisory Commission on the review of the Constitution of Rhodesia and Nyasaland* (1960) (chairman, Lord Monckton).

[20] C. Palley, *The Constitutional History and Law of Southern Rhodesia, 1888–1965, with Special Reference to Imperial Control* (Oxford: Clarendon Press, 1966).

[21] For details, see HMSO, *Cmd 8754: Southern Rhodesia, Northern Rhodesia and Nyasaland; the Federal Scheme Prepared by a Conference Held in London in January, 1953*.

[22] Most notably, Max Beloff (letter in *The Times*, June 19, 1952).

[23] See Margery Perham's letter to *The Times*, Mar. 4, 1952.

the FCB called upon the commonwealth relations minister Lord Addison to veto proposed Southern Rhodesian legislation.[24]

The black majority of the northern protectorates were convinced neither by the arguments for federation, nor the proposed safeguards. Their opposition to any involvement with the white south had been expressed as early as 1932 and at least one member of the pre-war Bledisloe Commission on Closer Association recognized that it was based not on ignorance nor fear of change[25] – both charges repeated *ad nauseam* when the federal scheme was floated – but on a genuine fear that Southern Rhodesian "native policy", in their view not too different from South African racial segregation, would be embedded north of the Zambezi. Nevertheless, Creech Jones's successor in the dying days of Labour's post-war administrations, Jim Griffiths, embarked on the task of selling it to the newly-formed African congresses in the northern territories, with a request that became a mantra, repeated by Labour and Conservative ministers over the next two years: if you don't like federation, suggest an alternative.[26] As the recently-retired provincial commissioner Thomas Fox-Pitt, adviser to the NRANC, rightly pointed out, one real alternative was to make no change.[27]

Black nationalists felt they had been betrayed by the British abandonment of black paramountcy, and repudiated the new partnership policy as a pious fraud, designed to entrench white-settler interests while misleading the British public. Inspired by the grant of internal self-government to the Gold Coast in 1951, both northern congresses set their sights on the same goal – black majority rule within the shortest possible time – thus in effect refusing to accept the Britain's distinction between West, and East/Central, "white settler", Africa. Their anger was stimulated further by the humiliation of colour-bar practices in public accommodations, racial discrimination in employment and a system of funding for education that disadvantaged the black majority, all set against a background of rapidly increasing white (British as well as Afrikaner) immigration into

---

[24] The campaign launched against post-war Southern Rhodesian-proposed "native" legislation by the FCB and other pressure groups is reviewed in M. Steele, *The Challenge of Rhodesia to European Liberal Thought, 1893–1953* (M Litt diss., University of Edinburgh, 1968), 358–98. On the FCB delegation, see FCB Box 27/2A: SR: Deputation to Lord Addison, 1946, ff 1–175.

[25] T. Fitzgerald's note, Bledisloe Commission, 250.

[26] G. Griffiths's rather testy comment cited in the *Central African Post* (Lusaka), Sep. 13, 1951: "I am still waiting for the alternative".

[27] T. Fox-Pitt to Marjorie Nicholson, Aug. 5, 1951, FCB: Box 101/6: NR: General Corresp., 1951–55, f 95.

both Rhodesias after 1945.[28] The exclusive, "Africanist", character of congress policy vexed many Labour MPs and alienated others. One of these, Stanley Evans, had led a Commonwealth Parliamentary Association delegation to central Africa in 1951 where he reprimanded the NRANC leader, Harry Nkumbula, for offering no alternative proposals to federation, and after his return home had become a prominent advocate of federation on the Labour benches. Nkumbula passed on his opinions of Evans to the FCB as someone who had "had too much Sundowns [sic] and forgot his duty", a reference to the Rhodesian "Sundowner" as a form of white-settler hospitality.[29]

However, Griffiths was spared any further ministerial anguish by the prorogation of parliament in the autumn of 1951, and Labour's subsequent electoral defeat. His successor, Oliver Lyttelton, who came with personal City connections, embraced the scheme with fervour as a chance to build "a British bloc in Central Africa", founded on the platform of racial partnership.[30] It was a view that echoed the new sense of optimism in Britain following post-war economic recovery and was to see the Central African Federation coming into existence, symbolically, in coronation year, 1953. Also, it was a view that tended to read too much into the emergence of a few green shoots of settler liberalism towards Africans, while ignoring the groundswell of illiberalism that at all times threatened to wither them.

As its original architects, Labour ex-ministers felt they could not, and indeed should not, back away from the principle of federation, however much noise black nationalists might make. Nor had they been encouraged by the totally rejectionist views of the African delegations when they arrived for the federal conference in London during the spring of 1952. The delegates' decision to boycott the conference, following the instructions given by their parties, spread dismay amongst its allies in Britain, such as the FCB. The Bureau's secretary, Marjorie Nicholson, set out her concerns in a letter to the veteran missionary-poet, Arthur Shearly Cripps. In advising the delegations:

> we have not been able to make them understand that a purely negative line of policy is not the most effective in the context of *British* politics. They will get support from the Parliamentary Labour Party and from general liberal opinion in this country even if they persist in not putting forward

---

[28] See the very extensive correspondence between the NRANC and Fox-Pitt with the Bureau in Box 101/6.
[29] Nkumbula to Nicholson, Sep. 21, 1951, FCB: Box 101/6, f34.
[30] As reported in *The Times*, Nov. 22, 1951.

any constructive ideas of their own, but it does not have as good an effect as it would have done if they had gone into the Conference and fought for their own point of view all along the line. It will be difficult to maintain support for this negation over any long period. ... What we have all realised is that they are very frightened, and it is clear that this fear in itself is an argument against federation. They are, however, very inexperienced and not very skilful.[31]

In the same paternalist spirit, the FCB did its utmost to isolate African delegates not just from the Communist Party of Great Britain, but also from organizations it considered almost as undesirable, the League of People Against Imperialism and the Union of Democratic Control[32], ostensibly because any association with the far left would discredit their cause; and even tried (unsuccessfully) to stop them addressing public meetings in Britain.[33] Nkumbula later defended the delegates' actions as designed to give the Conservatives a guilty conscience, a purpose that could be said to have borne fruit a decade later when the Macmillan government wound up the Federation. In any case, participation even as observers in a conference closed to the general public and the media posed obvious hazards including the suspicion that despite their mandate, they had been sucked into negotiations. On his return, he reiterated his Africanist stance: "I have come to the conclusion that the best government for the Black people is Government fully manned and run by the Black people of Africa".[34]

Labour's National Executive Committee (NEC) delayed establishing its position on federation until the debate on the Rhodesia and Nyasaland Bill in the spring of 1953. In the meantime, Attlee visited Central Africa at the end of the 1952 parliamentary session on an invitation from the Northern Rhodesian settler leader Roy Welensky. Like Stanley Evans, he seems to have been less than patient with African opposition, refusing to meet the NRANC in a plenary session; advising Nkumbula not to "rush things" when he presented a four-stage plan for majority rule involving the immediate appointment of African members with portfolios; and taking

---

[31] Nicholson to Rev A. S. Cripps, May 9, 1952, FCB: Box 99/3: S[outhern] R[hodesia]: Corresp, and related papers, 1939–67, f41. On the role of "liberal" pressure groups in the campaign against Federation, see Steele, *Challenge of Rhodesia*, 442–89.

[32] Nicholson to Fox-Pitt, June 9, 1952, FCB: Box 101/6, f184.

[33] Nicholson to Fox-Pitt, Apr. 18, 1952 (handwritten note), School of Oriental and African Studies: Fox-Pitt papers: Corresp from others, early 1951 [onwards].

[34] [NR]ANC, "Statement at a public meeting held at the Mapoloto African Township, Lusaka, on 26th June 1952", FCB Box 101/3, f183.

umbrage at remarks made at a meeting of otherwise politically "moderate" chiefs, African representative council delegates and black members of the Northern Rhodesian Legislative Council.[35]

Whatever his feelings on his return, there was known to be firm support for the scheme shown by 20–25 members, who might go to the extent of voting with the government. Seventeen eventually did defy a three-line whip. But most Labour MPs agreed with the principle of federation, provided Africans could be persuaded as to its desirability and some progress in implementing partnership could be demonstrated. Arguably, this was the wrong approach: it committed Labour to the scheme, and made the fact of its imposition the major objection rather than the scheme itself. To this objection, Lyttelton and other Conservative ministers had a ready answer, to be voiced on many future occasions, the claim that nationalists were using intimidation to enforce their views on ordinary Africans, adding as a sideswipe at critics on the left that the FCB and similar organizations were providing them with ammunition to be used against the government. And to this was added the irrefutable argument that "father knows best": as Alan Lennox-Boyd, Lyttelton's eventual successor put it, "It is our opinion that it is the duty of a trustee while consulting them [Africans] also to make it perfectly plain what we think ought to be done".[36]

In the second reading of the Bill (May 6, 1953), Attlee committed his party to "make it [Federation] work to the best of our ability" if it was given parliamentary approval.[37] When the left attacked Attlee's acquiescence at the Margate conference later that year, he had a ready retort:

> it is not the job of a great movement such as ours to encourage resistance to Acts of Parliament passed at Westminster. (A cry of "shame", and cries of "Oh"). No, there is no shame in it at all. It is a democratic principle. If you want to change it, you must change the government.[38]

Constitutionally correct though it might be, Attlee's pledge to co-operate once the Federation came into being became a long-term liability, to be

---

[35] Wood, *Welensky Papers*, 297–9. The ANC document and associated papers are in FCB Box 101/3.

[36] See *House of Commons Debates, 513,* Mar. 24, 1953, c 793; *504*, 24 July 1952, c 789; *499*, 29 April 1952, c 1294.

[37] *House of Commons Debates, 515*, 6 May 1953, c 418.

[38] Labour Party, *Report of the 52nd Annual Conference held in Margate, Sep. 28–Oct. 2, 1953,* 153.

invoked and exploited by government ministers when Labour became too critical of federal politicians.

Labour and the Federal Reality

Labour's record during the early days of partnership indicates a range of activities and an avuncular (as opposed to a paternalistic) attempt to help black politicians and trade unionists build effective organizations through a number of agencies such as its International Department and commonwealth sub-committee, the British Trades Union Congress, and the co-operative movement. Most significant of these colonial trade unions was the Northern Rhodesian African Mineworkers' Union, under its capable leader Lawrence Katilungu, who took to heart the British labour movement's advice to avoid political strikes which could be used by the colonial authorities as an excuse to emasculate the fledging trade union movement, although in practice, in the colonial context, even "acceptable" industrial action tended to have a "political" character.[39] Meanwhile, the FCB's influence declined, both in relation to the Labour's panel of spokesmen on colonial affairs in the House and to African leaders themselves, the result of its decision to adhere to Attlee's pledge to make the Federation "work"[40], the Bureau's increasingly restricted resources which necessitated cutbacks in office staff, the rise of more radical voices such as Fenner Brockway's Movement for Colonial Freedom (MCF), and the Party's decision to adopt a more direct role in imperial matters by setting up the commonwealth sub-committee within its International Department. Through this latter instrument, Transport House maintained an extensive, though at times intermittent, correspondence with individuals and movements in central Africa. Following the appointment of John Hatch as "Commonwealth Officer" in July 1954, regular and very full reports on developments in the dependent empire were sent to the Party's NEC.[41]

---

[39] For instance, a Mineworkers' Union wage demand (late 1954) which, if successful, would have entitled many workers to claim the franchise: see M. R. Mwendapole, *A History of the Trade Union Movement in Zambia up to 1968* (Lusaka: University of Zambia, 1977) 20–1.

[40] [M. Nicholson to] J. Ralston, Mar. 22, 1954, FCB Box 99/4. S R: Corresp. IV: 1953–6, f 16.

[41] See correspondence and papers relating to the Labour Party International Department (LPID) and its commonwealth sub-committee held at the Labour History Archive and Study Centre [hereafter, LHASC], People's History Museum, Manchester, particularly three unsorted boxes: (N. Rhodesia [Zambia]); C. Afr.

The Labour Party itself up to 1957 seems to have restricted itself to issuing rather general statements about so-called "plural societies" and moved towards democratic self-government at a future, though unspecified time. Calls at Conference for the setting of target dates for independence were regularly remitted at NEC request, and more radical demands for immediate withdrawal rejected at its insistence.[42] So far as the Central African Federation was concerned, the Party's *Plural Societies* statement approved at the 1956 Blackpool conference somewhat incongruously included it – and Kenya – with Fiji and Malaya as colonies falling into that category, thus obscuring the essential difference between "settler" and ethnically-divided societies.[43] In much of this discussion one can perceive a continuation of the Fabian perspective of the late 1940s, that without significant moves towards a more egalitarian social structure, an over-rapid decolonization process might simply lead to the replacement of one (white) elite by another (black). The criterion of a reasonable degree of popular literacy as a prerequisite for internal self-government, suggested by Fabian essayist Margaret Wrong in 1945, was reiterated by Griffiths in 1957.[44] In addition, concerns about the exclusivist nature of black nationalism in Central Africa continued to be expressed: in her contribution to the *New Fabian Colonial Essays*, written just before the 1959 emergencies, Marjorie Nicholson blamed the blunder of the Federation, which might well "[transform] what should have been a progressive movement into reactionary racialism".[45] In effect, within the envelope of an outwardly "conservative" political agenda sceptical of radical nationalist demagoguery, the FCB was putting forward a radical programme of social and economic transformation that would not just extinguish white privilege but also propel merging modern African

---

Fed. (Nyasaland, N. and S. Rhodesia); Nyasaland (Malawi); Southern Rhodesia (Zimbabwe). Also the (catalogued) commonwealth sub-committee, minutes and documents, 1946–62 (LP/CSC/56, 57).

[42] For instance, see the debate on the USDAW resolution on colonial affairs at the 1954 Scarborough Conference. (Labour Party: *Report of the 53rd Annual Conference held in Scarborough, Sep. 27 – Oct. 1, 1954*, 126–38).

[43] The Labour Party, *Report of the 55th Annual Conference held in Blackpool, Oct. 1–5, 1956*, 155–70. See also Hatch's preliminary draft in LHASC LP/CSC/54/48ff.

[44] M. Wrong, "Is Literacy Necessary in Africa", in R. Hinden, ed., *Fabian Colonial Essays* (London: George Allen and Unwin, 1945), 146; and "Report back on Mr Griffiths' address, 28 May 1957", Labour Party Archives: Commonwealth Labour Conference: 1957–63 (LHASC LP/CSC/8).

[45] "Political objectives and developments", in A. Creech Jones, ed., *New Fabian Colonial Essays* (London: Hogarth Press, 1959), 70.

societies towards a more socially progressive, if not socialist, model prior to granting independence.

Meanwhile, the Labour left reorganized itself behind the MCF, formed in 1954, which campaigned unequivocally for the ending of imperial rule and settler privilege in Africa, and soon displaced the FCB as the first port of call for African nationalists and anti-colonial activists. It provided platforms round Britain for visiting African politicians such as Nkumbula and his deputy, Kenneth Kaunda, to address the wider British public.[46] Their cause was strongly endorsed by the 1957 Commonwealth Labour conference, a gathering of overseas socialist and nationalist representatives organized by Labour's International Department, which passed a resolution condemning the creation of Federation "against the wishes of the people" and demanded full adult suffrage.[47] The anti-federal campaign was aided by the failure of the federal and territorial authorities to take any meaningful steps towards implementing partnership beyond a few token gestures, a criticism voiced by MPs such as the veteran spokesman on colonial affairs, James Johnson. Some Party officials, like John Hatch, were now finding it prudent to distance Labour from the federal scheme and claim, implausibly, it had been opposed from the start.[48] But many on the Labour left were convinced that the Federation was beyond redemption, a belief that culminated in *Tribune's* call (December 13, 1957) for the dissolution of the Federation when Labour returned to office.[49] However, the Party's leadership was not prepared to endorse this line, declaring in a March 1958 statement that the Federation could still "work" if full democracy and equal rights in the future were guaranteed and opportunities for advancement created, adding – though this appeared rather late in the drafting process – that dominion status, full self-government, should only be conferred when everyone wanted it.[50] Clearly, even five years on, with growing disillusion about the Federation, Attlee's 1953 pledge still carried weight in the higher reaches of the Party.

From this point onwards, the political pace in central Africa quickened, and Labour found itself having to cope with a rapidly deteriorating situation there. A number of contributory factors can be identified. First,

---

[46] See F. Brockway, *Towards Tomorrow* (London: Hart-Davis, MacGibbon, 1977).
[47] Commonwealth Labour Conference [1957]: 'Declaration of Principle', n. D., LHASC LP/CSC/8/23.
[48] Letter to the *Observer*, Aug. 12, 1956. Colin Legum's following note, referring to Attlee's pledge, is a more accurate representation of what happened in 1952–3.
[49] "Listen to the Leaders or Face the Gunmen!",*Tribune*, Dec. 13, 1957.
[50] Labour Party: Commonwealth Sub-Committee: Minutes and Documents, 1957–62: LHASC LP/CSC/57/36–8, refers.

Labour's growing domestic popularity after the Suez crisis stirred up African hopes for a change of government at the next election, and a new deal, which included the ending of the Federation: "We believe and hope that the Labour Party will soon be in a position to exercise great influence on events in central Africa", the Southern Rhodesia African Youth League leaders James Chikerema and Paul Mushonga remarked in a personal letter to Griffiths.[51] John Hatch was at pains to dampen down these hopes: "One of the things it is essential to avoid is to mislead the Africans into believing that the next Labour Government will solve all their problems".[52] Secondly, and in response to these expectations, the anxiety federal politicians felt about what such a government might do. This had been expressed as early as August 1956, when in a notorious and much-quoted address prime minister Godfrey Huggins had suggested that his government might have to follow the example of the North American colonies if it was faced with a "stupid government in the United Kingdom".[53] Thirdly, the withering of the few green shoots of white liberalism, with the gathering strength of segregationist forces in Southern Rhodesia and the wipe-out of Garfield Todd's more progressive United Rhodesia Party in the 1958 territorial election. Fourthly, the approach of the year 1960, set as the earliest date for a federal review conference, and taken by white opposition parties in central Africa as the last opportunity to get dominion status and so bring to an end CO (and for Southern Rhodesia, CRO) controls over African policy; this was a goal beyond Welensky's more pragmatic objective of securing full Commonwealth membership with the concession of some form of imperial oversight over black rights north of the Zambezi. Finally, and most dramatically, the rapid evolution of mass black nationalism in all three territories, set alight by economic recession and growing urban unemployment but fanned into flame by the ambition of white politicians. Especially in the northern territories, black nationalists called for the destruction of federation; and, inspired by Ghanaian independence and the Accra conference, they demanded full adult suffrage and internal self-government within the shortest possible time.

The eventual outcome of this course to collision, the 1959 emergencies in each of the component territories, raised the very real prospect of a growing wave of black violence and matching white counter-violence that would draw the imperial government into yet another military commitment on the scale of the Malaya, Kenya and Cyprus emergencies.

---

[51] In LPID: Unsorted Box SR (Zimbabwe): Corresp, 1956–60.
[52] Secretary's Report, Feb. 1958, Labour Party: LHASC LP/CSC/57/35.
[53] *East Africa and Rhodesia*, Aug. 30, 1956.

Gaitskell and his colleagues might – and did – condemn the handling of the emergencies, and in particular the use of (federal) white conscripts flown into Nyasaland to restore order. The Albert Hall protest meeting of April 8, 1959,[54] and debates on the Nyasaland emergency held in both Houses of Parliament,[55] brought the issue of federation before the British public and attracted wide media coverage. However, even at this stage James Callaghan, now the Party's shadow Colonial Secretary, felt constrained to refer to Attlee's pledge to give the Federation a fair trial, while insisting that African policy in the two northern territories should remain a British responsibility.[56] Otherwise, Transport House could do little but to wait on events: to encourage black leaders, while counselling them to urge their followers at all times to employ non-violent forms of protest; to publicize what was happening in Central Africa; and to feed information to MPs that could be used for the basis for parliamentary questions. Some of this impotence was of course the result of Labour being in opposition at Westminster, but arguably the constitutional basis of the federation, set out in Lyttelton's 1952 House of Commons declaration that abolition would be specifically excluded from the remit of the Review process,[57] and reinforced by the oft-repeated statement that it would require the consent of all four governments anyway, was a more significant factor. The picture darkened further in the autumn of 1959, when Labour lost its third general election. Its potential influence on black nationalists was correspondingly reduced, although the tone of their correspondence with Labour's Commonwealth Office and FCB indicates a growing self-confidence and a belief that at the end, majority rule would have to be achieved through their own efforts.[58]

It is perhaps ironic that the Labour leadership should use the boycott instrument, decried as "negative" when employed by African delegates to the 1952 conference, in its approach to the Monckton Commission, set up

---

[54] News item in *The Times*, Apr. 9, 1959

[55] See especially *House of Lords Debates, 215,* 24 March 1959, cc 198-362, of interest because of the number of speakers with direct Central African connections.

[56] Labour Party press release for Apr. 8, 1959, in LPID: Unsorted Box Nyasaland (Malawi); Documents 1956–1964.

[57] *House of Commons Debates, 513,* 24 March 1953, cc 669,689.

[58] See in particular Kaunda's correspondence with Transport House in LPID: Unsorted Box N. Rhodesia (Zambia). The general tone of statements and correspondence received by Labour and its organizations seems to have been moderate: outbursts, such as Frank Chitambala's in the FCB papers (Box 103/2 NR: Memoranda 1956–62, ff. 82–3) and ending with the comment that Conservative and Labour had the same colonial policy and were "just two sides of the same coin" are surprisingly rare.

by Macmillan to assess progress in central Africa ahead of a federal review conference. Labour decided not to participate, believing that the commission would simply endorse the continuation of the federation,[59] though after the event the FCB privately acknowledged the role of Kaunda and other nationalists in influencing its executive, and that of the party, in reaching its decision.[60] In fact, Monckton surprised everybody, reporting not just the "almost pathological"[61] hatred Africans felt towards it, but also mooting the possibility of territories seceding, thus kicking out the first block from the federal edifice. It is a further irony that in declining to be involved in the commission's proceedings, Labour left the federation's eventual dismantler, the Conservative government, alone to bear the opprobrium of betrayal Welensky and his colleagues heaped on it when it ended in 1963. However, whatever credit Labour had unexpectedly gained was rapidly forfeited when its turn came to handle the Rhodesian crisis from 1965 onwards.

Conclusion

In assessing Labour's central African record, any claim that it played a significant role in bringing about its destruction should be set aside. That claim rightly belongs to the African majority, and to a Conservative administration that at last realized that its latter-day exercise in imperial state-building was now doomed and could only be sustained through the use of force, an expedient that had become increasingly unrealistic as well as unpopular. There can be little doubt that a large part of the Labour Party had been complicit, indeed active, in its creation, sheltering behind the admittedly important issue of its imposition when the black majority expressed their opposition. It nevertheless believed that once it came into existence, with goodwill on all sides, it could be made to work, and the black majority eventually persuaded by the economic benefits that would "trickle down". Their thinking was not far removed from that of the Conservatives, reflecting the continuing consensus over colonial policy that had operated since the War. East and Central Africa were seen to be "different" from west Africa; time would be needed to elevate the black majority, while immigrant communities should be considered permanent features as their skills and entrepreneurship would be essential to bring

---

[59] Labour's plan to set up its own shadow commission failed to get off the ground: see LPID: Unsorted box C Afr Fed: Nyasaland (Malawi): Central African Commission.

[60] FCB to Kaunda, Oct. 7, 1960, FCB Box 102/3: NR: Corresp., 1956–61, f 265.

[61] Monckton Commission Report, 116.

this about. However, the post-war flood of white immigrants had the effect of further distorting expenditure on social services such as education, in effect exacerbating racial division and making it more and more difficult for the majority to gain the level of education and skills regarded as essential for substantial political progress. Labour's colonial ministers in office, and later in opposition had identified the underlying problem: the skewing of educational and other social services provision towards the white minority, and had a solution – the end to all colour-bar practices. But no one was prepared to grasp the nettle until the end of the 1950s, by which time the end to empire was in sight. In the meantime, like black nationalist calls for immediate universal adult suffrage, the demands of the Labour left for a rapid exit from empire in "settler", as well as "black", Africa, fell on deaf ears until the crisis period following the 1959 emergencies.

From the start, anxious about a possible backlash from white voters, the federal government had failed to advance at more than a glacial pace towards partnership, even though the Labour leadership, in the spirit of Attlee's 1953 pledge, still remained in hope. The tide turned from early 1958, with a series of events in central Africa which the Party could do little to influence; in particular the revival of, and the winning of mass support for, black nationalist parties that now had much less need for the succour bodies like the FCB had given a decade before. As Goldsworthy notes, Labour's advice to nationalists in this final stage was acceptable only insofar as it was seen as contributing to the cause of colonial freedom,[62] and at the final juncture, roles were reversed, with the patron following the client's lead over participation in the Monckton Commission. Nevertheless, the value of this fraternal assistance, and the more paternalistic contribution of the FCB and other organizations in the important formative period of the 1940s and early 1950s, should also be acknowledged, along with their traditional role of publicizing shortcomings in the exercise of imperial trusteeship overseas while at the same time keeping the British public and their representatives informed.

---

[62] Goldsworthy, *Colonial Issues,* 347–8.

LABOUR, EUROPEAN INTEGRATION AND THE POST-IMPERIAL MIND, 1960–75[1]

C. M. M. COTTON

Writing just before the 1964 general election, Harold Wilson made a pointed reference to what he described as a "clash of philosophies" between the foreign policies of the Labour party and Sir Alec Douglas-Home's Conservatives. The latter, he claimed, could not "rid themselves of their imperialist yearnings"; Labour, by contrast, was deemed instinctively to "recognise the character of the post-colonial age in which we live".[2] The question of Britain joining the European Community (EC), dormant since General de Gaulle vetoed Harold Macmillan's application in 1963 but gradually reactivated after Labour entered office the following year, went to the heart of this debate about the nature of Britain-after-empire.[3] This was on two counts, both related to the future role of the Commonwealth. First, accession to the EC would place Britain within the EC's common external tariff, thereby overturning not only the Ottawa agreement, which had shaped Britain's trade with the dominions since 1932, but the oceanic bias evident for centuries before that. Second, and more broadly, joining the EC suggested a re-orientation of Britain's diplomatic focus towards western Europe – a final contraction from Africa, Asia, and Australasia, with an apparent invitation for Commonwealth countries to look to their own locales, rather than to the mother country, for political and economic succour.

The issues of Europe, commonwealth, and empire were equally entangled for Labour, not least because both sides of the party's debate

---

[1] I am grateful to Jon Lawrence, Peter Mandler, Helen Parr, and Geraint Thomas, as well as to the editors of this volume, for reading this chapter in its various incarnations. Thanks also to Martin McLean and Gareth Nellis for their comments.
[2] H. Wilson, *The Relevance of British Socialism* (London: Weidenfeld and Nicolson, 1964), 81.
[3] For Labour's early stance on western Europe, see H. Parr, *Britain's Policy Towards the European Community. Harold Wilson and Britain's World Role, 1964–1967* (London: Routledge, 2006), chaps. 1–2.

over the Common Market sought to legitimate their conclusions with reference to the "imperialism" supposedly evident in the other's stance. Those opposed to accession, for example, frequently decried the EC's arrangements with its Associated Overseas Territories – members' former colonies – as a blatant form of economic imperialism which cast them as perpetual suppliers of primary goods. The EC wished to transform Africa into "its Latin America", wrote Frank Judd.[4] His colleagues, meanwhile, tarred the EC by association with the imperial records of some of its members – particularly France and Belgium, whose recent actions in Algeria and the Congo were said by Hugh Gaitskell to reveal the sustained "pro-colonial" instincts of the Europe which some in the party sought to join.[5] The Community itself was portrayed as a tool of American cold-war "military imperialism", with Konrad Adenauer and Walter Hallstein its chief anti-Soviet warriors. For their part, pro-Marketeers depicted their opponents' concern for maintaining commonwealth imports as reminiscent of the very worst traditions of "cheap colonial food".[6] Labour anti-Marketeers' continuing pre-occupation with the Commonwealth was, in Roy Jenkins's words, simply imperialism "with a quasi-modern twist".[7]

Such insults were predictable, for the lead protagonists in the European debate naturally vied to manoeuvre themselves on to the right side of Labour's belief in its historic anti-imperialism. They nevertheless point to the party's continuing desire, even during the final throes of the British empire, to define itself against what it had always seen as the component values of imperialism: militarism, nationalism, racial and cultural superiority, and distaste for democracy. When it came to mobilizing support for or against accession to the EC, even the indirect association of one's rivals with these bogeys was a compelling tactical ploy. Though the force of such rhetoric dimmed somewhat in the 1970s, this was true even during the European referendum campaign of 1975. Around this time, indeed, Tony Benn started to hitch his broader political critique to anti-imperial language, clearly eager to derive capital from a trope which still possessed powerful resonance. Britain itself was becoming a colony, he said – of the EC, as well as the "American global defence system", multinational corporations, and the International Monetary Fund. It therefore faced a "national liberation struggle", as much as had any of its

---

[4] *Labour Weekly*, Oct. 22, 1971.
[5] *Labour Party Annual Conference Report* (*LPACR*), 1962, p. 165.
[6] For example, Maurice Edelman in the *Coventry Evening Telegraph*, June 4, 1965.
[7] Labour History and Archive Study Centre, Manchester (LHASC), pamphlets: 328.5101, "Europe – the choice before us", pubd. Labour Committee for Europe (LCE), 1970, 6.

own former territories.[8] Others also took up this theme. Clive Jenkins, for instance, told an audience at Imperial College that Britain was the "victim" of a "determined drive towards a super-state dominated by a Franco-German alliance, in which our role would be... near-colonial".[9] Such talk was pinned on the hope that anything successfully branded as "imperial" – no matter how vaguely – would be immediately discredited within the party.

It is true that this apparently rigid line could not always be inferred from Labour's international policies, for opposition to "imperialism" had never translated straight-forwardly into opposition to empire – especially not to the British empire. Some members of the party had, of course, been positive enthusiasts. Jimmy Thomas, for example, apparently entered the Colonial Office in 1924 determined that there be "no mucking about with the British empire".[10] As foreign secretary, Ernest Bevin actively sought to extend it into areas of east Africa liberated from the Italians, whilst his plans for a Euro-African imperium preceded the turn to an Atlantic cold-war strategy.[11] More generally, Labour's management of the empire between 1945 and 1951 has come under heavy fire. For despite overseeing Indian independence, and Clement Attlee's initial desire to withdraw from the Middle East, Labour's treatment of Britain's tropical colonies has been widely censured. The encouragement of intensive monoculture export (and dollar-raising) industries, alongside the post-1945 tightening of the sterling area, has been judged particularly exploitative. In spite of some countervailing pressure, such as the work of Arthur Creech Jones, the result was a package which Stephen Howe claims "may well have been the most oppressive form of economic imperialism yet seen in the British tropical colonies".[12] Later, Wilson's governments in the 1960s disappointed

[8] For a broader explication of this case, see T. Benn, *Arguments for Democracy*, ed. Chris Mullin (Harmondsworth: Penguin, 2nd edn., 1982), 6–17.
[9] Modern Record Centre, University of Warwick (MRC), Mss.79/AS/3/8/28, press release pubd. Association of Scientific, Technical and Managerial Staffs (of which Jenkins became general secretary in 1970), May 29, 1975.
[10] G. Blaxland, *J. H. Thomas: A Life For Unity* (London: F. Muller, 1964), 170.
[11] J. Kent and J. W. Young, "British policy overseas, the 'Third Force' and the origins of NATO – in search of a new perspective", in B. Heuser and R. O'Neill, eds., *Securing Peace in Europe, 1945–62: Thoughts for the Post-Cold War Era* (Basingstoke: Macmillan, 1989), 41–61.
[12] S. Howe, *Anticolonialism in British Politics. The Left and the End of Empire* (Oxford: Clarendon Press, 1993), 145. See also P. S. Gupta, *Imperialism and the British Labour Movement, 1914–1964* (London: Macmillan, 1975), chaps. 9–10. More generous readings of Attlee's record are offered by H. Pelling, *The Labour Governments, 1945–51* (London: Macmillan, 1984), chap. 3; and K. O. Morgan,

many of the party's most committed anti-colonialists, especially with their policies towards Southern Rhodesia and Biafra.[13] Most recently, Tony Blair has been deemed to offer "implicit approval" of Britain's imperial past whilst embracing a new "liberal imperialism" of his own.[14]

This apparent disjunction between government action and party rhetoric is not just another manifestation of the many tensions which divided leaders and those they led, it also forged one of the great leitmotifs of labour history. Rather, it concerns a deeper aspect of Labour's political culture which had always produced highly ambiguous attitudes towards the British empire at all levels of the party. This was an ambiguity which reconciled sincere use of the language of anti-imperialism, and a "simple gut feeling" against empire,[15] with enthusiasm for the potential virtues of the British empire when managed according to the party's principles. Ramsay MacDonald insisted that Labour would not have wished the empire into existence, and regretted that the party would never enjoy the luxury of working from first principles on imperial questions.[16] But the party's origins in late nineteenth-century liberalism had caused it to imbibe the Gladstonian tradition of rational self-enlightenment in foreign policy, which always outweighed the Marxist mantra of "the workers have no country". Crucially, this caused many members of the new party to echo the Liberal imperialist tendency to see in the British empire a putative vanguard for the spread of wholesome values and customs, such as free trade, commerce, and liberalism. It would also preach Christianity, in a "civilising mission" which appealed to Labour's evangelical flank. The British empire could thus be something novel and special, not reflective of "imperialism" as historically practised. This distancing was evident in Labour's early use of the language of "commonwealth" – very much a

---

Labour in Power, 1945–1951 (Oxford: Clarendon Press, 1984), chaps. 5–6. See also chap. 6 in the current vol.

[13] J. W. Young, *The Labour Governments, 1964–70*, vol. 2: *International Policy* (Manchester: Manchester University Press, 2003), chaps. 7–8.

[14] P. Ward, *Britishness Since 1870* (London: Routledge, 2004), 111; P. D. Williams, *British Foreign Policy under New Labour, 1997–2005* (Basingstoke: Palgrave Macmillan, 2005), esp. chap. 8. For a Marxist account which generalizes the accusation that Labour has pursued "imperialist" foreign policies, see R. Clough, *Labour: A Party Fit for Imperialism* (London: Larkin Publications, 1992).

[15] K. O. Morgan, "Imperialists at Bay: British Labour and Decolonisation", *Journal of Imperial and Commonwealth History* 27, no. 2 (1999), 233–54.

[16] See esp. J. R. MacDonald, *Labour and the Empire* (London: George Allen, 1907).

case of "Imperialism is dead, long live the Empire". As John Callaghan recounts, *rapacious* imperialism was "firmly associated with foreigners".[17]

Labour's faith that the empire could be recruited in support of such a benevolent mission rested upon what the party saw as the unique capabilities of the metropolis. MacDonald made this explicit in his talk of the "Imperial standard". This was, as Paul Ward notes, "very much a British standard", which would endow the colonies with Britain's own criteria for "untainted administration of justice, fair trials, [and] law resting on consent".[18] Crucially, after 1945 this belief in a British global presence was buttressed by the conviction that, amongst the European powers, the United Kingdom had executed an outstandingly voluntary and peaceful decolonization. Historians now largely dismiss the idea of a coherent plan for "administrative transfer" unprompted by external pressure; Bill Schwarz, for example, describes it as "an extension of the familiar Whig conception, remodelled for empire" which "fails on every count".[19] Nevertheless, it quickly became a key tenet of Labour orthodoxy, and the metamorphosis of empire into commonwealth inspired confidence across the party that the end was not nigh for the role which many considered Britain still able to play.

When deliberations about EC membership began in earnest in the early 1960s, this was the crux. It remained so over the course of the decade, before the "domestication" of the European debate in the early 1970s shifted its spotlight to the home-policy implications.[20] We have seen that each side deployed anti-imperialism in support of its cause. As in previous decades, however, the execution of such an apparently uncompromising posture was not unproblematic. This chapter therefore considers how the anti-imperial rhetoric used in the 1960s ran parallel to ideas and other types of language, on both sides of the divide over EC membership, which might be described as quasi-imperialist. There is no suggestion that

---

[17] J. Callaghan, *The Labour Party and Foreign Policy: A History* (Abingdon: Routledge, 2007), 11.

[18] P. Ward, *Red Flag and Union Jack. England, Patriotism and the British Left, 1881–1924* (Woodbridge: Boydell Press, 1998), 70.

[19] B. Schwarz, "The end of empire", in P. Addison and H. Jones, eds., *A Companion to Contemporary Britain, 1939–2000* (Oxford: Blackwell, 2005), 482–97. For the case made by prominent Labour adherents to the "administrative transfer" model, see C. R. Attlee, *Empire into Commonwealth* (Oxford: Oxford University Press, 1961) and P. Gordon Walker, *The Commonwealth* (London: Secker and Warburg, 1962).

[20] On "domestication", see L. J. Robins, *The Reluctant Party. Labour and the EEC, 1961–1975* (Ormskirk: G. W. and A. Hesketh, 1979), 77–80.

anybody in the Labour party sought the restoration of formal colonial overlordship: as is evident from the displacement of the Fabian Colonial Bureau by the Movement for Colonial Freedom in the mid 1950s, there was even by then little truck with anything but general decolonization.[21] Nevertheless, the claims on anti-imperialism made by both sides sat alongside the kind of rhetoric which had earlier been used to qualify Labour attitudes towards disbanding the British empire. Expressions of trust in Britain's special global mission and peculiar capabilities had underpinned this ambiguous position; and so too in the 1960s, when both pro- and anti-Marketeers sought to harness the belief that Britain, especially with a Labour government at the helm, still possessed a uniquely constructive global role. One heterodox wing of the pro-Market coalition denied this and urged a scaling back of Britain's horizons. So too did some on the Labour left who, like Richard Crossman, sometimes wished Britain to retire as a "socialist offshore island". Yet identifying how most others fought against this prospect, and continued to exalt the morality of a global vision, demonstrates the ongoing complexities of Labour's relationship with "imperialism". It also reveals one way in which the study of European integration can be retrieved from a paradigm which only sees Labour ripped apart by the question of EC membership, whilst neglecting how the debate frequently forced the protagonists to contend for certain key ideas which still united the mass of the party.[22]

Anti-Marketeers: Europe as a Threat

At the beginning of the 1960s, most Labour anti-Marketeers' key objection to the EC rested upon a formulation that was to endure throughout the decade. This, as John Stonehouse told the 1961 party conference, was that more Common Market meant less Commonwealth.[23] A year later, Gaitskell posed a question which confirmed why this was both important and dangerous: "where would our influence be", he asked, "without the Commonwealth?"[24] The Commonwealth, thus, was key to Britain's international position and anti-Marketeers were loath to abandon it. On one level, this was a crude matter of status. In fact, in the early 1960s many in the party had believed that the Commonwealth, and therefore Britain, would soon become more significant, as issues of race

---

[21] Howe, *Anticolonialism*, chap. 2.
[22] On this, see C. M. M. Cotton, "The Labour Party and European Integration, 1961–1983" (PhD diss., University of Cambridge, in progress).
[23] *LPACR*, 1961, p. 211.
[24] Ibid, 1962, p. 161.

and poverty superseded East-West relations as the focus of global politics. This would furnish Britain with "a leading role as far ahead as it is possible to see", concluded Labour's research department.[25] Never one to recoil from hyperbole, Denis Healey forecast that the Commonwealth – with Britain at its centre – could become "the spinal column of a new world order".[26] Yet as Douglas Jay complained at the end of the decade, Britain in the EC would be "less important" in world politics.[27]

It was such an attitude that led Tom Nairn to accuse Labour anti-Marketeers of valuing the Commonwealth only as a means to national posturing.[28] There is some truth here. Nevertheless, it is helpful to move beyond such scepticism (which Labour's pro-Europeans purposefully fuelled) and to identify more specifically what kind of world role anti-Marketeers believed the Commonwealth would allow Labour in power to pursue. For the issue here is not a "delusion of grandeur" like that of which Wilson's first governments have been accused,[29] because the Commonwealth was not promoted primarily as an instrument of power politics. In fact, most left-wing anti-Marketeers eschewed the historic military and financial bases of Britain's international position. It was for this reason that most had long pressed for withdrawal from East of Suez; as *Tribune* alleged, Britain clung to its overseas bases only to "make some people feel frightfully important".[30] Meanwhile, the Tribune Group's early support for devaluation was based partly on the belief that it would encourage adjustment to a "post-imperial economic role".[31] There was also much talk, including from Wilson, about rededicating Britain to the United Nations and undertaking never to fight independently of it.

Together, such language distanced the anti-Market left from the postures typical of an imperial metropole. It was not, however, suggestive of a new humility regarding Britain's place in the world. Rather, Britain

---

[25] Labour Party National Executive Committee (NEC) papers, RD.126/Mar. 1961, "Britain and Europe", 21.
[26] *LPACR*, 1962, p. 175.
[27] *Guardian*, Mar. 12, 1969.
[28] T. Nairn, "British Nationalism and the EEC", *New Left Review*, 69 (1971), 3–28. See also idem, *The Left Against Europe* (Harmondsworth: Penguin, 1973), chap. 5.
[29] E. G. F. S. Northedge, *Descent From Power: British Foreign Policy, 1945–1973* (London: Allen and Unwin, 1974), chap. 8; D. Sanders, *Losing an Empire, Finding a Role: British Foreign Policy since 1945* (London: Macmillan, 1990), chap. 5; D. Reynolds, *Britannia Overruled: British Policy and World Power in the Twentieth Century* (Harlow: Longman, 2nd. ed., 2000), chap. 8.
[30] *Tribune*, Dec. 1, 1961.
[31] LHASC, LP/Rich/3/2/17, unrefd. Tribune Group statement, "Make Devaluation Work: An Immediate Policy for the Labour Government", n. D. [1967].

would continue to act out a uniquely constructive role through the Commonwealth, and it is here that the quasi-imperialist nature of anti-Market rhetoric becomes apparent. As we have seen, MacDonald had argued that Labour would not have created the empire but could nevertheless work for the greatest good possible from the existing imperial set-up. Labour, of course, proudly claimed paternity of the New Commonwealth, but the anti-Marketeers' determination to pursue a similar mission through it links them to what their predecessors wanted to achieve with the empire. So too is their certainty that Britain alone was suited to the task, on the basis of the knowledge, expertise, and compassion derived from its colonial past. Thus, Judith Hart would claim even in 1975, when making an explicit comparison with the Six, that "Britain has a very special role [and] a certain amount of greater wisdom, frankly ... I think we have a better contribution to make."[32] This echoed Jennie Lee's scolding of conference delegates in 1968 for appearing to lose confidence in the party's "profound conviction" that "we knew what was best for our country and best for the world".[33]

This was, in some respects, classic platform hyperbole. Nevertheless, it played to beliefs that Britain retained a distinctive function in the world. The European debate brought out the specifics of this, which were articulated in terms of two key geographical axes: North-South and East-West. They concerned how Britain and the Commonwealth would contribute to aid, multiracial harmony, and nuclear détente.

Development policies of the type Labour took to voters in 1964 were one aspect of the North-South mission: they promised a new "war on want" and focused on capital investment, commodity price agreements, and a world food board.[34] According to Clive Jenkins a few years earlier, Britain must say to the emerging African nations, "Join us. We can give you help with goods, factories, and universities."[35] Hart echoed this sentiment more than a decade later.[36] Aiding individual countries in this way grounded a view of Britain as a dynamic force, driving up standards of living across the third world and helping to build stable post-colonial

---

[32] BBC Written Archive Centre, Reading (BBC WAC), *Newsday*, tx. May 30, 1975.

[33] Churchill Archive Centre, Cambridge (CAC), Stwt/7/6/2, Labour Party News Release, "Chairman's Address to Conference", Sep. 30, 1968.

[34] I. Dale, ed., *Labour Party General Election Manifestos, 1900–1997* (London: Routledge, 2000), 120–1.

[35] *LPACR*, 1961, p. 214.

[36] J. Hart, *Aid and Liberation: A Socialist Study of Aid Policies* (London: Gollancz, 1973), esp. chap. 9.

polities. It also emphasised a global role based on responsibility and celebrated the moral dignity implicit in leading a group of under-developed nations. This vision remained evocative into and beyond the 1970s, despite successive Labour governments' failure to meet the totemic "1%" aid target and the undoubted slippage of third world issues down the hierarchy of party concerns.

Much was also made of the Commonwealth, and therefore Britain, as a "bridge" between North and South. This meant between both rich and poor and, in Attlee's words, "the black, the brown, the yellow, and white races".[37] As an influence for good and for peace, Britain's leadership would contribute to harmony between competing continents and races. Indeed, Labour's *Speakers' Handbook* for the 1970 election still played up Britain's ability to tackle "the twin challenges of world poverty and race".[38] Despite the reverses of the 1960s – Wilson's traumas over Rhodesia, most obviously – faith in Britain's capacity to achieve such goals remained strong. Indeed, it is striking how Britain was still readily characterized as the valiant protector of the weak abroad in dealings with its continued dependencies. This led even to dissent from the UN, which was otherwise almost untouchable in Labour circles. Michael Stewart, for example, found it necessary as foreign secretary in 1965 to reassure conference delegates that the government "by no means" agreed with all of the conclusions reached by the UN's Committee of 24, which had been installed as uncompromising custodian of the General Assembly's recent proclamation against colonialism. Soon after, the 1966 manifesto pledged Labour's support to those colonies "unlikely to be able to stand on their own two feet".[39] More strongly, Hart in 1970 dismissed the applicability of the UN's analysis to the "tiny red dots" in the Pacific and Caribbean. Britain must protect Gibraltar from Spanish fascism, she added.[40]

There was also a cold war dimension to this moral mission, important for revealing another application of Britain's continuing global reach. The vision again hung on the Commonwealth, which was thought to provide Britain with a signal role in bringing the superpowers together. This was articulated most clearly by the section of the anti-Market left most hostile to NATO. The neutrality of much of the New Commonwealth undergirded this, meaning that Britain could act (in the words of Konni Zilliacus) as

---

[37] House of Lords Debates, Aug. 3, 1961, vol. 234, col. 232.
[38] CAC, Stwt/9/5/2, "Draft chapters for *Speakers' Handbook*", sent by Peter Shore (as minister without portfolio) for Stewart's comments.
[39] Dale, *Manifestos*, 151.
[40] LHASC, Hart/10/07/1, unrefd. draft article on the withdrawal by Edward Heath's government from the Committee of 24, n. D.

"proud leader of a united Commonwealth working for peace through the United Nations". The African and Asian commonwealth would, Zilliacus went on, "gladly follow our lead".[41] They and other non-aligned countries were "dying for the leadership this country can give them", Alex Kitson told the 1965 conference: Britain would direct those "prepared to become the balance of power in the world".[42] The *New Left Review* likewise promoted Britain's pivotal input to "negotiating the end of the cold war".[43] Later, and despite the stabilization of East-West relations in the early to mid 1970s achieved by the Brandt-Schmidt *Ostpolitik*, left-wing anti-Marketeers continued to endow Britain with a central part in ending the cold war. This was evident particularly in the output of the Tribune Group and increasingly of the NEC, which maintained that a re-evaluation of Britain's relationship with NATO – including possible unilateral withdrawal – was key to unravelling the regional pacts which supposedly impeded a sustainable détente.[44] Without straining the analogy, just as Keep Left, the Socialist Vanguard Group, and the Fabian International Bureau believed in the 1940s that only Britain could lead a third force, so a current of Labour thinking in the mid 1970s continued to attribute a similar capacity to Britain when it came to laying a path between the superpowers. Sceptics easily ridiculed these pretensions: Wilson found this out when he attempted to engineer a mediating role for the Commonwealth over Vietnam. But what is important is that an entrenched intellectual framework within the party demanded he do just this, in line with Labour's faith in Britain as a lead promoter of global peace and prosperity.

Anti-Market internationalism in the 1960s and 1970s saw Britain very much in these terms, for Britain's capacity to establish Labour values across the world was central to its expression. The reasons deemed to compel Labour's retention of the empire had been articulated in a similar way, with the benevolent nature of the party's values again functioning to reconcile any conflict between its ambitions and a congenital impulse against "imperialism". In respect of the projection of a British role in third-world trade and aid, one might consider many of Labour's anti-

---

[41] LHASC, LP/Rich/3/2/18, Tribune Group discussion paper, "Britain and the EEC", n. d. [1966].

[42] *LPACR*, 1965, p. 183.

[43] E. G. "This Week – A New Left Bulletin. Labour party conference, Brighton, 1962", pubd. *NLR*, n. D. [Oct. 4/5, 1962].

[44] E. G. LHASC, LP/Rich/3/2/27, Tribune Group, "Statement on defence and foreign policy. A critique of policy for 1976", July 1976; LP/Rich/3/2/28, unrefd. paper written by Stan Newens, "A socialist policy towards the world", June 1979.

Marketeers as the heirs of a pre-war group which Howe labels as the
"constructive imperialists".[45] These individuals, like those in the later
Movement for Colonial Freedom, explained independence as only the
beginning of "true liberation", after which Britain retained both the
obligation and the skill to improve its former subjects' health, education,
and housing. The Commonwealth was therefore supposed to meet a task
that much of Labour had always seen for Britain after its colonies had
gained independence – a sequel to what the party had considered the
imperial mission to be and which had to be protected from the harm which
accession to the EC would inflict. More broadly, the Commonwealth
would also allow Britain to apply its talents to the healing of divisions
between North and South as well as East and West. Yet this was,
inevitably, another task which the EC would frustrate. As one *Tribune*
contributor wrote in 1961, Britain could never facilitate détente whilst
tethered to "a Commission of… veteran cold warriors". A full twenty
years later, Barbara Castle – by then a recalcitrant member of the
European Parliament – would still criticize the EC as a "closed shop for
western privilege".[46]

Pro-Marketeers #1: Europe as Ballast

Anti-Marketeers' fixation on the Commonwealth was dismissed by
Norman Hart in 1962 as an "empire complex".[47] This jibe was deployed
into the 1970s, whilst Tony Benn, during his brief pro-Market phase,
argued that Britain should enter the EC precisely to eradicate this kind of
thinking. The country needed to "cut Queen Victoria's umbilical cord", he
said as Wilson's move towards the EC gathered pace in 1967.[48] The
implication of such remarks seemed to be that Britain should trim its
foreign policy sails, contract its ambition, and reconcile itself to a future as
a second-rank, regional power. As we shall see, some pro-Marketeers
strongly adopted this position. Most, however, did not promote accession
on these grounds. Rather, in elucidating their vision of Britain in Europe
they mobilised many of the ideas about Britain's global leadership role
and unique qualities evoked by their anti-EC colleagues. This was
frequently conveyed in the same moral language of altruistic endeavour,

---

[45] Howe, *Anticolonialism*, 47–8.
[46] *Tribune*, Dec. 1, 1961; LHASC, Hart/08/44/623, cutting from *Europe '81*
magazine.
[47] *Tribune*, June 29, 1962.
[48] T. Benn, *Out of the Wilderness. Diaries, 1964–1967* (London: Hutchinson,
1987), 496 [Apr. 30, 1967].

even though there were also echoes of the more status-conscious case for membership presented by the foreign office in this period. As Helen Parr has shown, this centred on the warning that Britain risked reducing itself to a "greater Sweden" should it remain outside the EC.[49] The rhetoric of the Labour pro-Marketeers determined to avert this fate combined three main themes, stressed to varying extents across the pro-Market coalition. First, that Britain would lead and reform the EC; second, that it would augment its geo-political influence through the EC; and, third, that it would maintain an independent extra-European role. The assumption that Britain exercised such weight both naturally and rightfully, and that good for all would spring from it, was explicit. This echoed the belief of many early Labour integrationists that Britain had something to teach Europe and the world, as victory in 1945 had proved.[50] In the 1960s, the mainstream case made for British accession demonstrated either that some pro-Marketeers were as hidebound by the past as they claimed their opponents to be, or that they believed successful persuasion to depend upon the projection of past national greatness into a European future.

Predictably, George Brown provided the most vigorous echo of anti-Marketeers' focus on the ongoing British capacity for international leadership. Soon after leaving office, he wrote with tremendous bombast of Britain as "the leader of a new [European] bloc in the world" – specifically, "a bloc with the same power and influence as the old British Commonwealth in days gone by". Rejecting Dean Acheson, he declared, "We have a role: our role is to lead Europe"; this had been so, apparently, since the days of King Alfred. With neither France nor West Germany trusted to assume the tiller, Europe could look only to Britain.[51] Now, Brown probably hammed up his rhetoric in order to present a more boisterous front to a public audience, but his words reflected the case he put to the party. He also clumsily took the message to Europe itself: as Willy Brandt recalled, Brown as foreign secretary had badgered him to ease Britain's way into the Community with the plea, "You must get us in so we can take the lead".[52]

As important as this fact of British leadership were the fruits it would bear, for they plugged the case for accession into the same ethical

---

[49] This phrase was used by Con O'Neill, then Britain's ambassador to Brussels. See Parr, *Britain's Policy Towards the European Community*, 20.

[50] R. M. Douglas, *The Labour Party, Nationalism and Internationalism, 1939–1951* (London: Routledge, 2004), 237–8.

[51] G. Brown, *In My Way, by George Brown: The Political Memoirs of Lord George-Brown* (Harmondsworth: Penguin, 2nd edn., 1972), 202–3, 208–9.

[52] W. Brandt, *My Life in Politics* (London: Hamish Hamilton, 1992), 420.

internationalism which animated its opponents. It is usually forgotten that pro-Marketeers were quite candid about the flaws in Community policy, even though in some circumstances, such as when agricultural policy was under discussion, candour was the only credible strategy. But the "join and reform" line to which this gave rise held for international affairs with particular force: Labour would transform the EC so that it came to reflect the party's own internationalist virtues. Just as British membership would foster socialism and democracy in the EC, so it would somehow encourage the Community to become (in the ubiquitous phrase of the time) "outward-looking". Labour's moral calling was therefore not denied, but the EC enlisted in support – just as, in fact, had the League of Nations between the wars.[53]

There was also a more defensive aspect to these claims, which stressed the need for European support in pursuit of Labour's development objectives. Britain alone, the argument ran, simply could not afford to make good the party's aspirations and would be better able to do so from within the EC, thanks to the economic growth which access to the single market would induce. Yet such humility was unrepresentative of the self-confident language in which the pro-Market case was generally framed. This contended that, once in, Britain would endow the Six with the wisdom of its oceanic perspective. Ironically, some hung this directly on the Commonwealth. Jeremy Bray, for instance, told party workers that British entry would "strengthen the EC's worldwide commitments through the Commonwealth". Even when still unsure about joining, Patrick Gordon Walker conceded that "bringing our world responsibilities into the Common Market" might help it become "really outward-looking".[54]

Labour's pro-Marketeers stuck closely to this theme over the 1960s, especially as the party launched its own application for membership in 1967. But only in 1975 were they able to make it more concretely, thanks to the signing of the Lomé Convention in February that year. The treaty reset the EC's economic relations with its Overseas Territories and was a stroke of good fortune for the pro-Market camp, for it came in time to be subsumed into the referendum campaign. Importantly, it offered concessions beyond those contained in the previous Yaoundé treaties,

---

[53] J. F. Naylor, *Labour's International Policy. The Labour Party in the 1930s* (London: Weidenfeld and Nicolson, 1969), 7.
[54] CAC, Bray/610/641, hand-written draft press release, n. D. [Sep.–Oct. 1962]; *Daily Mirror*, Apr. 1, 1965. Only a year later did Gordon Walker tell Wilson that he was "beginning to change his mind" on the Market. See his *Political Diaries, 1932–1971*, ed. Robert Pearce (London: Historians' Press, 1991), 307 [Apr. 19, 1966].

including the dropping of demands for reverse preferences, a new deal for Caribbean and Indian sugar, and a mechanism for the stabilization of associates' export earnings.[55] Coming just a year after Wilson regained office, it was eagerly hailed as proof that, under Labour's influence, the Community was re-orientating its gaze towards the developing world and channelling resources towards Labour's historic concerns. Reg Prentice claimed to have been converted to the EC by Lomé alone: it "shows what can be done", he gushed. No longer did accession mean "forgetting the rest of the world", as he had once fretted.[56] As Wilson insisted in April 1975, Labour's crusade against poverty, illiteracy, and disease now bound it to Europe. Not afraid to try his luck, James Callaghan proclaimed the convention as "a piece of socialism" – with Labour to thank.[57]

So the European Community would be, and then had been, brought in to line with Britain's long-standing mission to ameliorate living standards in the third world. In this respect, the pro-Marketeers put themselves directly behind the Anglo-centric ethical vision articulated by their rivals. This process also manifested itself in the way Stewart pushed the view that accession to the EC would allow Britain to reassert its leadership of the Commonwealth. In the wake of the Rhodesian crisis, this was a potentially enticing argument. Of particular concern, Stewart argued in the mid 1960s, was that many of Britain's former African colonies were seeking their own bilateral relations with Brussels, and thereby playing into de Gaulle's attempt – blessed by the Commission – to usurp British influence. He insisted that the way to reverse the drift was to join the EC, for only the diplomatic and economic fillips of entry would allow Britain to reassert its relevance to these countries.[58] In this way, Stewart aligned his case for

---

[55] For an explanation and endorsement of Lomé's provisions, see S. Holland, *UnCommon Market. Capital, Class, and Power in the European Community* (London: Macmillan, 1980), 162–4.
[56] British Library of Political and Economic Science, London (BLPES), Prentice/2/7, speech to a Britain in Europe rally at Newham Town Hall, May 5, 1975; *Newham Recorder*, Oct. 16, 1969. One should keep in mind the possibility that extolling Lomé's virtues was a convenient cover for Prentice's shift from a position on the EC increasingly incompatible with his ideological progress across Labour's ranks and, eventually, over the party divide. Benn, of course, was frequently accused of using the campaign for a European referendum as camouflage for his own change of view on EC membership.
[57] *Report of the Special Conference on the Common Market*, 1975, pp. 7, 25.
[58] P. Alexander, "The Commonwealth and European Integration: Competing Commitments for Britain, 1956–1967" (PhD diss., University of Cambridge, 2002), 287–92. See also M. Stewart, *Life and Labour* (London: Sidgwick and Jackson, 1980), 162, 199, 259. Jim Callaghan later speculated that this process

Europe with both the anti-Market vision of British stewardship of the Commonwealth and what Labour was supposed to achieve with it.

In being so explicit about rebuilding Britain's leadership of the Commonwealth, Stewart paddled his own canoe. But it was standard practice to insist that EC membership did not preclude an extra-European role, and, like Stewart, pro-Marketeers talked about this in terms of the objectives upon which their opponents focused. Even after converting to the EC, Wilson never hinted that he was ready to forfeit his place on the world stage. Addressing the City of London soon after announcing his application, for instance, he maintained that the party would contribute to disarmament and détente, mediation over Vietnam, and the GATT Kennedy Round – all matters which preoccupied anti-Marketeers – independently of the EC. On these issues, he told his MPs, Labour and Britain would be "on the field and not the touchline".[59] Significantly, both Wilson and Stewart accepted EC membership without initially extrapolating accession to the need for full withdrawal from East of Suez. Stewart, indeed, continued to oppose some defence cuts on the grounds that they would destroy Britain's influence in the Middle and Far East.[60] Wilson later admitted to being a "slow learner" as far as military retrenchment was concerned.[61] Yet both he and Stewart took inordinate care to present their party with a vision in which "Europe" did not displace "the world".

Other pro-Marketeers were equally judicious in denying any hint of mutual exclusivity. Even Brown, whose geo-political interests were largely confined to the Atlantic alliance, insisted that Britain need not forsake its "wider interests and commitments" in order to join the EC.[62] Others spoke of the survival of the sterling bloc in similar terms.

---

might have turned Gaitskell towards the Market: see his *Time and Chance* (London: Collins, 1987), 149–50.

[59] BBC WAC, unrefd. transcript of Wilson's address to the Lord Mayor's Banquet, Nov. 14, 1966; LHASC, PLP minutes, Apr. 27, 1967.

[60] See the reports of the relevant cabinet meeting in B. Castle, *The Castle Diaries, 1964–70* (London: Weidenfeld and Nicolson, 1984), 142–5; and R. Crossman, *The Diaries of a Cabinet Minister*, vol. 1: *Minister of Housing, 1964–66* (London: Hamilton, 1975), 569–70 [both July 14, 1966].

[61] Including on Richard Crossman's television chat show. See BBC WAC, *Crosstalk*, tx. Jan. 21, 1973. According to the continuity announcer, Crossman invited "eminent contemporaries to discuss with him some of the interests and issues that have concerned him during his forty years in public life". Other guests included Enoch Powell and W. H. Auden.

[62] CAC, Stwt/7/1/2, PLP/4, "The Common Market. Information document: political implications", Apr. 1967, 4.

Admittedly, the idea of a European reserve currency was usually advertised as something into which sterling would be incorporated, giving rise to (in effect) common reserves and shared liabilities. Some, however, claimed to envisage it guaranteeing British liabilities – that is, propping up the sterling area. This was enough to prick an interest even in an instinctual anti-European like Callaghan, who in his dark days at the Treasury reconciled himself to Wilson's application as a means to avert devaluation and thereby maintain Britain's international financial standing. Always with an eye on Labour's commonwealth lobby – which, as we shall see, remained sturdier than most writers allow – pro-Marketeers eagerly linked this to the need to uphold Britain's obligations to its commonwealth depositors.[63]

How Labour pro-Marketeers rebuffed their opponents' claims about British accession to the EC thwarting the resolution of the cold war is also important. Supporters of membership certainly took constant care to locate the Community in a narrative of détente. For a start, they reminded their party that Adenauer and Hallstein were not immortal: their hyper-aggressive mentalities would die with them. They also gave a consistently wide berth to any notion of collectivizing western European nuclear defence and warmly welcomed the EC's contribution to the NATO Harmel Exercise of 1966–7. Their case went beyond legitimating the EC's own approach to the conflict, however, and invested in Britain the significant role in détente which anti-Marketeers insisted it possessed. Thus, Maurice Edelman in particular argued that only the further consolidation of western Europe – especially British membership of the EC – would allow negotiations with the Soviet Union to be conducted from the necessary position of strength.[64] The invasion of Czechoslovakia in 1968 naturally added salience to this case. Pro-Marketeers also claimed that British accession to the EC would smooth the latter's relations with the East. This line of reasoning was pursued into the 1970s. Stewart, for example, argued in 1973 that further integration – again, British accession – would reduce fears in eastern Europe of a West German lunge for its "lost territories".[65] By 1975, Shirley Williams could note that, since

---

[63] Alexander, "The Commonwealth and European integration", 242–51; Castle, *Diaries*, 93 [Nov. 9, 1966]. See also R. Hattersley, *Fifty Years On. A Prejudiced History of Britain since the War* (London: Little, Brown, 1997), 159.

[64] MRC, Mss.125/2/11/1, speech by Edelman to the assembly of the Western European Union, "Britain, the European Free Trade Area and the European Economic Community", n. D. [1965].

[65] M. Stewart, "Now we are in, what are we going to do?", *Political Quarterly* 49, no. 1 (1973), 1–8.

Britain had settled terms with the Commission, China had appointed its first ambassador to Brussels and Russo-EC trade had expanded rapidly.[66] Not only was the EC far from the cold warrior of anti-Market imagination, therefore, but British membership would (and then did) put its pursuit of détente into even sharper focus. As one trade union resolution prophesized in 1967, the EC with Britain inside would not only be "against poverty" but also "for peace".[67]

The pro-Marketeers considered here acknowledged that states like Britain were becoming weaker in relation both to the superpowers and new regional blocs like the European Community. This, indeed, was part of their claim to recognize "reality" and "the modern world". Yet although these concerns about Britain's diminished international influence dominated Whitehall and cabinet discussions about the EC, they emerged only *sotto voce* in the pro-Market case presented to Labour audiences, overwhelmed by the idea that Britain's unique virtues qualified it to lead, and to mould in its own image, the bloc to which isolation forced it. The palpable sense of crisis and retreat evident in official deliberations was largely absent, as most Labour pro-Marketeers instead concentrated their rhetoric on essential continuities in the party's foreign policy: leadership, both of Europe and the Commonwealth, and a prominent role in third-world development and détente. In each instance, the pro-Market case bound itself to the aims and principles targeted by its rivals. Hart's invocation of Britain's "greater wisdom" could have come from the mouth of any of these Labour pro-Marketeers. Though Europe rather than the Commonwealth was appointed as lead support, charges that Britain would be "submerged" or "corralled" within it were refuted: as far as Labour should be concerned, the world was still to be Britain's stage and the EC its new pulpit. In this respect, the magnitude of the policy change involved in the turn to the EC was rarely obvious in the case for membership placed before Labour. Across the 1960s, pro-Marketeers consistently threatened their opponents with the disjunction in Britain's international standing, and consequent threat to Labour's goals, which continued abstention would bring about. Revealingly, officials pressing for accession in the late

---

[66] BBC WAC, *Panorama*, tx. May 19, 1975; LHASC, uncatd. Colin Beever papers, LCE weekly briefing notes, no. 5, May 5, 1975.

[67] NEC, "Agenda for the Sixty-Sixth Annual Conference of the Labour Party", 29 (res. no. 127, National Union of General and Municipal Workers). Also see H. Parr, "Anglo-French relations, détente and Britain's second application for membership of the EEC, 1964 to 1967", in N. P. Ludlow, ed., *European Integration and the Cold War: Ostpolitik-Westpolitik, 1965–1973* (London: Routledge, 2007), 81–104.

1960s believed that the best way to cajole sceptical Labour ministers was to do just this.[68] This message was distinctly un-*communautaire*, echoing what anti-Marketeers claimed was best about Britain and encapsulated in Brown's boast of "as much arrogant patriotism... as anybody else".[69]

Pro-Marketeers #2: Europe as Departure

In 1969, Norman Hart repeated his taunt that anti-Marketeers' world view amounted to little more than "latter-day imperialism".[70] By then, however, Roy Jenkins already felt that the attitude of some pro-Europeans was no less anachronistic, and later recalled that Brown and others had in 1968 "defended Britain's worldwide role with an attachment to imperial commitments worthy of a conclave of Joseph Chamberlain, Kitchener of Khartoum, and George Nathanial Curzon".[71] It is revealing that this was the charge for which Jenkins reached almost twenty-five years after the event. His attack, furthermore, points to the cleavage within Labour's pro-Market flank, one section of which positively disavowed the presumptions of British exceptionalism which had shaped Labour's approach first to the empire and then the Commonwealth. The aberrant group orbited Jenkins, was distinctly social democratic in its leadership, and organized itself through the body founded in 1962 as the Labour Common Market Committee (soon to become the Labour Committee for Europe [LCE]).

It would be misleading to exaggerate the divergence among Labour's pro-Marketeers, for they were united by common despair of Britain's current travails and a conviction that the country would become poorer and weaker outside the European Community. All therefore followed a revivalist theme which exploited ever-more pervasive narratives of national decline. They also insisted that European unity was about more than the "price of butter", even though most did not hoist overtly idealistic colours in front of party audiences. Nor were the social democratic pro-Marketeers wholly immune to the message of their centrist and centre-right colleagues. Tom Bradley, for instance, once enthused about Britain "transforming the entire European scene", whilst Anthony Crosland declared even in the mid 1970s that "we owe it to... the world to exert maximum influence".[72]

---

[68] Alexander, "The Commonwealth and European Integration", 269–70.

[69] Brown, *In My Way*, 202.

[70] N. Hart and E. Wistrich, "Europe: out of the impasse", Fabian Tract 398 (1969), 2.

[71] R. Jenkins, *A Life at the Centre* (London: Macmillan, 1991), 224–5.

[72] MRC, Mss.79/AS/3/8/23, interview with Bradley distributed by the LCE for inclusion in trade unions' in-house journals, June 1967; BLPES, Crosland/13/33/1-

Nevertheless, Jenkins and his acolytes emphasised national frailties, and stressed the essential sameness of Britain and Europe, much more heavily than did Labour's other pro-Marketeers. Britain was to have no unique or even special global mission. As Stanley Henig – one-time leading light in the LCE – told his parliamentary colleagues in 1967, "only through the Community" did Britain have any hope of exercising international influence. Labour was also warned against grasping EC membership as the means to re-establish pre-eminence in Europe and beyond: it was not "ballast for national policy", rebuked Bradley.[73] Perhaps most heretically, the LCE's *Europe Left* newsletter even denied any special relationship between Britain and the third world. "Viewed from the turmoil of Africa and Asia", it claimed in 1967, "Britain looks very much like any other white, wealthy, and western nation". Far from Britain having withdrawn from empire in a wholesome and dignified way, "no former colonial power has left so unhappy a memorial... as this country has in South Africa".[74] A special role in détente was a "myth and a pipedream", concluded Crosland in the early 1960s, whilst Jenkins later expressed the hope that Labour might one day want to help the third world without seeking to lead it.[75] Even in the early 1990s one long-standing social democrat was keen to write off such aspirations as having been "fantasy".[76]

This kind of talk, especially from Jenkins, arose partly from a world-weariness associated with the desire to deflate all kinds of political overstatement. Nevertheless, the effect was explicitly to disassociate the LCE from Labour's acute sense of British exceptionalism. Indeed, one particularly brutal edition of *Europe Left* accused Britain of having

---

9, hand-written notes, "What sort of Community?", n. D. [1974–6]. Bradley was parliamentary private secretary to Jenkins in the 1960s and president of the Transport Salaried Staffs' Assocn. between 1964 and 1977. He defected to the SDP in 1981. Crosland had, of course, by the mid 1970s largely broken with Jenkins and his coterie, on Europe as well as on other issues. See G. Radice, *Friends and Rivals: Crosland, Jenkins and Healey* (London: Abacus, 2nd edn., 2003), chaps. 9–11.

[73] T. Bradley, "Europe and the trade unions", pubd. Trade Union Committee for Europe, n. d. [pre-Oct. 1971].

[74] *Europe Left*, Oct. 1967. See also *Newsbrief* (the predecessor of *Europe Left*), Oct. 1962, on the Central African Federation.

[75] BLPES, Crosland/4/9/6-15, hand-written notes, "The case for Britain joining", n. d. [1962]; *Into Europe*, Oct. 1970 (quoting Jenkins' address to an LCE rally at the 1970 party conference).

[76] G. Radice, *Offshore. Britain and the European Idea* (London: I. B. Tauris, 1992), 23.

become a "sorry mess" whilst standing aloof from European integration.[77] This involved loading 1940 and 1945 with negative connotations – quite a contrast to Labour's usual celebration of these years. Jenkins, for example, dismissed Peter Shore's appeal for the party to marshal the "spirit of 1940" against the EC with the observation that "few things have done us more harm in the past twenty-five years than this belief that we have some... special position, away from the rest of Europe".[78] He had already proposed that Britain run down sterling and encourage the assumption of comparable reserve responsibilities by France, West Germany, and Italy.[79] This much more self-effacing vision required Britain to play a role equal to its European partners, and not use them to bolster itself in the manner some other pro-Marketeers aspired. As one social democratic pro-Marketeer and SDP defector later wrote, the idea of Britain leading Europe went "beyond the fanciful to the ludicrous".[80]

The most strident statements of the social democratic case for Europe came from the relatively closed world of the LCE and its journal. The message also came across powerfully when put to the party at large, but it is worth considering how it varied by audience and with time. Changing rhetoric about the Commonwealth illustrates both cases. It is evident that Labour's social democratic pro-Marketeers had lost patience with the Commonwealth even by the early 1960s, and that it was seen largely as a geo-political encumbrance. Soon after the 1962 party conference, for instance, Gaitskell reported to the Campaign for Democratic Socialism (CDS) with evident irritation that John Diamond had been heard asserting that he "didn't care a damn" for it. Jenkins apparently said something similar at a Fabian tea party.[81] For its part, *Newsbrief* raised an eyebrow at the "exaggerated distress signals" coming from the old dominions, whilst Jenkins noted that Canada was "most full of complaint" at the prospect of Britain's move to Europe yet nevertheless "recoiled with distaste" at the

---

[77] *Europe Left*, Feb. 1975.

[78] PLP minutes, July 19, 1971. For a sceptical critique of this popular theory, see N. P. Ludlow, "Paying the price of victory? Post-war Britain and the ideas of national independence", in D. Geppert, ed., *The Postwar Challenge: Cultural, Social and Political Change in Western Europe, 1945–1958* (Oxford: Oxford University Press, 2003), 259–72.

[79] LCE, "Europe – the choice before us".

[80] S. Haseler, *The English Tribe. Identity, Nation and Europe* (Basingstoke: Macmillan, 1996), 130.

[81] BLPES, Crosland 6/1/102-6, "Meeting of Hugh Gaitskell with CDS, post-Brighton, Oct. 62", memorandum written by Bill Rodgers.

idea of an Anglo-Canadian free trade area.[82] Such criticisms sometimes possessed a hard partisan edge, with one CDS publication decrying John Diefenbaker and Robert Menzies as "Tory prime ministers who have lacked... the will to do much for Britain when their own economic interests have been at stake".[83]

In more inclusive Labour forums, however, most social democratic pro-Marketeers initially adopted a much less antagonistic stance. As Hugo Young has written, paying homage to the Commonwealth remained "the acme of political correctness" within the party.[84] This was true at least in public, as evidenced by the way Jenkins at party conference in 1962 only gently pointed to the dangers of being "more pro-Commonwealth than the Commonwealth".[85] A year earlier, Brown had insisted with his usual bluster that he would "give way to nobody's feelings of loyalty to the... Commonwealth".[86] There was also an affected tone of sorrow that Britain alone did not have the resources to lead a commonwealth development plan, rather than ridicule that it should even try. But this kind of talk faded as the 1960s went on, as anger that the Commonwealth remained a drag on Britain's move to Europe dented pro-Marketeers' willingness to pander to the loyalties still held to it. The consequence was a more heated insistence that the Commonwealth itself had a declining political and economic interest in Britain. It did not wish to be Britain's "alternative" to Europe, wrote Williams.[87] The Kennedy Round was taken as ample evidence of this, as the old dominions traded British preferences for opportunities in American and Japanese markets. Soon after, the idea of sections of the Commonwealth actively conspiring against British interests broke into the party conference. In 1967, only in private had Crosland condemned Australia and Canada as "rich, ruthless, and blackmailing".[88] Yet in 1970, Joe Gormley, speaking on behalf of the NEC, openly suggested that "perhaps we should ask the Commonwealth to have a little regard for us now and again: it might help our economy".[89] *Europe Left* later described

---

[82] *Newsbrief*, July 1962; *Statist*, Nov. 24, 1961.

[83] *Campaign*, no. 14, issued by the Labour Manifesto Group, CDS, Mar. 1962.

[84] H. Young, *This Blessed Plot. Britain and Europe from Churchill to Blair* (London: Macmillan, 1998), 156.

[85] *LPACR*, 1962, p. 173.

[86] Ibid, 1961, p. 266.

[87] LHASC, uncatd. Colin Beever papers, LCE minutes, Mar. 16, 1965.

[88] BLPES, Crosland/4/9/16, hand-written notes, 1967.

[89] *LPACR*, 1970, 198.

the idea of support from the Commonwealth during any future economic crisis as a "sick joke".[90]

This shift has led many writers to dismiss the relevance of the Commonwealth to Labour after the mid 1960s, especially given that Wilson – unlike Macmillan – never intimated any sort of commonwealth veto over his EC application. Lynton Robins, for instance, concludes that by 1967 there was only a "Commonwealth problem".[91] Others have looked beyond the European issue to chart a declining commitment – to the 1968 legislation on Kenyan Asian immigration, for example.[92] Writing on the Commonwealth itself, moreover, emphasises how its members came to develop more exclusively national conceptions of self-interest.[93] Yet it remains dangerous to lose sight of the Commonwealth after the mid 1960s. Philip Alexander recently demonstrated this by reasserting the importance of commonwealth policy in the late 1960s.[94] It is, however, necessary to take the story well into the 1970s.

This is because Labour pro-Marketeers were clearly aware of a commonwealth gallery to which they felt compelled to play during the 1975 referendum campaign. Wilson especially sought to attract pro-commonwealth sentiment to the Yes camp, by strenuously promoting the positive outcomes of the pre-referendum renegotiation for the antipodeans, the sugar producers, and those covered by Lomé. More broadly, he placed great store by his supposed revitalization of commonwealth relations since March 1974. All this probably came naturally to Wilson, for the political sensibilities which had convinced him to support the principle of EC membership since 1966 (including through the obfuscations of Opposition after 1970) never overwhelmed his strong emotional attachment to the Commonwealth.[95] What is more striking is that the LCE now also made a concerted effort to sell the EC on commonwealth grounds in 1975. As it

---

[90] *Europe Left*, Feb. 1975.

[91] Robins, *Reluctant Party*, 22. See also Callaghan, *Foreign Policy*, chap. 8.

[92] R. Hansen, "The Kenyan Asians, British politics, and the Commonwealth Immigration Act, 1968", *Historical Journal* 42, no. 3 (1999), 809–34.

[93] E. G. S. Ward, "A matter of preference: the EEC and the erosion of the old Commonwealth relationship", in A. May, ed., *Britain, the Commonwealth, and Europe: the Commonwealth and Britain's Applications to join the European Communities* (Basingstoke: Palgrave, 2001), 156–80.

[94] P. Alexander, "A Tale of Two Smiths: the Transformation of Commonwealth Policy, 1964–70", *Contemporary British History* 20, no. 3 (2006), 303–21.

[95] B. Donoughue, *Downing Street Diary. With Harold Wilson in No. 10* (London: Jonathan Cape, 2005), 393, 402 [May 29 and June 6, 1975]; M. Falkender, *Downing Street in Perspective* (London: Weidenfeld and Nicolson, 1983), 192, 194; J. Haines, *Glimmers of Twilight* (London: Politico, 2nd edn., 2004), 200.

eagerly pointed out, both Gough Whitlam – "Australia's Labour P. M." – and Bill Rowling, prime minister of New Zealand and "also a Labour man", supported British membership. So too did the African members of the Commonwealth, it went on, and anti-Marketeers should not patronize them by claiming to know their interests better than they did.[96]

Labour's most prominent pro-Marketeers also engaged their opponents on commonwealth territory in the public referendum campaign, where this much more forgiving rhetoric was again evident. Thus, Jenkins now generously declared that the old dominions had "grown up" and that Britain must not act like "a parent... complaining about his children getting married".[97] "Once upon a time the Commonwealth, now Europe", Williams told *Midweek* viewers as she gently nudged them towards the EC.[98] This shift is significant, for it implies that the pro-Market campaign felt it necessary to neutralize its opponents' pleadings on behalf of the Commonwealth despite what most historians describe as a marked lack of public interest in it.[99] Likewise, the way in which the internal Labour campaign for Europe resumed its previous indulgences of commonwealth loyalties suggests that it recognized how many in the party still clung to them as an important expression of purpose for both their party and their country.

Without this direct electoral imperative, however, Labour's social democratic pro-Marketeers were ready to disregard the Commonwealth and to contradict a key part of Labour's ethos by denying a unique British vocation beyond Europe. It is worth reflecting that many of those prepared to defy this cardinal aspect of Labour's tradition in the 1960s were those who broke away from the party in the early 1980s, for the overlap between the LCE and the SDP was sizeable. We might also consider that the social democrats' attitude towards the British imperial legacy lends them a serious claim on the mantle of Labour progressivism, in contrast to the reputation as rather lukewarm socialists which burdened them within the party.

---

[96] LHASC, uncatd. Colin Beever papers, "Labour Campaign for Britain in Europe: speakers' notes".
[97] BBC WAC, Britain in Europe television broadcast, tx. May 29, 1975.
[98] BBC WAC, *Midweek*, tx. Apr. 10, 1975. For more on this aspect of the pro-Market campaign, see C. M. M. Cotton, "The British Labour Party and the 1975 European Referendum" (article in preparation).
[99] E. G. R. Weight, *Patriots: National Identity in Britain, 1940–2000* (London: Pan, 2nd edn., 2003), 340–2; and W. Webster, *Englishness and Empire, 1939–1965* (Oxford: Oxford University Press, 2005) esp. chap. 6.

Beyond Empire?

The European debate functioned as a forum in which Labour fought over its political identity and purpose. In the 1960s and 1970s, it permitted a rhetorical reaffirmation of the commitment to "anti-imperialism" as both sides fought to harness it to their respective causes. The same applied to Germanophobia and anti-Americanism, as well as to Labour's commitment to some eventual form of "world government".[100] At a deeper level, however, the debate about EC membership also showed how attitudes which had earlier rendered Labour ambivalent about disbanding the empire shaped the party's responses to European integration. In particular, Britain continued to be exalted as uniquely able to contribute to the sum of world harmony, through both economic development and superpower détente. There was, of course, a serious divide between those who argued that this was most likely to be achieved through the Commonwealth – the scion of empire – or the European Community. Beyond this, however, the debate about Europe forced the main protagonists to compete for the allegiance of those holding quite homogeneous views of Britain's place in the world and their party's foreign policy aims. By doing so, it confirmed their centrality to Labour's political sense of self.

---

[100] Cotton, "Labour and European Integration", chap. 3.

"A COMPLEX QUESTION ABOUT THE REMNANTS OF EMPIRE":[1] THE LABOUR PARTY AND THE FALKLANDS WAR[2]

DAVID STEWART

The Falklands War of 1982 was the last military conflict to be fought independently by Britain. Although it occurred in a post-colonial era in which the United Kingdom had ceased to be a "Great Power", the prominence of imperial imagery was a feature of the conflict.[3] It was presented by the media and the Conservative Party as atonement for the humiliation of the 1956 Suez Crisis, signalling the reversal of Britain's perceived decline. The war also represented a turning point in the Thatcher era, acting as a launch pad for a generation of Conservative Party hegemony. Debate, led by Max Hastings, Simon Jenkins, Richard Thornton, Hugo Bicheno and Lawrence Freedman, has tended to focus on the diplomatic and political origins of the conflict and the conduct of the military campaign.[4] Social scientists, such as Paul Whiteley, Harold Clarke, William Mishler, David Sanders, Hugh Ward, and David Marsh have concentrated on the conflict's role in reinvigorating Margaret Thatcher's premiership.[5]

---

[1] Tony Benn, *The End of an Era: Diaries 1980–90* (London: Arrow, 1994), 202.

[2] I would like to thank Stephen Meredith, Billy Frank and Craig Horner for their comments on earlier drafts of this chapter.

[3] John M. MacKenzie, *Propaganda and Empire: The Manipulation of British Public Opinion, 1880–1960* (Manchester: Manchester University Press, 1994), 258.

[4] Max Hastings and Simon Jenkins, *The Battle for the Falklands* (London: Pan, 1983).

[5] Harold Clarke, William Mishler and Paul Whiteley, "Recapturing the Falklands: Models of Conservative Popularity, 1979–83", in *British Journal of Political Science* 20, no. 1 (1990), 63–81; David Sanders, Hugh Ward and David Marsh,

Yet despite Stephen Howe's contention that the Falklands conflict "prompted a host of [centre-left] historians to start thinking about... patriotism and national identity in Britain",[6] the Labour Party's responses to the war have largely been overlooked. No in-depth study of Labour Party strategy has been published, leaving interested scholars dependent on the highly partisan memoirs, diaries and biographies of leading Labour Party protagonists, and Anthony Barnett and Clive Christie's brief contemporary accounts of the British left and the Falklands War.[7] Although labour historians and social scientists' preoccupation with internal Labour Party factionalism and domestic policymaking during the 1980s is understandable, an examination of the party's response to this pivotal event in the Thatcher era is long overdue. The conflict posed a stern challenge to the Labour Party's often inchoate anti-imperialist, democratic socialist and pacifist traditions. Indeed, the party leader Michael Foot, and his foremost left-wing opponent Tony Benn embodied this dilemma.

This chapter seeks to place the Labour Party's responses to the Falklands War in the context of the party's historic anti-imperialism and post-war foreign policy. The positions of the party leadership, backbench MPs, Constituency Labour Parties (CLPs), and trade unions are considered, revealing the extent to which Labour's handling of the Falklands crisis was shaped by left/right divisions and factional alliances. The contrasting personalities of Foot and Benn underpin the chapter. Emphasizing the importance of media coverage in influencing popular attitudes towards the conflict, it also scrutinizes the Falklands campaign's impact on Labour's electoral fortunes. The chapter begins by outlining the nature of the British-Argentine dispute over the Falkland Islands.

Labour and Empire: Labour Party Foreign Policy and the Origins of the Falklands Conflict, 1945–75

Argentina's claim to the Malvinas, which were situated 8,000 miles from the United Kingdom in the South Atlantic, stemmed from its sporadic occupations of the Islands in the period 1820–9, when Spanish imperial

---

"Government Popularity and the Falklands War", *British Journal of Political Science* 17, no. 2 (1987), 281–313.

[6] Stephen Howe, "Internal Decolonization? British Politics since Thatcher as Post-Colonial Trauma", *Twentieth-Century British History* 14, no. 3 (2003), 293–4.

[7] Anthony Barnett, *Iron Britannia* (London: Allison and Busby, 1983); Clive Christie, "The British Left and the Falklands War", *Political Quarterly* 55, no. 3 (1984), 288–307.

power was dissolving in South America.[8] The Falkland Islands officially became a British colony in 1833, acting as a fuelling station for the Royal Navy. Its small population primarily consisted of Scottish and Welsh sheep farmers shipped there by the British government to provide a permanent presence. From 1875 the Falklands was controlled by the Falkland Islands Company, which owned two-thirds of the farms on the Islands. In 1880, Argentina requested the return of the Falklands, establishing a diplomatic pattern in which its claim was raised at thirty-year intervals.[9] During this period, Argentina became a British economic and commercial dependency, attracting a sizeable British settler population. Following Argentina's assertion of sovereignty over South Georgia in 1927, however, British-Argentinean relations gradually deteriorated, and during World War Two Argentinean support for the Axis powers led Britain to send troops to protect the Falklands.

After 1945, the decline of the British Empire combined with the rise of Peronism to heighten Argentine interest in the Islands.[10] Peronism, which united trade union and industrial interests behind the cause of Argentine economic modernization, took its name from the Argentine President, General Juan Peron, who propounded a xenophobic form of "integral nationalism". By harnessing nationalist sentiment over the Malvinas, Peron added to his popular appeal and diverted attention from Argentina's stagnating economy. Despite Peron's exile in 1955, the Malvinas remained a frontline issue in Argentine politics, and in 1965, the United Nations (UN) recognized Argentina's right to negotiate with Britain over sovereignty.

The 1964–70 Labour government was unprepared for this development. The Prime Minister, Harold Wilson, was drawing from a shallow pool of distinctive Labour Party foreign policy ideas. Labour's belief in its historic anti-imperialism, based upon the party's perceived opposition to militarism, nationalism, racism, and dictatorships, was central to the Labour Party's self-image. However, post-war Labour foreign policy had been shaped by pragmatic internationalism, placing particular emphasis on collective security, and the upholding of democracy and human rights. Rhiannon Vickers asserts that these sentiments owed

---

[8] Hastings and Jenkins, *Battle for the Falklands*, 6–7.
[9] Lawrence Freedman, *Britain and the Falklands War* (Oxford: Blackwell, 1988), 19–25.
[10] J. C. J. Metford, "Falklands or Malvinas? The Background to the Dispute", *International Affairs* 44, no. 3 (1968), 463.

more to radical nineteenth-century liberalism than socialism.[11] Despite notable decolonizations in India and Palestine, the Attlee governments favoured colonial development over self-determination. Labour's preference for a paternalistic commonwealth was built upon the imperialist assumption of a British global role. The party adopted an Atlanticist stance in the cold war, and sanctioned a British nuclear weapons programme. Labour was also a founder of the UN in 1947 and the North Atlantic Treaty Organization in 1949.[12] This set the framework for a loose political consensus on foreign policy, embracing collective security, Atlanticism and a nuclear deterrent, intended to maintain Britain's "Great Power" status.

Although the Labour Party leadership's pragmatism provided British foreign policy continuity, reassuring the electorate of Labour's patriotism,[13] it undermined the pursuit of socialism by diverting public expenditure away from the welfare state and nationalized industries, thereby inhibiting redistribution. The imperialist financial underpinnings of the party's opponents in the City of London were overlooked. Even left-wing opponents of the consensus, such as Foot, who had forged his political and journalistic reputation through the condemnation of appeasement in *Guilty Men*,[14] operated on the premise that Britain was a "Great Power", wielding international influence that should be used to promote democratic socialism and nuclear disarmament. Foot's vision blended "regretful but firm anti-communism" with unwavering commitment to parliament, the Commonwealth and the UN.[15] Consequently, a coherent socialist post-imperial foreign policy failed to emerge. Instead, Labour differentiated itself from the Conservatives by denouncing doctrines of racial superiority, affirming the brotherhood of man, and advocating redistribution of wealth from the richer to poorer countries.[16]

---

[11] Rhiannon Vickers, *The Labour Party and the World*, vol. 1: *The Evolution of Labour's Foreign Policy 1900–51* (Manchester: Manchester University Press, 2004), 192–3.

[12] Kenneth O. Morgan, *Labour in Power, 1945–1951* (Oxford: Oxford University Press, 1984), 238–9, 279–84.

[13] Stephen Howe, "Labour Patriotism, 1939–83", in Raphael Samuel, ed., *Patriotism: The Making and Unmaking of British National Identity*, vol. 1: *History and Politics* (London, Routledge, 1989), 132–3.

[14] Michael Foot (with Peter Howard and Frank Owen), *Guilty Men* (London: Gollancz, 1940).

[15] Kenneth O. Morgan, *Michael Foot: A Life* (London: Harper Collins, 2007), 125.

[16] John Callaghan, *The Labour Party and Foreign Policy: A History*, (Abingdon: Routledge, 2007), 193-4.

The Suez Crisis acted as a watershed, altering the nature of the consensus. After a period of prevarication, the Labour Party leader, Hugh Gaitskell, opposed British military action, calling for a UN settlement.[17] Suez exposed Britain's financial reliance on America, undermining its claim to "Great Power" status. Thereafter, decolonization became integral to the foreign policy consensus. Assumptions of British "Greatness" were gradually eroded, as foreign policy focused on managing the retreat from Empire, and locating a new world role. The Wilson governments bid for European Economic Community (EEC) membership, refused to commit troops in the Vietnam War, and established the Department for Overseas Development (DFOD), which provided financial assistance to New Commonwealth and third-world countries. As C.M.M. Cotton demonstrates, rhetorical anti-imperialism remained central to the Labour Party's moral self-image, and the DFOD won widespread acclaim from party members anxious to atone for Britain's imperial past. Wilson also initiated military withdrawal from east of Suez, reducing Britain's cold war commitments. The failure to implement commonwealth sanctions against the apartheid regime in South Africa and the government's impotence following Southern Rhodesia's unilateral declaration of independence, however, were condemned by a cross-section of the Labour Party. John Young concludes that although Wilson 'created a sustainable policy', he did so 'more by muddle and a collapse of alternatives than any long-term vision'.[18]

When the Falklands issue arose in 1965 it was deemed of peripheral significance.[19] Labour highlighted the rights of the 1,800 islanders, who wished to remain British, while initiating a gradual process of disengagement. Wilson's Conservative successor, Edward Heath, encouraged Argentina to improve transport communications with the Falklands in the hope of eroding the Islanders' opposition to Argentine control. During 1974 the new Labour foreign secretary, Jim Callaghan, discussed joint British-Argentinean development of the Falklands' oil reserves.[20] The previous year, British entry to the EEC raised the prospect of a new post-imperial role as the bridge between Europe and America. At the 1975 EEC Referendum, however, left-wing opponents of membership, such as Foot, MP for Ebbw Vale, and Benn, MP for Bristol South East,

---

[17] Philip M. Williams, *Hugh Gaitskell* (Oxford: Jonathan Cape, 1982), 278–92.
[18] John W. Young, *The Labour Governments 1964–1970*, vol. 2: *International Policy* (Manchester: Manchester University Press, 2003), 226.
[19] Ibid, 12–13.
[20] Kenneth O. Morgan, *Callaghan: A Life* (Oxford: Oxford University Press, 1997), 461–2.

condemned the prospect of abandoning the Commonwealth for a "rich man's club".[21] Benn had been moving rapidly leftwards since 1970 and his Marxist-influenced views differed significantly from Foot's 'undoctrinaire ethical socialism'. Benn laid claim to the mantle of anti-imperialism by associating British entry to the EEC with an establishment project to "transform the troublesome natives of Britain...into the subjects of a new imperialism".[22] Arguing that Britain had become the "last colony in the British Empire" through the surrender of sovereignty to America, the EEC and multinational companies, Benn called for the Labour movement to lead a "national liberation struggle".[23] The Labour Party was split, precipitating bitter internal divisions and jeopardizing the foreign policy consensus.

End of Consensus: The Path to War, 1976–82

In the midst of this uncertainty, the Falklands issue became increasingly volatile. In 1976, a quasi-fascist military junta seized power in Argentina, executing Marxist opponents and arresting socialists and trade unionists.[24] That year the former Labour leader of the House of Lords, Lord Shackleton, published a report recommending £13 million of investment in the Falkland Islands' infrastructure to facilitate economic expansion and greater independence from Britain.[25] Coinciding with the International Monetary Fund crisis and substantial reductions in public expenditure, Shackleton's proposals were rejected by the Labour government.

Meanwhile, an Argentine bid to purchase the Falkland Islands Company was blocked, and the British ambassador was withdrawn from Buenos Aires after the Argentine navy fired on a British Antarctic survey ship. When British intelligence uncovered Argentine plans to invade the Islands in 1977, the prime minister, Callaghan, sent a nuclear submarine and two frigates to the South Atlantic to warn off the Junta.[26] Callaghan's actions were welcomed by the Labour Party, which supported the British Argentina Support Campaign, pressing for a ban on arms sales to the

---

[21] Morgan, *Michael Foot*, 274.

[22] Tony Benn, *Arguments for Socialism* (London: Jonathan Cape, 1979), 164.

[23] Tony Benn, *Arguments for Democracy* (London: Jonathan Cape, 1981), 3–17.

[24] Richard Thornton, *The Falklands Sting: Reagan, Thatcher, and Argentina's Bomb* (Washington DC: Brassey's, 1988), 4–19.

[25] Hastings and Jenkins, *Battle for the Falklands*, 28–30.

[26] Morgan, *Callaghan*, 594.

Junta, and a policy of providing refuge to Argentine political prisoners.[27] The trade unions, which formed the organizational and financial hub of the Campaign, demanded that diplomatic pressure be exerted on Argentina to reintroduce basic trade union and human rights. Callaghan suspended negotiations over a proposed lease-back arrangement on the grounds of excessive Argentine belligerency, and introduced a Latin-American refugee scheme, but continued to permit arms sales to the regime.

Diplomatic relations with Argentina remained frozen until Margaret Thatcher's victory at the 1979 general election. Rejecting the inevitability of post-imperial decline, Thatcher forcefully pledged to renew Britain's nuclear capability and revitalize British-American relations. She envisaged Britain as America's foremost partner in the cold war and had little interest in the Commonwealth, which "provided a stage for post-colonial posturing by nationalist leaders happy to squeeze as much aid as possible from Britain".[28] In Thatcher's eyes, the Conservative Party was leading a post-colonial mission to destroy the preconditions for socialism on a national and global basis. If successful this mission would reverse British decline. Her primary imperial concerns were reaching settlements over Rhodesia and Hong Kong.[29] The Conservatives' Falklands' strategy was guided by America, which viewed the Junta as a bulwark against the spread of socialism in South America.[30]

Thatcher's government accelerated arms sales to the Junta, removed the amnesty for political prisoners and restarted negotiations over sovereignty.[31] The junior Foreign Office minister, Nicholas Ridley, a close ally of Thatcher, favoured a leaseback arrangement, whereby Britain would transfer sovereignty to Argentina while continuing to govern the Islands in the medium term. In 1981, the Nationality Act removed Falkland Islanders' rights to full British citizenship, further complicating the sovereignty question. That year, a Defence Review recommended the

[27] Labour History Archive and Study Centre (LHASC), Judith Hart Papers, Hart 6/11, *Argentina: The Trade Unions Fight On* (London, British Argentina Campaign, 1978).
[28] John Campbell, *Margaret Thatcher*, vol. 2: *The Iron Lady* (London: Jonathan Cape, 2003), 319.
[29] Margaret Thatcher, *The Downing Street Years* (London: Harper Collins, 1995), 71–8, 259–62.
[30] Modern Records Centre (MRC), University of Warwick, Trades Union Congress (TUC) Archive, International Department Files on Latin and South America 1981–1982, MSS.292D/980/3. The International Confederation of Free Trade Unions (ICFTU) attributed the Junta's growing confidence to the right-wing Republican, Ronald Reagan's election as American President in November 1980.
[31] LHASC, Michael Foot Papers, MF/L19, Events Leading up to the Conflict.

withdrawal of the sole naval patrol ship HMS *Endurance* from the South Atlantic by the autumn of 1982. Richard Thornton contends that these actions were part of an elaborate "sting", devised by American President, Ronald Reagan, and Thatcher, to encourage an invasion of the Falklands, which could be used as a pre-text for military intervention to topple the Junta, which was close to developing a nuclear weapons capability.[32] This would strengthen Thatcher's domestic standing, preserving New Right leadership on both sides of the Atlantic.

Thornton's analysis, however, is questionable, as America possessed the economic leverage to undermine the Junta without resort to a proxy war. Furthermore, British military success was not guaranteed, and it was not in America's strategic cold war interests to destabilize its relations with South America. Argentina invaded the Falkland Islands on April 2, 1982, facing minimal resistance. When parliament was recalled the following day, for its first Saturday sitting since the Suez Crisis, Thatcher, already beset by record post-war unemployment, unrest in the "inner-cities" and the lowest poll ratings of any previous prime minister, was in an exposed position. Her decision to despatch a naval taskforce to the South Atlantic, 8,000 miles from the United Kingdom, represented a huge military and political gamble. On the surface, it appeared an ideal opportunity for the opposition to exploit.

Speaking for Britain? Labour Party Strategies, April 3–21, 1982

The Labour Party, however, had descended into bitter left/right in-fighting following the 1979 general election defeat. The future ideological trajectory of the party was at the heart of debate. A left-wing grouping on the National Executive Committee (NEC), led by Benn, sought to transform Labour into a vehicle for radical economic and social change through NEC control of the election manifestos and mandatory reselection of MPs.[33] In contrast, moderates and revisionists were intent on constructing a cross-class coalition to resurrect the social democratic consensus. Following the establishment of the Social Democratic Party (SDP) in March 1981 by senior "liberal revisionists", the Labour Party's status as the main

---

[32] Thornton, *Falklands Sting*, xvii–xxv.
[33] Leo Panitch and Colin Leys, *The End of Parliamentary Socialism* (London: Verso, 2001), 168–76.

opposition party appeared in jeopardy.[34] The SDP highlighted infiltration of the Labour Party by the Trotskyite Militant Tendency, presenting Labour as infested with left-wing extremists. Militant encouraged social democrats and socially conservative CLP members to leave the Labour Party, exacerbating internal divisions.[35]

Foreign policy was a central issue, with the debate over nuclear disarmament and EEC membership forming symbolic fault-lines. The Bennite left promised a decisive break with the consensus on foreign policy, condemning American policy in Latin America as imperialist and lending vociferous support to the Anti-Apartheid Movement.[36] Foot, who had been elected as Labour Party leader in 1980, was suspicious of the Bennite left's 'anti-parliamentary tendencies', and focused on maintaining party unity, seeking to create an atmosphere of tolerance and trust. In pursuing this goal, however, Foot struck uncomfortable compromises with left-wing and moderate opponents, generating a sense of indecision and allowing internal divisions to fester. By April 1982, Foot's ability to lead the party was under scrutiny.[37]

Foot adopted an unexpectedly belligerent stance over the Argentine invasion of the Falklands, unequivocally supporting the decision to send a naval taskforce to the South Atlantic.[38] He asserted that Britain had a "moral duty, a political duty and every other kind of duty" to ensure that the islanders' "association" with Britain was sustained.[39] Barnett argues that Foot's rhetoric discredited his internationalist credentials and exposed

---

[34] Ivor Crewe and Anthony King, *The Birth, Life, and Death of the Social Democratic Party* (Oxford: Oxford University Press, 1997), 93; John Golding, *Hammer of the Left: Defeating Tony Benn, Eric Heffer and Militant in the Battle for the Labour Party* (London: Politico, 2003), 178–84; Stephen Meredith, *Labours Old and New: The Parliamentary Right of the British Labour Party, 1970–79 and the Roots of New Labour* (Manchester: Manchester University Press, 2008), 13–18.
[35] Diane Hayter, *Fightback! The Labour Party's Traditional Right during the 1970s and 1980s* (Manchester: Manchester University Press, 2005), 28–31.
[36] Stephen Howe, "Labour and International Affairs", in Duncan Tanner, Pat Thane and Nick Tiratsoo, eds., *Labour's First Century* (Cambridge: Cambridge University Press, 2000), 143.
[37] In May 1982, National Union of General and Municipal Workers (GMWU)-sponsored MPs discussed the possibility of removing Foot as party leader before the next general election. See Giles Radice, *Diaries 1980–2001: From Political Disaster to Election Triumph* (London: Orion, 2004), 70.
[38] LHASC, Labour Party Archive (LPA), Parliamentary Labour Party (PLP) Parliamentary Committee (PC) Minutes, Apr. 3, 1982; Interview with Michael Foot on Dec. 12, 2007.
[39] *Hansard Parliamentary Debates* (Apr. 3, 1982), col. 638.

him as a liberal imperialist.[40] Yet Foot viewed the Junta's actions as unwarranted fascist aggression. He was convinced that challenging the Junta was in the international interest and contended that Argentine democratic socialists would welcome Britain's statement of intent. Foot envisaged Labour's primary role in the dispute as ensuring parliamentary scrutiny of the government in order to expose Thatcher's compliance in allowing the invasion to occur. With this objective in mind, Foot declined Thatcher's offer to share military intelligence with the party.[41] Demanding a UN-brokered settlement, Foot's strategy rested on the principle of collective security. He hoped that the party would unite behind this dual-track approach.

The strategy, however, reflected the extent to which Foot was torn between two conflicting interpretations of the dispute. On the one hand, his commitment to anti-appeasement and democratic socialism led him to oppose all fascist aggression, while on the other hand, Foot felt anxious over the parallels with the Suez Crisis, which he had so forcefully condemned whilst editor of *Tribune*.[42] Labour's deputy leader and shadow foreign secretary Denis Healey was privately concerned by Foot's intervention, fearing that it would limit the party's room for manoeuvre.[43] He had been in Greece, and had not been contacted by Foot to clarify tactics. Healey drew direct parallels with the Suez Crisis. He was convinced that America would not allow British military intervention in the Falklands to destabilize its relations with South America.[44] Nevertheless, Healey supported Foot's stance in order to maintain party unity.

Within the shadow cabinet and NEC, Foot paradoxically relied upon the support of moderates and revisionists engaged in bitter anti-left conflict to provide him with a majority. Revisionists, such as the shadow home secretary Roy Hattersley, MP for Birmingham Sparkbrook, tended to believe that Britain was obliged to intervene to uphold democracy.[45] Giles Radice, MP for Chester-le-Street, described the revisionists' watchwords as "no moral gestures, no mock heroics and no blank cheques".[46] With the local elections looming, they were determined that the party avoid being perceived as unpatriotic or pacifist. The shadow

---

[40] Barnett, *Iron Britannia*, 32–3.
[41] LPA, PLP PC Minutes, Apr. 14, 1982.
[42] Michael Foot Papers, MF/L19, scribbled notes on Falklands Crisis.
[43] Denis Healey, *The Time of My Life* (London: Penguin, 1990), 496.
[44] LPA, PLP PC Minutes, Apr. 14, 1982.
[45] LPA, PLP PC Minutes, Apr. 5, 1982.
[46] Radice, *Diaries*, 66.

chancellor Peter Shore, MP for Stepney, adopted a similar stance, while the shadow education secretary Neil Kinnock, MP for Bedwellty, then on the centre left of the party, supported the taskforce as a bargaining chip to achieve a diplomatic settlement.[47] Moderates, such as John Golding, MP for Newcastle-under-Lyme, sought to appear in touch with working-class sentiment by adopting a combative, anti-fascist interpretation of the dispute.[48] In Golding's eyes, the Falklands debate represented another shibboleth of the internal war against the Bennite left. Describing the dispute as "a complex question about the remnants of empire", Benn contended that the "real interest there is the oil" and condemned the prospect of military conflict.[49] Eric Heffer, the shadow minister for European and community affairs and MP for Liverpool Walton, was the only NEC member associated with the Bennite left to deviate from outright opposition to the taskforce.

The leadership sought to vindicate its stance by highlighting official Labour Party policy, which linked the transfer of sovereignty with the restoration of democracy in Argentina. In doing so, however, Foot found himself at odds with the Labour-supporting *Daily Mirror* and *Labour Weekly*, which opposed sending the taskforce, arguing that "the blood that needs to be spilt is the blood of political reputations".[50] Indeed, the Socialist International Committee for Latin America, the General Confederation of Labour of the Argentine Republic, and Argentine human-rights groups attacked the Labour Party's support for the taskforce, arguing that the campaign for democracy in Argentina was unrelated to the Malvinas.[51] Meanwhile, by denouncing opponents of the taskforce as "appeasers", Healey and the moderates unwittingly endorsed the position of New Right-influenced tabloids, such as the *Sun*, which were intent on using the crisis to popularize Thatcherism. The *Sun* asserted that "A British citizen is either on his country's side – or he is its enemy", communicating the simple message that Britain, "can still...be 'Great'", to its predominantly working-class readership.[52]

[47] LPA, PLP PC Minutes, Apr. 5, 1982.

[48] Golding, *Hammer of the Left*, 241–3.

[49] Benn, *The End of an Era*, 202–5.

[50] *Daily Mirror*, Apr. 5, 1982; *Labour Weekly*, Apr. 8, 1982.

[51] Michael Foot Papers, MF/L19, Labour Party News Release, May 26, 1982; TUC Archive, MSS.292D/901/21, International Committee Minutes, 10 May 1982; Judith Hart Papers, HART 6/1, Letter from the Committee for Human Rights in Argentina on May 6, 1982.

[52] *Sun*, May 7, 1982; Eric Hobsbawm, "Falklands Fallout", *Marxism Today* (Jan. 1983), 19.

Developments amongst Foot's traditional centre-left allies in the Tribune Group were crucial to the balance of opinion within the party. At the previous year's party conference, a "soft left" Tribunite faction, led by Kinnock, had broken away from the Bennite left and aligned itself with the moderates and revisionists in defence of the party leadership.[53] The Falklands dispute was the first serious challenge to the cohesion and purpose of the anti-Bennite, Tribunite "soft left". Despite scepticism over the despatch of the taskforce, the editor of *Tribune*, Dick Clements, gave the newspaper's approval to Foot's dual-track strategy.[54] Within the Parliamentary Labour Party, however, there was substantial opposition towards sending the taskforce, centring on the belief that its presence in the South Atlantic would heighten the prospect of escalation to full-scale war with Argentina.[55] Given heightened cold war tensions, there was also concern that the Soviet Union would intervene, widening the conflict. Others condemned the prospect of islanders being caught in military crossfire, and feared retribution against British nationals in Argentina. Unlike Foot's dual-track strategy, opponents of the taskforce favoured UN financial and economic sanctions to exploit Argentina's dependence on foreign loans and emphasised that the UN should take full responsibility for brokering a peaceful resolution to the dispute. The overwhelming majority of CLP motions endorsed this interpretation of the dispute, pressing Foot to use the invasion to highlight the limited deterrent offered by nuclear weapons.[56]

Foot's tactics were reliant on America vetoing British military intervention, or the achievement of a diplomatic settlement, closely associated with Labour Party policy, which could be used as a platform from which to expose the Conservatives' incompetent handling of the dispute. Reagan, however, privately supported Britain, and the Junta was unwilling to engage in constructive dialogue, playing into the hands of Thatcher, who hoped to use successful military action to revitalize her premiership.

---

[53] Hayter, *Fightback!*, 19–22.
[54] Mervyn Jones, *Michael Foot* (London: Gollancz, 1994), 489.
[55] LPA, PLP Minutes, Apr. 22, 1982.
[56] Judith Hart Papers, HART 6/10, CLP Motions on the Falklands War.

Searching for Peace and Unity: The Outbreak of War and Internal Labour Party Dissension, April 21 – June 14, 1982

Following the outbreak of hostilities in South Georgia on April 21, Foot and Healey became increasingly desperate to broker a UN settlement, as a tidal wave of media-generated jingoism swept Britain.[57] However, by calling for a conditional ceasefire, dependent on Argentine withdrawal from the Islands, Foot confused his earlier belligerent rhetoric, creating a general sense of incoherence. The Labour Party also appeared impractical and unpatriotic to be insisting on a diplomatic settlement, entailing UN trusteeship of the Islands or shared sovereignty, when British forces were making advances. Christie argues that "the Labour leadership's hesitant and unconvincing support for the war exemplified the point that Labour has never managed to work out a consistent and distinctive view of Britain's place in the world".[58] In contrast, Thatcher formed a war cabinet and deployed "Churchillian" rhetoric to emphasize the independent nature of Britain's actions, combining "resonances of Victorian 'gunboat diplomacy' [with]…the popular experience and memory of the Second World War".[59] Joe Ashton, the Tribunite MP for Bassetlaw, sought to use his column in the Daily Star to puncture Thatcher's "furious flag-waving patriotism" by querying her World War Two service record, but the rest of the media would not carry the story.[60]

Friction now began to emerge amongst revisionists, moderates and the "soft left" over the islanders' right to self-determination, and the prospect of a full-scale British invasion. Hattersley rejected the Falklanders' right to a "veto" over British defence and foreign policy, but the shadow health secretary Gwyneth Dunwoody, MP for Crewe, and George Robertson, MP for Hamilton, insisted that the islanders' wishes should be paramount.[61] Kinnock opposed an invasion on the grounds that it would sabotage diplomatic negotiations, while Healey, resigned to the loss of British sovereignty over the Falklands, insisted that a full-scale invasion was not feasible. In contrast, Shore argued that Britain was "morally in the right", and that Labour should not be seen as a "peace at any price party".[62]

---

[57] LPA, PLP PC Minutes, Apr. 28, 1982.

[58] Christie, "British Left and the Falklands War", 301.

[59] Robert Gray, "The Falklands Factor", Marxism Today (July 1982), 10.

[60] Joe Ashton, Red Rose Blues: The Story of a Good Labour Man (London: Macmillan, 2000), 298–9.

[61] LPA, PLP PC Minutes, Apr. 21, 1982; PLP PC Minutes, Apr. 26, 1982.

[62] LPA, PLP PC Minutes, Apr. 28, 1982.

Although it was evident that the leadership's strategy was unravelling, the revisionist-moderate-"soft left" coalition on the NEC held, defeating a motion by Benn, urging immediate withdrawal of the taskforce, by fifteen votes to eight.[63]

The TUC was vital in defending Foot's position. It issued a supportive press statement and secured international endorsement of Foot's strategy from the ICFTU and the Commonwealth Trades Union Congress.[64] The TUC justified its stance on the basis of solidarity with the Falkland Islands General Employees' Union, which opposed a transfer of sovereignty to Argentina. In reality, its approach was shaped by moderate and "soft left" unions intent on maintaining Labour Party unity and marginalising the Bennite left. Indeed, moderate and "soft left" unions, such as the GMWU, National Union of Railwaymen (NUR) and Transport and General Workers' Union (TGWU), limited official discussion of the issue at their conferences to conceal the undercurrent of unrest amongst left-wing trade unionists.[65] Official opposition towards the taskforce was largely restricted to the "hard left" National Union of Mineworkers (NUM), Fire Brigades Union and National Union of Public Employees.[66]

During this period, opponents of the conflict became more vocal. Judith Hart, Tribunite MP for South Lanark, established the cross-party Ad Hoc Committee for Peace in the Falklands, which worked in tandem with Labour Action for Peace and the British Peace Assembly, campaigning for an unconditional ceasefire.[67] The Committee was bolstered by the selection of a leading Bennite, Chris Mullin, as *Tribune's* new editor.[68] Under Mullin's stewardship *Tribune* became anti-war, printing a reworded

---

[63] LPA, NEC Minutes, Apr. 28, 1982.

[64] TUC Archive, MSS.292D/20/15, General Council Minutes, Apr. 28, 1982; MSS.292D/901/21, International Committee Minutes, May 10, 1982; LHASC, *TUC Congress Report 1982*, (London: TUC, 1982), 214–5.

[65] MRC, GMWU Archive, Executive Council Minutes, May 22, 1982; *Report of 1982 GMWU Congress* (London: GMWU, 1982), 34–5, 45; TGWU Archive, General Council Minutes, June 7, 1982; NUR Archive, MSS.127/NU/1/1/111-112, General Secretary's Report to Annual General Meeting, June 28, 1982.

[66] John Prescott, shadow regional affairs spokesman and MP for Hull East, then a Tribunite, disassociated himself from his union sponsors, the National Union of Seamen, over their support for the taskforce. See Colin Brown, *Fighting Talk: The Biography of John Prescott* (London: Simon and Schuster, 1997), 198.

[67] Judith Hart Papers, HART 6/5, Falklands Crisis – Responses of the Peace Movements; HART 6/8, Labour Action for Peace Press Statement on Apr. 20, 1982; HART 6/2, British Peace Assembly Press Statement on May 5, 1982.

[68] Martin Westlake, *Kinnock: The Biography* (London: Little, Brown and Company, 2001), 192–4.

version of Foot's famous 1956 headline "Stop This Suez Madness", which proclaimed "Stop This Falklands Madness".[69] Mullin also published an open letter by former *Tribune* journalist, Anthony Arblaster, entitled "Will The Real Michael Foot Stand Up?", which accused Foot of being "carried along by [the] tide of revived imperialist fervour". Foot responded by highlighting his desire for a UN-brokered settlement and condemning the new regime's "infantile leftism".[70]

Christie contends that, "it was precisely that section of the Left that had for years been arguing...for a principled foreign policy who were now arguing against the war on basically pragmatic grounds".[71] However, he fails to appreciate that these groupings viewed the conflict as imperialist, seeking to revive jingoistic, militaristic and racist sentiment, which would be exploited by the Conservative Party. Arguments surrounding the anti-fascist nature of the war were condemned as hypocritical, given Britain's escalating arms sales to the Junta, enlistment of Chilean fascist support, and the City of London's ongoing handling of Argentinean financial transactions.[72]

Pragmatic opposition, led by Tam Dalyell, the shadow science spokesman and centrist MP for West Lothian, focused on the economic worthlessness of the Islands and the logistical difficulties surrounding the military operation.[73] Following the sinking of the Argentine cruiser *General Belgrano* on May 2, Dalyell played an increasingly prominent role in opposing the war. Meanwhile, Benn proposed evacuating the Falklands and compensating the islanders for their losses on the grounds that it would create the preconditions for a UN settlement, and be more cost efficient than fighting a war.[74] He contended that it was immoral to spend £4 billion on a war at a time of record post-war unemployment and widespread cuts in public services. The Scottish Trades Union Congress and the NUM supported this line of argument.[75] Following a parliamentary

---

[69] *Tribune*, May 7, 1982.

[70] *Tribune*, May 14, 1982; *Tribune*, May 21, 1982.

[71] Christie, "British Left and the Falklands War", 303.

[72] Judith Hart Papers, HART 6/8, Campaign Against Arms Trade Press Statement on Apr. 6, 1982; *Tribune*, May 7, 1982.

[73] Michael Foot Papers, MF/L19, Letter from Tam Dalyell to Michael Foot on May 22, 1982.

[74] Judith Hart Papers, HART 6/11, *Tony Benn on the Falklands War* (Nottingham: Bertrand Russell Peace Foundation, 1982), 2–14.

[75] Glasgow Caledonian University Research Collections, Scottish Trades Union Congress (STUC) Archive, General Council Minutes, July–Sep. 1982, Press Statement on June 22, p. 002862; At the 1982 NUM Annual Conference, the NUM President, Arthur Scargill, argued that Thatcher's "mad adventure of colonialism

debate on May 20, thirty-three Labour MPs voted against the war. In a vain effort to assert leadership authority, Foot sacked Dalyell and the shadow arts spokesman Andrew Faulds, MP for Warley from their frontbench positions on May 24. However, this only served to prompt the resignations of the shadow home affairs spokesman John Tilley, MP for Lambeth Central, and the shadow food, agriculture and fisheries spokesman Gavin Strang, MP for Edinburgh East.[76]

The Militant Tendency attacked the Ad Hoc Committee for Peace in the Falklands as being detached from the confrontational reality of working-class life, concluding that Thatcher "would merely shrug her shoulders and laugh" at its pacifist demands.[77] Indeed, anti-war demonstrations tended to be confined to London, attracting crowds of 2,000–10,000.[78] Some protestors displayed banners proclaiming "Victory to the Argentine Junta", embellishing the media-generated perception that the labour movement was unpatriotic.[79] Kenneth O. Morgan accurately surmizes that "the jingoism of wartime seldom helps a party of the left".[80] At the 1982 local elections, the Labour Party suffered a net loss of forty-seven council seats.[81] The "Falklands effect" was felt most heavily in southern England, London, and parts of the Midlands, which were integral to the electoral balance of power. The party made limited progress in northern England, reinforcing its grip on South Yorkshire, but failing to retake Liverpool, whilst suffering heavy losses in Leeds and Bradford. In

---

[would] produce yet another round of closures as our share of the burden". See *National Union of Mineworkers Annual Conference Report 1982* (London: NUM, 1982), 344–5.

[76] John Tilley was a Co-operative Party-sponsored MP. Although the Co-operative Party leadership endorsed Foot's strategy, there was some discontent amongst the Co-operative Parliamentary Group and considerable opposition towards the war at Local Co-operative Party level. See National Co-operative Archive, *Co-operative Congress Report 1982*, (Manchester: Co-operative Union, 1982), 50–1, 63.

[77] Michael Foot Papers, MF/L19, Ted Grant, *Falklands Crisis: A Socialist Answer* (London: Militant, 1982).

[78] The Peace Pledge Union called a Day of Action on 1 May that involved a variety of small-scale protests in over 30 towns, including the occupation of a Royal Navy recruiting office in Sheffield. See *New Statesman*, May 28, 1982.

[79] Eric Heffer, *Never a Yes Man: The Life and Politics of an Adopted Liverpudlian* (London: Verso, 1993), 195–6.

[80] Morgan, *Michael Foot*, 414.

[81] *Labour Weekly*, May 14, 1982.

Scotland, results were more encouraging, reflecting the less jingoistic Scottish response to the conflict.[82]

Foot's complex diplomatic argument, which contrasted sharply with Thatcher's populist jingoistic rhetoric, had limited appeal in an increasingly polarized wartime climate. The Labour Party's strategies were built upon the principle of collective security, and acceptance of Britain's diminished post-imperial status. By creating the perception that Britain could still operate as an independent international power, Thatcher's victory in the Falklands tapped a rich seam of dormant Anglo-British nationalism, which celebrated the United Kingdom's imperial past. Divided and bereft of a credible alternative, the Labour Party was unable to counter this upsurge in jingoism. The sole political beneficiary of the conflict was the Conservative Party, which linked victory in the Falklands with Thatcher's efforts to overturn the post-war consensus and restore British "Greatness".[83] Presenting the labour movement as an unpatriotic vested interest, inhibiting economic recovery and national unity, Thatcher harnessed the "Falklands Factor" to win a landslide victory at the 1983 general election.[84]

A Lost Cause: The Labour Party's Falklands Campaign in Perspective

The Falklands conflict presented the Labour Party with a post-imperial foreign policy conundrum that neither the leadership nor anti-war opponents could solve. The reinstatement of democracy in Argentina was supported by the entire labour movement and British victory in the Falklands helped to achieve this goal. However, the previous Labour government had armed the Junta and, during the conflict, fascist Chile assisted the British war effort, discrediting notions of an anti-fascist crusade. Indeed, arguments surrounding British sovereignty and the islanders' right to self-determination were complicated by the Falklands' control by a private company. Although anti-war campaigners' interpretation

---

[82] Jimmy Allison, *Guilty by Suspicion: A Life and Labour* (Glendaruel: Argyll, 1995), 95, 99.

[83] Thatcher, *The Downing Street Years*, 235.

[84] Speaking in Cheltenham on July 3, 1982, Thatcher proclaimed, "We have to see that the spirit of the South Atlantic – the real spirit of Britain – is kindled not only by war but can now be fired by peace…We know we can do it…That is the Falklands Factor…We have ceased to be a nation in retreat. We have instead a newfound confidence born in the economic battles at home and tested and found true 8,000 miles away."

of the conflict, which drew on the Labour Party's belief in its historic anti-imperialism, corresponded with CLP and Argentine socialist opinion, their acceptance of short-term Argentine control of the Falklands risked strengthening the Junta, which was persecuting fellow socialists and trade unionists. Furthermore, anti-war opponents were out of touch with working-class and public opinion, which overwhelmingly approved of Thatcher's action. Viewed through the prism of jingoistic media coverage, victory in the Falklands rendered Benn's contention that Britain was the "last colony in the British Empire" implausible.

John Golding's deluded assertion that the conflict "probably saved the Labour Party", by discrediting Benn and undermining support for the SDP, is testament to the depth of feeling generated by internal factionalism.[85] Although the revisionist-moderate-"soft left" alliance on the NEC remained intact, laying the preconditions for the Kinnock/Hattersley "dream ticket" leadership,[86] the war weakened the popular appeal of the Labour Party. Waning support for the SDP-Liberal Party alliance was at best of marginal benefit to Labour, which became increasingly debilitated as the conflict progressed. Existing divisions were deepened, new internal wounds inflicted, and the party's public image further tarnished. Foot's dual-track strategy could only succeed if a diplomatic agreement was reached or the taskforce was defeated or suffered heavy casualties, leaving the Labour Party leadership ill-prepared for British military advances. After hostilities commenced, they appeared impractical and incoherent, continuing to support the taskforce, while arguing in favour of a ceasefire and UN trusteeship of the Falklands when British troops were successfully fighting to recover the Islands.

Foot's strategy also took insufficient account of the media's role in presenting Labour Party policy. The overwhelmingly hostile media gave the party leadership little credit for supporting the taskforce, whilst castigating Foot for proposing a negotiated settlement. Indeed, in the public consciousness, extensive media coverage of Labour Party opponents of the war led the party to become associated with pacifism and appear unpatriotic, sabotaging Foot's delicate political balancing act. To compound matters, Foot found himself at odds with the pro-Labour press and his CND support base, further weakening his leadership authority and accentuating internal divisions. In effect, British military success in the Falklands left the Labour Party in a no-win situation, galvanizing Thatcher's post-imperial mission to destroy socialism.

---

[85] Golding, *Hammer of the Left*, 243.
[86] Hayter, *Fightback!*, 23–7.

CONTRIBUTORS

Hester Barron is a lecturer in history at the University of Sussex. She specializes in twentieth-century British social history and is particularly interested in labour history and the history of the working classes in the early part of the century. Her book *The 1926 Miners' Lockout: Meanings of Community in the Durham Coalfield* was published in 2009.

C. M. M. Cotton is a research student at King's College, Cambridge, working on Labour and European integration from the 1960s to the 1980s. He has been awarded a Scouloudi Research Fellowship at the Institute of Historical Research for 2009–10.

Mary Davis FRSA is Professor of Labour History at London Metropolitan University where she heads the Centre for Trade Union Studies, and is the Deputy Director of the Working Lives Research Institute. She has written, broadcast and lectured widely on women's history, labour history, imperialism, and racism.

Billy Frank is a senior lecturer and course leader in the School of Education and Social Science at the University of Central Lancashire (UCLan). His doctoral thesis examined Britain's colonial development policy in Central and Southern Africa in the trans-World War Two period with special reference to Barclays Bank (Dominion, Colonies and Overseas). He is currently researching the lives and careers of empire bankers, developers and "experts" in post-1945 southern Africa.

Craig Horner is co-editor and book reviews editor of the *Manchester Region History Review*. His doctoral thesis was on the middling sorts of eighteenth-century Manchester; and he has published *The Diary of Edmund Harrold, a Manchester Wigmaker* (Aldershot: Ashgate, 2008). He guest-edited the *Manchester Region History Review* special volume on early modern Manchester (2008) and is now researching early motoring and society in the United Kingdom prior to World War One.

Neville Kirk is Emeritus Professor of Social and Labour History at Manchester Metropolitan University. His recent and current interests embrace the comparative and transnational labour history of Australia, Britain and the United States, and global labour history. His publications include *The Growth of Working-Class Reformism in Mid-Victorian England* (1985), *Labour and Society in Britain and the USA*, 2 vols. (1994), *Comrades and Cousins: Globalization, Workers and Labour Movements in Britain, the USA and Australia from the 1880s to 1914* (2003), *Custom and Conflict in the Land of the Gael: Ballachulish 1900–1910* (2007). He has recently held Visiting Fellowships at the University of Sydney and the Australian National University. In 2007 he took up a Leverhulme Study Abroad Fellowship at the University of Toronto, Canada. In the past year he has delivered papers at the Universities of Toronto and New Brunswick in Canada, the University of Reading in England and most recently at Lochaber College, part of the University of the Highlands and Islands, in Fort William, Scotland. He is about to take up a Visiting Fellowship at the National Europe Centre, the Australian National University.

Nicholas Mansfield has been Director of the People's History Museum in Manchester, United Kingdom, since 1989. An honorary staff member at the Universities of Manchester, Salford and Central Lancashire, he has published over forty journal articles and chapters and is the author of *English Farmworkers and Local Patriotism, 1900–1930* (Aldershot: Ashgate, 2001).

Christopher Prior is a lecturer in imperial history at the University of Leeds. His two main research interests are the British imperial state in Africa, with a specific interest in Sudan, and the interactions between popular culture and empire from 1870 to the present day. His PhD was concerned with colonial officials' mindsets in inter-war Africa. He is currently working on an expanded book-length version of the thesis, to encompass the period from the end of the 'Scramble for Africa' through to the outbreak of World War Two.

Murray Steele, who has now retired from teaching, was Head of Afro-Asian Studies at the former Edge Hill HE College, now University, where his main area of expertise was the colonial history of southern Africa. He has taught and researched in Zimbabwe and Canada, as well as the United Kingdom. His publications cover a number of fields in Zimbabwean history, including race relations, labour and missionary history, rural studies and comparative local government, and have included more recently studies of the legacy of slavery and colonialism for Liverpool.

David Stewart is BA (Hons.) History course leader at UCLan and, through his position as joint UCLan-People's History Museum Research Fellow, has played an integral role in developing their institutional partnership. His research interests traverse twentieth-century political history, labour history and Scottish history. An innovative research monograph, based upon his PhD thesis, *The Path to Devolution and Change: A Political History of Scotland under Margaret Thatcher*, was published by I. B. Tauris in 2009.

INDEX

Accra Conference 144
Acheson, Dean 160
Ad Hoc Committee for Peace in the
    Falklands 186, 188
Addison, [Lord] 137
Adenauer, Konrad 150, 164
African Affairs Board 136
Alexander, Horace 72
All-India Trade Union Congress 74
All-India Trade Union Federation
    71, 74
Amalgamated Weavers' Association
    67–8, 74, 78, 81, 86
Anglo-Boer Wars 14, 21, 23, 25–6,
    30–2, 34, 36–7, 53–6
Arblaster, Anthony 187
Armitage, G. W. 82
Ashton, Joe 185
Ashurst, T. 86
Associated Overseas Territories
    150, 161
Attlee, Clement 95, 107, 118, 121,
    132–3, 139–41, 143, 145, 147,
    151, 157, 176
Australian Labor Party 44, 52, 55,
    57–8, 62
Barclays Bank (Dominion, Colonies
    and Overseas) 122
Battershill, [Sir] William 115
Bax, Ernest Belfort 27–8
Baxter, G. H. 134
Benn, Tony 9, 150, 174, 177–8,
    180–1, 183, 186–7, 190
Bentinck, [Lord] 15
Besant, Annie, ix
Bevin, Ernest 95, 151
Blair, Tony 152
Blandford, John 119
Blatchford, Robert 24, 34, 54, 61–3

Bledisloe Commission on Closer
    Association 137
Bolton and District Weavers and
    Winders' Union 77
Bolton Operative Spinners'
    Association 75
Bowen, Walter 99, 102
Bradley, Tom 166
Brandt, Willy 158, 160
Bray, Jeremy 161
Brazier, John 103
Bright Reform Club 75
Britannic Alliance 91
British Argentina Support
    Campaign 178
British Commonwealth and Labour
    Conference 91, 143
British Peace Assembly 186
Brockway, Fenner, ix, 141
Brook, [Sir] Norman 107
Brown, George 160, 163, 166, 169
Burgess, Joseph 35–6
Burns, John 29
Cabinet Committee on Colonial
    Development (CCCD) 113–14,
    121
Callaghan, James 145, 162, 164,
    177–9
Campaign for Democratic Socialism
    (CDS) 168
Campaign for Nuclear Disarmament
    (CND) 190
Castle, Barbara 159
Central Economic Planning Staff
    (CEPS) 111–14
Chamberlain, Joseph 166
Champion, Henry Hyde 43
Chancellor, [Sir] John 123
Chikerema, James 144

Citrine, Walter 94, 97
Clements, Dick 184
Cohen, Andrew 134
Colby, [Sir] Geoffrey 124–5
Colonial Advisory Committee
      (CAC) 92–3, 100
Colonial Development and
      Economic Council (CEDC) 109,
      112, 115, 124
Colonial Development and Welfare
      Act (CDWA) 95, 108
Colonial Development Corporation
      (CDC) 110, 117
Colonial Development Working
      Party (CDWP) 111, 113, 122–3,
      126
Colonial Dollar Drain Committee
      (CDDC) 112–13
Colonial Labour Advisory
      Committee (CLAC) 101, 104
Colonial Office 92, 94, 96, 100–1,
      103–5, 109, 111–12, 118, 120–
      2, 134, 144
Colonial Primary Products
      Committee (CPPC) 112–13
Comintern 90–1
Commonwealth Immigrants' Act 94
Commonwealth Relations Office
      (CRO) 112–13, 134, 144
Commonwealth Trades Union
      Congress 186
Communist Party of Great Britain
      96–8, 139
Communist University of the
      Toilers of the East 90
Conference (shipping line) 123
Conservative Party, colonial policy
      103, 179, 187; Falklands War
      strategy 179, 189
Cotton Spinners and Manufacturers'
      Association 86
Creech Jones, Arthur 93, 95, 109–
      10, 112, 115, 118–21, 128, 133–
      5, 151
Cripps, [Sir] Stafford 107, 111
Cripps, Arthur Shearly 138

Crompton, Henry 36
Crosland, Anthony 166–7, 169
Crossman, Richard 154
Curtin, John 60–1
Curzon, George Nathaniel 166
Dalgleish, Andrew 102
Dalton, Hugh 95, 113
Dalyell, Tam 187–8
Darwen Weavers, Warpers and
      Winders' Association 84
Davies, [Mrs] J. P. 70
De Gaulle, [General] Charles 149,
      162
Diamond, John 168
Diefenbaker, John 169
Douglas-Home, [Sir] Alec 149
Dugdale, John 135
Dunwoody, Gwyneth 185
East Africa Groundnuts Scheme
      110, 117–20
East African Trades Union
      Confederation (EATUC) 100
Easter Rising 57
Edelman, Maurice 164
Eden, Anthony ix
Edwards, Owen Morgan 32
Ellam, John E. 63
European Economic Community
      (EEC) 5, 149–50, 153–5, 159–
      60, 162–5, 167–8, 170–2, 177–
      8, 181
Evans, Stanley 138–9
Fabian Colonial Research Bureau
      95, 108–9, 135–43, 145, 147,
      154, 158
Fabians/ Fabian Society 99–100,
      142
Fairfield Commission 96
Falkland Islands General
      Employees' Union 186
Falklands War 173–4, 177–8, 180–
      1, 185, 189–90
Faulds, Andrew 188
Federation of Master Cotton
      Spinners' Associations 75
Fire Brigades Union 186

Fisher, Andrew 44, 59
Fitzgerald, C. L. 28
Foggon, [Sir] George 92
Foley, Alice 77
Foot, Michael 174, 176–8, 181–90
Foreign and Commonwealth Office
    (FCO) 92, 104
Fox-Pitt, Thomas 137
Gaitskell, Hugh 145, 150, 154, 168,
    177
Gallipoli campaign 48, 57
Game, [Sir] Philip 49, 57
Gandhi, Mahatma 65, 67–9;
    personal safety 68–9; in
    Lancashire 68, 76; Gandhi-Irwin
    talks 67; spinning 70;
    cultivating image 76–7
General Agreement on Tariffs and
    Trade (GATT), Kennedy Round
    163, 169
General and Municipal Workers
    Union (GMWU) 186
General Belgrano 187
General Confederation of Labour of
    the Argentine Republic 183
George V, [king] 57, 59
gold standard 65
Golding, John 183, 190
Gordon, [Sergeant-Major] 16
Gordon Walker, Patrick 128, 161
Gormley, Joe 169
Great Harwood Weavers'
    Association 68, 71, 76
Griffiths, Jim 137–8, 142, 144
Hallstein, Walter 150, 164
Hannington, James 25
Hardie, Keir, ix, 24, 29, 43, 60–2
Hart, Judith 156–7, 186, 165
Hart, Norman 159, 166
Hatch, John 141, 143–4
Hattersley, Roy 182, 185, 190
Havelock Wilson, J. 29
Healey, Denis 155, 182–3, 185
Heath, Edward 177
Heffer, Eric 183
Henig, Stanley 167

Henty, G. A. 30
Hinden, Rita 95, 108–9, 128
Hindle, J. 86
Hitchman, E. A. 113
Howell, George 29
Huggins, Godfrey 132, 144
Hurst, [Sir] Gerald 78
Hyndman, H. M. 24, 33–4, 61
Imperial Advisory Committee, see:
    Imperial Affairs Sub-Committee
Imperial Affairs Sub-Committee 91
Imperial Conference 58–9
Indian National Congress 67, 74, 86
Indian Rebellion 38
International African Friends of
    Abyssinia 93
International African Service
    Bureau 93
International Committee of Negro
    Workers 90
International Confederation of Free
    Trade Unions (ICFTU) 97–8,
    101–2, 105, 186
International Federation of Textile
    Workers' Associations 74
International Monetary Fund 150
James, C. L. R. 93
Jameson Raid 23, 30, 38
Jay, Douglas 155
Jenkins, Clive 151, 156
Jenkins, Roy 150, 166–9, 171
Johnson, James 143
Joint Committee of Cotton Trade
    Organizations 65
Katilungu, Lawrence 141
Kaunda, Kenneth 143, 146
"Keep Left" 158
Kenworthy, [Commander] J. M. 83
Kenyatta, Jomo 90, 93
Kinnock, Neil 183–5, 190
Kitchener, [Field Marshall] Horatio
    Herbert 166
Kitson, Alex 158
Kubai, Fred 100
Labour Action for Peace 186

Labour Party 52, 60, 66; minority
government 56, 65; conferences
73, 140, 142–3, 145, 154, 156–
7, 158, 168–9, 184; stance on
cotton boycott 81; manifestos
and policy statements 60, 91,
157; colonial policy 93, 95–7,
103, 105, 131, 149–50; African
policy 107; National Executive
Committee (NEC) 139, 141–2,
158, 169, 180, 182–3, 186, 190;
International Department 141,
143; Labour Common Market
Committee/ Labour Committee
for Europe (LCE) 166–8, 170–
1; response to Falklands War
174, 184, 189; 1982 elections
188
Labour Representation Committee
53–4, 62
Lang, Jack 49, 57
Langford, Benjamin Franklin 17
Lawson, Wilfrid 30
League of Nations 114, 161
League of People Against
Imperialism 139
Lee, Jennie 156
Lennox-Boyd, Alan 140
Lester, Muriel 78
Lomé Convention 161–2, 170
Lugard, Frederick 26
Lyttelton, Oliver 135, 138, 140, 145
Macara, Charles 75
MacDonald , Margaret 43
MacDonald, Ramsay 43, 57–60, 65,
152–3, 156
Macmillan, Harold 103, 146, 149,
170; government 132, 136, 139
Makonnen, Ras 93
Malan, D. F. 96
Mann, Tom 43
Marquand, H. 114
Mau Mau, ix
Menzies, Robert 169
Militant Tendency 181, 188

Monckton, Walter Turner 145;
Monckton Commission 145,
147
Montgomery, [Field Marshall Lord]
110–11
Morris, William 24, 26–7, 35, 37
Morrison, Herbert 95
Movement for Colonial Freedom
(MCF), ix, 98, 141, 143, 154,
159
Moyne Commission, see: West
Indies Royal Commission
Mullin, Chris 186
Mushonga, Paul 144
Mwanga, [Kababa of Buganda] 25
Naesmith, Andrew 78, 86
Nairn, Tom 155
National Executive Committee
(NEC), see: Labour Party
National Union of Mineworkers
(NUM) 186–7
National Union of Public
Employees (NUPE) 186
National Union of Railwaymen
(NUR) 186
Nationality Act 179
"New Commonwealth" 47–8, 55,
59, 156, 177
Nicholson, Marjorie 138, 142
Nkumbula, Harry 138–9, 143
North Atlantic Treaty Organisation
(NATO) 157–8, 164
Northern Rhodesia African National
Congress (NRANC) 135, 137–
9, 176
Northern Rhodesian African
Mineworkers' Union 141
Northern Rhodesian Legislative
Council 140
"Numquam", see: Blatchford,
Robert
O'Connor, T. P. 32
Oliver, P. M. 80
Orde-Brown, [Major] 94
Ottawa Agreement 149

Overseas Food Corporation (OFC)
110, 117–20
Overseas Resources Development
Act 110, 117
Padmore, George 90, 93
Pan-African Congress 93
Pan-African Federation 93
Pan-African Movement 90
Pasha , Emin, Relief Expedition 26
Passfield, [Lord], see: Webb,
Sidney; Passfield Memorandum
92
Pearman, [Sergeant] John 19
Peron, [General] Juan 175
Pitblado, D. B. 123
Plowden, Sir Edwin 123
Plummer, Leslie 118–19
Prentice, Reg 162
Priestley, J. B. 72
Radice, Giles 182
Reagan, Ronald 180, 184
Red Flag Riots 57
Red International of Labour Unions
90
Rees-Williams, David 115–16
Review of Programmes and of
Colonial Capital Investment
Requirements Committee 112–
13
Rhodes, Cecil 110
Richards, Frank 20
Ridley, Nicholas 179
Robertson, George 185
Roll, Edward 112–13
Round Table Conference 65
Rowling, Bill 171
Rust, William 81
Samuel, [Sir] Herbert 72
Schmidt, Helmut 158
Scottish Trades Union Congress 187
Scullin, James 57–8
Shackleton, [Lord] 178
Shaw, George Bernard 34
Shaw, Tom 74
Shirer, William 69, 78, 80
Shiva Rao, B. 71, 74

Shore, Peter 168, 183, 185
Simon Commission 74
Singh, Makhan 100
Smalley, Henry 75
Snowdon, [Lord] Philip 60
Social Democratic Federation 24
Social Democratic Party (SDP) 171,
180–1, 190; SDP-Liberal Party
Alliance 190
Socialist International Committee
for Latin America 183
Socialist League 24
Socialist Vanguard Group 158
Southern Rhodesia African Youth
League 144
Spencer, Herbert 30
Statute of Westminster 65
Stead, W. T. 32
Sterling Area Development
Working Party (SADWP) 112–
13
Stewart, Michael 157, 162–4
Stonehouse, John 154
Strachey, John 118–20
Strang, Gavin 188
Suez Crisis 173, 177, 180, 182
Sunderland, J. W. 68, 76–7
Thatcher, Margaret 173, 179–80,
185, 188–90
Theodore, Ted 57
Thomas, Jimmy 151
Tilley, John 188
Todd, Garfield 144
Tout, William 82
Trades Union Congress (TUC) 74,
141; stance on cotton boycott
81; colonial policy 92–3, 95, 97,
99–105; stance on communism
97–8, 101; International
Committee 93, 102; stance on
Falklands War 186
Transport and General Workers'
Union (TGWU) 186
Tribune Group 155, 158, 184
tsetse fly 114–16
Twining, [Sir] Edward 115

Unilever, see also: United Africa
   Company (UAC) 117, 120
Union of Democratic Control 139
United Africa Company (UAC) 117
United Nations 155, 157, 175, 185,
   187, 190; Colonial Aspects of
   the Economic Activities of the
   United Nations Committee 112–
   13
United Textile Factory Workers'
   Association 81
Wakefield, A. J. 117, 120;
   Wakefield Commission 117–20
Wallace Johnson, I. T. A. 93
Webb, Beatrice 43
Webb, Sidney 29, 43, 91, 133
Welensky, Roy 139, 144–5
Wellington, [Duke of] 11

West Indies Royal Commission 94
"White Australia" policy 47, 55
White Mutiny 17
Whitlam, Gough 171
Williams, Shirley 164, 169, 171
Wilson, Harold 149, 155, 157–9,
   162–4, 170, 175, 177;
   government 151, 155, 177
Wolseley, [Sir] Garnet 26
Woodis, Jack 96
Woolf, Leonard 91
World Federation of Trade Unions
   (WFTU) 98
Wrong, Margaret 142
Yamba, Dauti 132
Yaoundé treaty 161
Zilliacus, Konni 157–8
Zinoviev, Grigory 90